News across Five Continents

Text and Social Context

Series Editors

Alison Moore
University of Wollongong

Rebekah Wegener
University of Salzburg

Tom Bartlett
University of Glasgow

This series provides in-depth accounts of language use in social life that interrelate fine-grained analysis of texts and extensive analysis of the sociocultural context in which the texts are produced and interpreted. It brings together and consolidates the strengths of various sociolinguistic, textual and critical discourse approaches to linguistic analysis that are often treated in isolation. The series draws explicitly on functional accounts of language-as-action in specific social contexts both to analyse the social meaning of situated texts and to test and develop the theory against these accounts.

Books in this series provide a fuller and more adequate description of the social context than is often afforded by existing textual studies. Equal prominence is therefore given to descriptions of context, drawing on methods from disciplines such as ethnography, sociology and psychology, and to the language produced. Titles discuss not only significant patterns of linguistic choices in texts and their role in construing the context in which the texts function, but also the dynamics of language production and uptake.

News across Five Continents

Newspaper Language in the Context of
Regional and Functional Variation

Jennifer Fest

SHEFFIELD UK   BRISTOL CT

Published by Equinox Publishing Ltd.

UK   Office 415, The Workstation, 15 Paternoster Row, Sheffield, South Yorkshire S1 2BX
USA ISD, 70 Enterprise Drive, Bristol, CT 06010

www.equinoxpub.com

First published 2023

© Jennifer Fest 2023

All rights reserved. No part of this publication may be reproduced or transmitted in any form or by any means, electronic or mechanical, including photocopying, recording or any information storage or retrieval system, without prior permission in writing from the publishers.

British Library Cataloguing-in-Publication Data

A catalogue record for this book is available from the British Library.

ISBN-13 978 1 80050 289 5   (hardback)
         978 1 80050 290 1   (paperback)
         978 1 80050 291 8   (ePDF)
         978 1 80050 349 6   (ePub)

Library of Congress Cataloging-in-Publication Data

Names: Fest, Jennifer, author.
Title: News across five continents : newspaper language in the context of regional and functional variation / Jennifer Fest.
Description: Sheffield, South Yorkshire ; Bristol, CT : Equinox Publishing, 2023. | Series: Text and social context | Includes bibliographical references and index. | Summary: "This volume presents a thorough analysis of newspaper language from a regional and functional perspective. Based on a collection of 4,000 newspaper articles from five English-speaking regions and five different news domains, it discusses the benefit of register analysis in a systemic functional framework to comparing varieties and determining their developmental status"-- Provided by publisher.
Identifiers: LCCN 2022045100 (print) | LCCN 2022045101 (ebook) | ISBN 9781800502895 (hardback) | ISBN 9781800502901 (paperback) | ISBN 9781800502918 (pdf) | ISBN 9781800503496 (epub)
Subjects: LCSH: English language--Variation. | Functionalism (Linguistics) | Register (Linguistics) | Newspapers--Language.
Classification: LCC PE1074.7 .F47 2023 (print) | LCC PE1074.7 (ebook) | DDC 070.01/4--dc23/eng/20230105
LC record available at https://lccn.loc.gov/2022045100
LC ebook record available at https://lccn.loc.gov/2022045101

Typeset by Sparks – www.sparkspublishing.com

Contents

Acknowledgements	vii
Abbreviations	viii
List of tables and figures	ix

Part I: Theory

1	Regional and functional variation	3
2	Varieties of English – Concepts and previous work	6
3	The role of news and its language	27
4	A functional approach to variation in English	34

Part II: Methodology

5	Defining register for a quantitative analysis	43
6	Corpus Design	57

Part III: Results and what to learn from them

7	Field of discourse	67
8	Tenor of discourse	92
9	Mode of discourse	121
10	Regional and functional variation – What do we learn?	131
11	Concluding remarks	143

Appendix 1: Top ten keywords	148
Appendix 2: Top 20 place references per variety	153
Appendix 3: Ranges and deviations	155
Glossary	160
References	163
Index	183

Acknowledgements

A lot of people were involved in making this book possible. First of all, I would like to thank Stella Neumann, Thomas Niehr and Sven Kommer, who supervised the original PhD thesis from which this volume emerged. Monika Bednarek supervised me during a research stay in Sydney, and supported me with helpful feedback and advice that I am still very grateful for. The stay was funded by the German Academic Exchange Service (DAAD)[1], without which I could not have undertaken this adventure.

The editors of this series, Tom Bartlett, Alison Moore and Rebekah Wegener, accompanied me in the process of creating this book. Whenever I got stuck, they were there to help and to provide valuable comments. Paula Niemietz took on the task of editing the manuscript and giving me further feedback. Thank you for your work and, most of all, your patience.

A lot of good friends also supported me, during my PhD as well as my work on this volume. Whether I was in doubt, tired or just fretting, these people were always by my side, and I am very thankful for that.

Finally, I am immensely grateful for the constant and unconditional support I received from my family: my mother Brunhilde, my father Helmut and my brother Dennis. Thank you.

---

[1] This publication is based on data parts of which were collected during a research stay at the University of Sydney funded by the German Academic Exchange Service (DAAD).

Abbreviations

AUS	Australia
ECO	Economy
EFL	English as a foreign language
ENL	English as native language
ESL	English as a second language
HK	Hong Kong
HN	Hard news
ICE	International Corpus of English
KEY	Kenya
L1	English as a first language
L2	English as a second language
LIFE	Lifestyle
POL	Politics
TTR	Type/token ratio
RSF	Reporters without Borders
SCMP	*South China Morning Post*
SFL	Systemic functional linguistics
SPO	Sports

List of tables and figures

Tables

Table 1	Operationalization – Overview	56
Table 2	Corpus size (articles, words and tokens)	64
Table 3	Top ten keywords per domain	69
Table 4	Top ten keywords per variety	70
Table 5	Average type/token ratios	84
Table 6	3rd p. pronouns – Relative frequencies	89
Table 7	Frequencies of imperatives and interrogatives	93
Table 8	Amount of keywords – Domains	101
Table 9	Amount of keywords – Regions	102
Table 10	Frequencies of national and international place references	113
Table 11	Relative frequencies of nouns and nominalizations	117
Table 12	Pronouns – Absolute and relative frequencies	122
Table 13	Relative frequencies of coordinators (General and sentence-initial)	123
Table 14	Keywords – Domain-internal comparison	148
Table 15	Keywords – Variety-internal comparison	150
Table 16	Popular place references per variety	152
Table 17	Ranges and deviations for individual features	154

Figures

Figure 1	Ranks of press freedom based on the index by RSF (2020)	33
Figure 2	Distribution of tenses	72
Figure 3	References of time – Narrow scope	76
Figure 4	References of time – Wider scope	78
Figure 5	References of time – General	79
Figure 6	Lexical density – Distribution	81
Figure 7	Declarative mood – Relative frequencies	86

Figure 8	Declarative mood – Distribution	87
Figure 9	Modal verbs – Relative frequencies	97
Figure 10	Distribution of modal verbs	99
Figure 11	Distribution of boosting and minimizing lexis	105
Figure 12	Boosters and minimizers – Frequencies	107
Figure 13	1st and 2nd person pronouns – Frequencies	109
Figure 14	Frequencies of passive voice in % of all finite verbs	115
Figure 15	Distribution of contractions	125
Figure 16	Average distribution of word classes – Domains	128
Figure 17	Average distribution of word classes – Regions	129
Figure 18	Cumulative ranges and deviations from average – Domains	133
Figure 19	Cumulative ranges and deviations from average – Regions	136
Figure 20	Correlations of linguistic features and press freedom	141

PART I: THEORY

1 Regional and functional variation

1.1 About this book

This book is about the way newspaper articles are written in five different English-speaking regions: Australia, Kenya, Hong Kong, the USA and the UK. It combines two separate perspectives on language, that of regional and that of functional variation, and brings in the additional dimension of news language.

From the point of view of regional variation, this book will address questions of differences between native and L2 varieties and relate them to the socio-political and socio-economical particularities of their regions. Does newspaper language differ depending on the country? If so, does it differ across all types of news or does news in these regions vary only when addressing specific topics or audiences? What causes these differences? And do they display a pattern that would allow us to map them onto other regional varieties as well?

The idea of the news context – e.g. topic and audience – having an influence already implies the functional perspective. For this book, we will not consider newspaper language as one large category, but instead distinguish thematic areas of news which are commonly found in every newspaper and which reflect different possible functions of news language. Variation will be traced between these categories, and will be analyzed based on the contextual basis of these categories by making use of the systemic functional concept of register (e.g. Halliday & Hasan, 1985).

The next two sections will look more closely at the two types of variation and their interplay. Chapters 2 and 3 of this book will then give an introduction to all relevant terms and definitions and derive the theoretical bases of the register framework and news language. Part II will describe how the concept of register is operationalized for this study and what the dataset looks like. Finally, Part III will present the results and interpretation as well as methodological conclusions that can be drawn.

1.2 Why combine regional and functional variation?

As can already be seen, combining regional and functional perspectives leads to a complex network of analyses and results covering both types of variation. Why is this necessary? What do we gain from this? These, too, are questions that this book will address and repeatedly come back to.

The point of departure is the assumption that functional variation reflects the level of complexity a language has reached in a certain society (cf. Neumann, 2020; Neumann & Fest, 2016). When a topic is dealt with frequently in a speech community, or a social activity is beginning to institutionalize, the language used for it will become institutionalized, too, and form a recognizable register (i.e. a variety meant for the specific purpose) that differs from other registers in the language (cf. Halliday & Hasan, 1985, p. 56). This implies that the more registers a language (or one of its varieties) has formed, the wider its field of applications in the respective society.

In a country where English is an official language and the language of instruction and education and where most speakers are natives, English can be expected to have formed as many registers as there are situation types, as it is the prevalent language and is present in every aspect of life. If English is only a second language and maybe only one of several official languages, its function will be different: it may play only a minor role in the lives of most members of the society and not be used in every area of life. In this case it will have formed fewer registers as fewer situation types are institutionalized for English in this speech community.

Whether or not a variety has a distinguishable register in English for a certain topic can therefore be seen as an indicator of the frequency with which the language is used in this situation type. On a larger scale, this means that analyzing the functional diversity in a variety is a direct road to defining its developmental status (Mollin, 2007; Neumann & Fest, 2016). The combination of the two perspectives can thus be expected to be valuable for the field of variational linguistics, but has so far been realized only rarely in large-scale studies. In addition to defining regional and functional variation, this study will therefore also undertake to revise the method and suggest further improvements.

1.3 Why news language?

With the connection between the two types of variation defined, the question remains as to why newspaper language was chosen as the field of application. The main reason for this is simply that news language has been found to reflect our society in a way that few other instances of public language use do

(A. Bell, 1995). News producers and their audiences are in a constant negotiation cycle about what is relevant and adequate; while news producers choose the topics they intend to cover and define the news values along which they want to construct them (Bednarek & Caple, 2014, pp. 136–7), addressees decide which news outlets to follow and which newspapers to buy, thereby directly influencing the (financial) success of the producers – who will, in turn, tend towards the coverage of more popular topics. The same holds true for the style in which news is presented, which might or might not please the audience and trigger respective reactions.

In addition to this, language used in news reflects the language as it is understood by most members of a speech community at the time. Not everybody talks or writes like a journalist, but the reception and understanding of news should be possible for almost everyone, although intended audiences can differ. News language is mainstream language and more representative by far than other types of public language use, such as legal language or lectures, for example.

A further aspect of news language is that it reflects not only topics relevant within a community, but also restrictions and political mechanisms that are at work. Freedom of press is in very real danger in many parts of the world. This danger can manifest itself in explicit ways, e.g. in the form of concrete laws or threats against journalists; in this case, the violations of press freedom are obvious and are monitored and evaluated by organizations like Reporters without Borders (*Reporters sans frontières*, RSF) or Freedom House. However, it can also occur in the form of subtler constraints on journalistic norms and work, which often result in self-censorship, i.e. strategies news writers employ to avoid sanctions from the start (e.g. C.-C. Lee, 1998; F. L. Lee & Lin, 2006). These are harder to recognize and track from the outside, but the actual news texts produced under such circumstances can be expected to show linguistic particularities that indicate that press freedom might be threatened here.

All this makes news language an ideal example of an area of functional variation that depends not only on the immediate contextual configuration, but also on broader societal influences that originate from political decisions. Although the concept of press freedom has so far not been defined in linguistic terms, this book will look more closely at existing concepts in Chapter 3 and consider it as a factor for variation when interpreting the results.

Last but not least, news language of course encompasses not only newspapers, but radio, television and new media as well. For the current study newspapers were chosen because, in many parts of the world, access to TV, radio and also internet is very limited. Newspapers, on the other hand, are the most widely available form of media, thus addressing the largest potential audience.

2 Varieties of English – Concepts and previous work

The process of the expansion of English around the world has been discussed and analyzed from various perspectives, and has itself been influenced by societal and political changes both in the language's "home country", England, as well as its new territories. The history of English has countless dimensions depending on contact languages, cultures and ideologies, all of which are reflected in the research and the trains of thought that led to the understanding of English as a global language and the acceptance of varieties of English as legitimate forms.

In order to examine varieties of English, and fully grasp the implications of and conclusions from such an analysis, it is necessary to understand which concepts are involved and from which research traditions and times they originate. Although the field of World English is mainly focusing on the development and treatment of regional variation, beginning with colonial history and continuing through current stages and beyond, functional variation again plays a distinct role in defining the related terms and ideas, especially since digital variations have begun to emerge that no longer depend on physically existing regions.

This chapter will give a brief outline of the field of World English, tracing the development of major ideas and research streams. Since Kenya and Hong Kong are generally considered so-called New Englishes, we will also recapitulate the current situation regarding English use in these two regions and previous work analyzing their varieties. All these fields have accumulated a wide range of terminology, not all of which is always used consistently. This book does not claim to resolve terminological confusion or even settle ongoing debates; terms relevant for the analysis will be defined as clearly as is possible and necessary for the later discussions.

2.1 English in a global context – World English and World Englishes

English is now above all an international language, used or understood in most parts of the globe and in a great variety of circumstances. In today's world it serves as a means of expression and communication not only among people who have acquired it as their mother tongue but – on an even more remarkable scale – with and among non-native users, whose mother tongues are many and various. (Abbott, 1981, p. 1)

In this brief but exact introductory statement, taken from the editorial of the first issue of the newly founded *World Englishes*, Abbott touches upon several issues that were and still are crucial for researching the English language.

Since the publication of Abbott's editorial, the number of people who speak English has increased steadily. The mere counting of speakers has been given up as hardly feasible; instead, the formulation and discussion of abstract concepts, acceptance of new varieties and analyses of them as well as political and social implications have dominated the field.

After all, one does not have to know the exact number of English speakers globally in order to work with the assumption that there are millions, and that English is therefore a world language. Suggestions as to what that might mean and imply differ greatly however, and the ensuing discussions have revealed just how far-reaching and obscure the construct of English really is.

Early on, the idea of a world language was mainly a prescriptive one. It was not only taken to mean that many people speak English, but also that they should speak the same form of English, ideally an artificial one easy and fast to learn. Both A. M. Bell (1888, p. 40) and later Quirk (1981, pp. 155–6) suggested this concept, although with varying degrees of radicalness regarding how it might be put into place.

These approaches were based on the central notion that the same language should be imposed on everyone, and that this would solve communicative problems in the future. However, they underestimated or ignored several major consequences. On the one hand, speakers of English on a native or advanced level would face the problem of having to downgrade their language whenever they communicated with someone who had learned only a simplified version of English, a behavior which would be impossible to enforce. On the other hand, the factor of language change and the tendency for languages to develop differently depending on where and by whom they are spoken would very likely render fruitless all efforts to establish and retain a worldwide language. There is of course no empirical data to this effect[1], but evidence from the histories of other languages makes it more than likely that an

---

[1] The only constructed language for which data is readily accessible is Esperanto, a language developed by Zamenhof between 1872–85. Intended as an auxiliary language to simplify international communication, its number of speakers is estimated by Ethnologue (2016) at about 2,000,000.

artificially created world language would remain homogenous only for a very short time. It would start to change the moment it was introduced, through being adapted to social groups, formed to suit societies' needs and influenced by surrounding languages, ideologies, and geography (e.g. B. B. Kachru, 1985, p. 22; Eco, 1995, p. 292; Seargeant, 2012, p. 26; Strang, 1970, p. 17). In other words, it would form regional and functional varieties – something for which no artificial language is needed, because English is doing just that on a global scale already.

Recognizing this, the research field of World English experienced a slight shift from the attempts to establish (a version of) English on a global scale to analyzing the English that was already there. This of course presupposed accepting the fact that English differed greatly depending on where and by whom it was spoken. In his *A History of the English-Speaking Peoples* (1956-8), Churchill acknowledges this diversity within the English language, but regards the varieties as nothing more than slight alterations of the English spoken in England. Although the *Oxford English Dictionary* (2016) records the first instance of the word "Englishes" in the sense that it refers to regional varieties of the language English in the year 1910, it was not before the mid-20th century that the term became more frequent in scientific texts (Mesthrie & Bhatt, 2008, p. 3). A simple morphological analysis is enough to unveil the basic idea behind this new use:

> When we transform "English" (N1) into "Englishes" (N2) we change a "mass (or "uncountable")" noun into a "count (or "countable")" one, resorting to the well-known process of *functional shift* (or *conversion*, or *zero derivation*). It is the same when we speak of "Italian *cheeses*", "English *cheeses*" or "French *cheeses*": we are referring to different kinds/varieties of the same (though diversified) "thing", i.e. *cheese*. (Chevillet, 1993, p. 32; emphasis in original)

The birth of this concept, logical as it was, triggered the question of the future of the English language. Bailey (1985) and Maley (1985) painted two possible scenarios for this: either English would break up into various, eventually no longer mutually intelligible languages, as with Latin (see also Schneider 2007, p. 68); or it would remain united due to the fast exchange of communication and information made possible by modern technology. Eventually, Maley (1985, p. 32) settled for a compromise: "What I foresee then is the continuing development of local or specialist dialects, but within a framework of an internationally understood variety of English". This prediction raised other issues which he, too, was quick to add: "Where then will 'real' English be spoken? What will be recognized as the 'best' kind of English?"

These questions clearly show that, despite the insight that there were different varieties of English, the overall perspective was still fairly centered on one core language, located either in the USA (as suggested e.g. by McArthur, 1987) or Britain (Christophersen, 1988). This is mirrored in several attempts at visualizing the diversity and expansion of English. Strevens (1980, p. 86) presented a model that displays English as a family tree drawn across the map of the world, indicating which Englishes come from which English. The starting point is an abstract "English" outside the map, which then splits into American and British English as its "children". Strevens' model thus focuses on synchronic variation, but leaves no room to express the existing and potential interconnections between varieties and other contact languages, and entirely ignores functional variation of language. With these shortcomings, it appears too static and nonexpendable for a language which has affectionately been called "the living laboratory of World English" (McArthur, 1987, p. 10).

In contrast to this, McArthur (1987, p. 11) and Görlach (1990, p. 42) presented models in wheel structure that depict English and its variations as centered around a hub of one standard variety. Although both models concentrate on regional variation alone, they have the potential for further expansion that could include functional variation, too. The idea of a central "macro-English" as a point of reference (cf. also Mesthrie & Bhatt, 2008, pp. 27–9) is non-negotiable in all these models though.

The first attempt at modelling the English language without such a fixed anchor was made by Kachru in his "Three concentric circles of English". As the name suggests, the model consists of three circles: the smallest "inner circle", the medium-sized "outer circle" and the largest "extending (also "expanding") circle". The varieties in the inner circle are said to be "norm-providing", the ones in the outer circle "norm-developing", and those in the expanding circle are "norm-dependent".

The model has been slightly altered throughout Kachru's works (e.g. 1988, p. 5; 1992, p. 356, 2006, p. 196), but the basic idea behind it has remained constant and, in contrast to the preceding models, does not draw on an international variety of English. Like the wheels of McArthur and Görlach, the concentric circles contain space for future developments in the English language – the recent (2006) version even contains additional empty circles to demonstrate that it is not only likely for varieties to enter existing circles or shift from one to the other, but that entirely new dimensions of the English language can potentially emerge as well. Kachru's model is now more than 30 years old, and already one might argue that particular spheres, such as social networks, forums or online multiplayer games are developing their own varieties of English. These are neither dependent on any physically existing region nor is there any reliable way of determining the number of users or speakers.

The model also implies another major statement: the outer circle varieties do not just rely on the inner circle for their language, but develop norms of their own. This aspect is strongly emphasized by Kachru (e.g. 1985, 1991), who argues for a distinct autonomy of the outer circle varieties and suggests that, in the countries belonging to this category, the local varieties should be institutionalized as the languages used in education (cf. also Bolton, 2006, ch. 2 Modiano, 1999, p. 22). This would naturally lead to much diversification, but "the spread of a [...] language implies adaptation and nonconformity" (Widdowson, 1997, p. 140). There are too many local influences in the different countries in which English is spoken for it to remain static. Only a very basic common core can be expected to be shared by all varieties:

> A common core or nucleus is present in all the varieties so that, however esoteric a variety may be, it has running through it a set of grammatical and other characteristics that are present in all the others. It is this fact that justifies the application of the name "English" to all the varieties. (Quirk, Greenbaum, Leech, & Svartvik, 1985, p. 16)

The concept appears in the literature under different terms; Chambers (2004) and Sharma (2009) talk about "vernacular universals", and Kortmann and Szmrecsanyi (2004) specify "angloversals". In this sense, a shared "Englishness" is not only logical, but also observable in empirical studies, as for instance Nelson's (2006) large-scale analysis of the International Corpus of English (ICE) and numerous other studies following his example (e.g. Xiao, 2009; Yao & Collins, 2012) have demonstrated.

The scenario predicted by Maley and Bailey in 1985, namely a mutual intelligibility of all Englishes due to modern communication, therefore seems to have become a reality. To distinguish it from the idea of World English, this concept is mainly referred to as "English as an International Language" (EIL), which is essentially a functional variation of English. It serves the purpose of ensuring mutual intelligibility among all speakers of English, and facilitates communication in such matters as economy, politics, science, and education, but also across regions (Matsuda & Friedrich, 2011, p. 333; Seargeant, 2012, pp. 87–9). It is not the same as the concept of English as a lingua franca, since the latter is usually used to imply that at least one participant of the communication does not speak English as a first or native language, and English thus functions as "a means of communication between people who do not share a common language" (Seargeant, 2012, p. 191). EIL includes this possibility, but goes beyond it.

To what degree an individual might need EIL can of course vary; L. E. Smith (1992, p. 75) argues that "it is unnecessary for every user of English to be intelligible to every other user of English. Our speech/writing in English needs to be intelligible only to those with whom we wish to communicate in English". Looking at today's communicative networks and demands however, the need for EIL as well as its existence can hardly be denied. Its basis is the common core described by Quirk et al. (1985); yet to really function as a world-wide language in a number of settings, EIL has to go beyond that and thereby logically include linguistic features that are characteristic of some varieties, but not of others (i.e. departing from the common core).

Depending on the setting, these additional features vary, eventually leaving us with not one EIL, but several, world-wide, yet functionally specific registers. This trend is reflected in the scientific literature as studies analyzing functional varieties such as academic writing (e.g. Alméciga & Evans, 2014; Hützen, 2015; Hyland, 2002), social media English (e.g. Gillen & Merchant, 2013; Raguseo, 2010; Zappavigna, 2011), business communication in international settings (e.g. Barés & Llurda, 2013; Böttger, 2007; Du-Babcock, 2013) or legal English (e.g. Bhatia, 1993; Thomas, 1985). These registers vary with regard to their divergence from the common core – which enhancements are made to the basics depends on the function as well as the influence of individual varieties on the particular field. This differentiation of registers, of course, restricts the mutual intelligibility of all Englishes to a certain degree; particularly with regard to their lexicon – functional varieties are often specialized to a degree which renders them unintelligible to outsiders (Widdowson, 1994, p. 383; 1997, p. 144). In short, a person might be a very proficient speaker of English, but still find it difficult to follow, for instance, a medical conference, since the technical terminology is comprehensible only to members familiar with this particular register.

It can thus be said that while the term "World Englishes" refers to regional varieties of English, "Englishes as International Languages" (as it would have to be termed) describes functional variations of the language or the so-called "English for Specific Purposes" (ESP) (see Widdowson, 1997, p. 144). This distinction, although helpful from a terminological point of view, does not imply that the two categories do not influence each other – quite the contrary, they steadily interlace and shape the landscape of Englishes. Taking into account both functional and regional variation adds a helpful perspective to the long-lasting debate about the nature of the international status of English, but cannot solve another issue which was already touched upon above:

that of norms and rights of English. Does anyone own English? Can or should anyone enforce prescriptive rules? And who, if anyone, has the authority to decide what is to carry the label "English" and what is not?

After all, despite all research efforts and discussions, "the myth of a single 'golden' or 'pure' form of English dies hard" (Strevens, 1981, p. 3). The next section will therefore look more closely at the ideas of nativeness and English as a foreign or second language, and define the meanings of these concepts for the purpose of this work.

2.2 EFL, ESL and the concept of nativeness

When describing models like the ones presented in the previous chapter, it is unavoidable to work with terms such as *native speaker*, *mother tongue*, *foreign language* or *second language*. Statistics about language users usually employ these categories, too. In the literature concerned with the terminology, however, the meanings of these terms are far from clear, and with people becoming ever more mobile and linguistic biographies ever more diverse, new terms arise to describe new phenomena concerning language use.

To begin with, the frequently used idea of *nativeness* should be treated with a certain caution. Not only is the notion rather vague, but it is also often used synonymously with other concepts, especially with *first language* or *L1* and *mother tongue*:

> *Native* must surely be one of the most misleading and confusing terms ever employed in technical or semi-technical argumentation. Two other terms, partly synonymous with it, run it a close second or third: *mother tongue* and *first language*. A person's mother tongue is not necessarily his mother's tongue; nor is his first language always that which he learnt first, because *first* can mean "first in importance" as well as "first in time" and, alas, the two meanings are sometimes run together as if they were one and the same. All three terms, moreover, are surrounded by an aura of mystique and are heavily loaded with emotional connotations inimical to sober scientific investigation. (Christophersen, 1988, p. 15; emphasis in original)

Native language and *mother tongue* are used synonymously almost all through literature to refer to "the language that one acquires from birth" (Seargeant, 2012, p. 196; see also Mesthrie & Bhatt, 2008, p. 4), and will also be used that way in this study.

The concept of *first language*, however, is defined rather unsatisfactorily in most cases. To distinguish it from *native language* as clearly as possible, we will rely on a definition suggested by E. W. Schneider (2007, p. 17) according to which L1-speakers are "speakers who, after having acquired an indigenous mother tongue, have sooner or later shifted to using English only or predominantly in all or many domains of everyday life".

This is fairly close to the common idea of what a second language (L2) is (see e.g. Crystal, 1985). The main distinction is on the level of dominance. Widdowson (1997, p. 144) emphasizes the official character of an L2 as being used for institutional purposes. Seargeant (2012, p. 192) elaborates that English as a second language (ESL)[2] refers "to the use of English in countries where it has some official status (mostly due to the legacy of colonialism), or in which it is the predominant means of communication and is being learnt by people [...] from non-native speaking backgrounds".

English in the sense of ESL, then, is actively learned and in most cases an obligatory school subject due to the function of the language within the country in question. In contrast to English as L1, however, ESL is not necessarily dominant in a speaker's life, but might be restricted to official or institutional contexts. The most striking cases of this linguistic configuration can be found in former British or American colonies which, after their national independence, have kept English as an official language (E. W. Schneider, 2007, p. 12).

The dimension of the official status which is so important for ESL is usually missing for people who learn English as a foreign language (EFL). Apart from this, EFL and ESL have a lot in common, not least the fact that they are both, in most cases, learned at school. For those who learn English as a second language, it is also a foreign language, but with different implications. The two categories have therefore often been compared (e.g. Bongartz & Buschfeld, 2011; Szmrecsanyi & Kortmann, 2011), and many studies have treated them not as separate entities but as two ends of a continuum (see e.g. Gilquin & Granger, 2011; Hundt & Vogel, 2011).

From the perspective of language acquisition this makes sense, but it neglects the fact that, especially in former colonial areas, "English has become a part of the cultural heritage" (B. B. Kachru & Quirk, 1981, p. xix; see also Crystal, 1985, p. 9). Although taught at school, it is not just a language that is learned because of its usefulness, but because it has a historical implication for the country and more often than not works as a national language, i.e. a symbol of identity, as well as an official one (Mesthrie & Bhatt, 2008,

---

[2] This is also sometimes referred to as *English as an additional language* in order to avoid the impression that it has to be the second language (cf. Seargeant, 2012, p. 192).

p. 5; Seargeant, 2012, p. 196). Due to this, these varieties of English have a certain autonomy which EFL varieties do not display to that degree: by becoming institutionalized and constituting a part of the country's historical background, English is adapted to the society and will develop characteristics that set it apart.[3]

As we can see, this categorization is very detailed and requires a lot of disentangling of definitions and ideas. In contrast to this, Kachru (1981, 1983d) suggests splitting the varieties of English into just two categories, native and non-native ones. The native ones are those spoken in the USA, Australia, New Zealand and Canada, as English was "transplanted" there: that is, large numbers of native speakers settled there to stay (B. B. Kachru, 1981, pp. 16–17). The non-native varieties include everything else, both EFL and L2 varieties (although the distinction is emphasized), and are defined as having "mainly developed in 'un-English' cultural and linguistic contexts in various parts of the world" (B. B. Kachru, 1981, p. 15).

This distinction is clear from a historical point of view, and takes into account the different circumstances under which English reached foreign shores. Since then, however, things have changed; the emerging forms of ESL varieties in former colonies have developed and become distant from the native varieties as they have undergone processes of "de-Anglicizing" and "de-Americanizing" (B. B. Kachru & Quirk, 1981, p. xix). In many cases, processes of nativization (also sometimes called indigenization) can be observed, meaning that the language has developed "new linguistic features at all linguistic levels, features that would be considered deviant if used in countries where the 'native speaker' varieties of English [...] predominate" (Lowenberg, 1992, p. 109; see also B. B. Kachru, 1990, part 1; Mufwene, 2015, p. 8; J. C. Richards & Tay, 1981, p. 45).

These varieties of English display a sort of "functional nativeness" (B. B. Kachru, 1997, p. 68) due to being in frequent use and having been adapted to their environment. This raises the question of possible standards of English: If English is taught in an ESL country, should the local variety be given priority or should the teachers look to Britain or the USA for norms? Can someone be called a native speaker of English if they speak a variety other than British or American? Can a variety become a new standard, and at what point? In other words, which rights do these emerging varieties have, and does anyone "own" English?

---

[3] B. B. Kachru (1983c) uses the terms *institutionalized variety* and *performance variety* to emphasize this distinction.

The immediate answer to this must of course be: no. "Language is an immensely democratizing institution. To have learned a language is immediately to have rights in it. You may add to it, modify it, play with it, create in it, ignore bits of it, as you will" (Crystal, 2003, p. 172). Crystal's attitude is shared by many, as by B. B. Kachru and L. E. Smith (1985, p. 210), who state that "the language now belongs to those who use it as their first language, and to those who use it as an additional language, whether in its standard form or in its localized forms". It is inevitable that English changes the more it is used (cf. Strevens, 1981, p. 1), but it is natural that this poses a problem to the native speaker concept. Until then, it was generally meant to refer to a person who "fully commands a language and has proper intuitions on its structural properties" (E. W. Schneider, 2007, p. 17; see also Mesthrie & Bhatt, 2008, p. 36; Seargeant, 2012, p. 196). Christophersen (1988, p. 16) speaks of somebody who "is fully at home in the language, is confident in his use of it and is able to make judgments about usage with which other members of the language community will normally agree".

With diverging varieties of English, this agreement is not always guaranteed; native speakers might differ greatly in what they think is acceptable use of "their" language (Christophersen, 1988, p. 16; Romaine, 1992, p. 254). The diversity of definitions is very valuable to get a better understanding of the concepts, but since abstract ideas like "intuition" and "judgment" are too imprecise to be controlled for in a study, we will adhere to the more clear-cut and restricted concepts as follows:

- Native speaker/ENL: a speaker who has learned English from birth
- L1: a language learned after the mother tongue that has become the dominant language in a speaker's life
- L2/ESL: a language learned in school and used for official purposes, but not necessarily the dominant language for a speaker

In this sense, the categories of ENL and L2/ESL can be mapped onto the circles of Kachru's model. The inner, norm-providing circle mainly consists of speakers who speak English as a native language; the outer circle consists of the L2 varieties which are norm-developing and are gaining in independence from the inner circle varieties. The expanding circle includes all EFL speakers, who usually learn English based on the norms provided by the inner circle (see also Berns, 2005, pp. 86–7). In contrast to Kachru's distinction between native and non-native varieties, however, the categories in his model are flexible and allow varieties to change their status. The varieties at the core can be said to have their own standards, and to use them confidently in all domains of life; and varieties from the outer circle are, by varying degrees, approaching this status, too.

What is interesting is that English being a native language for most speakers ceases to be an exclusive criterion for the core circle – it just happened to be so until now as the inner circle equals the original set of native varieties. With the emerging varieties gaining more independence, there could soon be a group of varieties in the inner circle in which English functions as a first or second language, and yet has developed a functional standard for the country in question.

The original concept of two major standards, British English and American English, appears to have outlived its adequacy in the face of so many new varieties of the language, yet learners often request a standard (cf. B. B. Kachru, 1983d, p. 32), and especially in EFL contexts, this is still mainly sought in Britain or the USA. Furthermore, the original "owners" of English have from time to time shown themselves hesitant to give up their privileged status among speakers of English (B. B. Kachru, 1983a, pp. 234–5; Romaine, 1992, p. 254; Widdowson, 1994, p. 377).

This linguistic form of territoriality is curious, because the standards of British and American English have not always been unchallenged in their own countries. In Britain, the sophistication which has often been associated with speaking Received Pronunciation or "Queen's English" has been criticized for being segregational (B. B. Kachru, 1983b, p. 8), blocking the way up the social ladder for everybody underneath it. In the USA, the teaching of standard pronunciation at the cost of localized accents has been called "unintelligent" (Kenyon, 1924, p. 3), and it was feared that it threatened the identity of minorities. Both standards are spoken by a mere minority of people, and are in every sense abstract sets of rules and guidelines. And yet, they are sets of rules that are fixed in dictionaries and grammars, a step which many emerging varieties of English have not yet taken.

In today's linguistic landscape, at least, the way is paved for the acceptance of emerging varieties, and they are largely met with a sense of curiosity. It has become plain that the English language is no longer defined by the original native varieties, but that it has become "a public domain" (Modiano, 1999, p. 27). The terminology described above, the notions of ESL or L2, EFL, ENL, EIL and so on, are tools in the attempts to describe the diversity of English, although, as Strang (1970, p. 17) states, "language is human behavior of immeasurable complexity. Because it is so complex we try to subdivide it for purposes of study; but every subdivision breaks down somewhere, because in practice, in actual use, language is unified". Despite this obvious truth, the set of terms has been generally agreed upon as being helpful (Görlach,

1989, p. 279), and will be applied in this study in the senses outlined above. It should be kept in mind, however, that while referring to individual speakers allows a quite clear-cut distinction, whole varieties are often generalized. Today most countries are multilingual, and can thus not be classified entirely and as a whole as an EFL variety, or an L2 society (see E. W. Schneider, 2007, p. 13). When such terminology is used in this context, it refers to the majority of speakers in their use of English.

This holds true also for the five regions analyzed in this book. The Englishes spoken in Australia, the USA and Britain are what Kachru termed native varieties, and mainly consist of native speakers of English. The other two varieties, those spoken in Kenya and Hong Kong, will be treated as L2 varieties. Both belong to the so-called New Englishes, the varieties spoken in former colonies of Great Britain and, partly, the USA. This makes their situation very particular – in order to understand the analyses and conclusions later on in this book, the following sections will briefly revisit the concept of New Englishes and put the varieties of Kenya and Hong Kong in the contexts of their respective histories.

2.3   New Englishes

The term *New Englishes* was introduced to a larger audience by Platt, Weber, and Ho (1984). In the already vibrant market of technical terms relating to the study of the English language, this initially caused some confusion. The new term was used both as a synonym for *World Englishes* (see e.g. Mufwene, 1994) as well as a description of a subgroup of these, namely all varieties of English spoken in former colonies, before the latter definition finally won the upper hand in linguistic discourse. Yet "the obvious question of how many New Englishes there are and which countries belong to the various categories suggested cannot be answered precisely at this point. Any attempt at a comprehensive listing will require extensive discussions and unavoidably arbitrary decisions" (E. W. Schneider, 2003, p. 237).

These concerns are justified, but a list of certain countries, based on their colonial history, is generally agreed upon, including India, Singapore, The Philippines, Ghana, Hong Kong, Sierra Leone, Fiji, Cameroon, Barbados, Jamaica, Kenya, Sri Lanka, Puerto Rico, Tanzania, Trinidad and Tobago, Malaysia and Nigeria. Approaches differ, however, in their levels of distinction; while some studies look very closely at individual countries (e.g. Childs & Wolfram, 2004 for Bahamian English; Devonish & Otelemate, 2004 for Jamaican English; Asante, 2012 for Ghanaian English), others summarize countries under headings such as African (Y. Kachru & Nelson, 2006), East African[4] (e.g. C. Haase, 2004; Hancock & Angogo, 1986; Rooy, Terblanche, Haase, & Schmied, 2010; Schmied, 2006) or Caribbean English (e.g. Allsopp, 2003; Christie, 1989; Craig, 1983; Haynes, 1983; Lawton, 1986).

To define the still large category of New Englishes more exactly, Platt et al. (1984, pp. 2–3) name four criteria for a variety to be called a New English: namely that it (1) has been established in the education system of the country, (2) developed in a country were English was not originally the major language, (3) is used for various functions and, finally, (4) has adapted to the social and geographic environment and has therefore developed a number of characteristics of its own. These criteria are focused mainly on the synchronic status of a variety and do not include how it got there. To reflect this aspect, Schneider (e.g. 2003, 2007, 2014), over several years, formulated and refined a model to describe the evolution of such varieties. This "Dynamic Model" is exclusively meant for English in former colonies, and Schneider replaces *New Englishes* with *Postcolonial Englishes*[5] to give this aspect more prominence. The model suggests that emerging varieties, in this case of English, undergo five major phases:

1 **foundation**, in which English is established in a new area by colonial powers;
2 **exonormative stabilization**, in which the indigenous population and the new settlers increase their contact and external linguistic norms are accepted as the new, local English;
3 **nativization**, which is the central phase and is characterized by a desire for political and cultural independence as well as a rise in national pride which is taken over by the settlers' descendants;
4 **endonormative stabilization**, in the course of which national independence is gained and the local variety is institutionalized in dictionaries and grammars;

---

[4] Most studies that work with this grouping of East African English are based on the ICE-component East Africa and therefore do not argue for this combination, but rely on the data provided by the ICE collection.

[5] *New Englishes* and *Postcolonial Englishes* are not the only terms that have been suggested; Fishman, Conrad, and Rubal-Lopez (1996) talk about *Post-Imperial English*, Moag (1983) uses the term *Third World Englishes*, and Mazrui and Mazrui (1996) analyze *imperial language*. All these can be said to roughly equal the concept of *New Englishes*, but are by far less frequently used.

5 **differentiation**, during which the new variety itself experiences a movement towards diversity through the emergence of accents and dialects.

The two schemata do not contradict or exclude each other; rather, the criteria defined by Platt et al. (1984) can be mapped onto stages 3–5 in Schneider's list. The model certainly goes a long way in explaining the development of language varieties in colonial and postcolonial settings; but, like other models before it, it neglects functional variation as an important indicator. Stage 5 will only be reached when a variety goes beyond a purely pragmatic purpose – as long as it is the country's language of choice predominantly in matters such as politics, media and education, any form of differentiation, as expected in the last stage, would be counterproductive. For internal diversity to become a reality, it must be accompanied by the language being used in more forms of social interaction, in other words to form more institutionalized registers apart from purely formal ones. In this sense, stage 5 should refer not only to regional but also functional differentiation.

The factor of institutionalization – as the language of education as well as in grammars and dictionaries – is in line with Kachru's call for increased autonomy of the varieties, and roughly corresponds to the outer circle and thus norm-developing varieties. Still, as helpful as these categorizations are, it should be kept in mind that no variety exactly equals another, neither in its diachronic development, nor in its developmental stage or its status within its society. The situation is different in every individual case, and the two varieties which are part of this study, the Englishes of Kenya and Hong Kong, show this quite clearly. They can be called both *Postcolonial Englishes* and *New Englishes*, as they fit both definitions; we will refer to them as *New Englishes* in this book.

To create a common ground for the analysis and discussion, we will briefly look at the historical development of English in Kenya and Hong Kong. How did English get there and why? For which purposes was it intended, and which did it really serve? And, of course, why are these two varieties useful for a study such as this one?

2.3.1 Kenyan English

Kenya is, of course, by far the larger of the two regions, with 45.5 million inhabitants spread out over about 581,000 km². Of those of 15 years or older, 81.5% are registered as literate (UNESCO Institute for Statistics, 2021).

The two most frequently spoken languages in the country are English and Kiswahili; in total, however, there are 67 living languages in the country and, apart from English and Kiswahili, 10 others are used in educational contexts (Lewis, Simons, & Fennig, 2015, p. 6). The linguistic situation is thus very diverse, and always has been so. The vast majority of these 67 languages (and in fact several more that are now extinct) were spoken in the area long before English arrived. Kiswahili functioned as a shared language among the people of eastern Africa as early as the 8th century, and remains one of the most widespread languages in Africa today (Skandera, 2003, p. 9). English first reached this part of Africa in the 16th century, but the interest of the British exceeded mere trade only in the late 19th century, during what is often called the "scramble for Africa". European colonial powers had discovered the continent as a new market with rich resources and huge economic potential, and claimed various parts for themselves. Finally, as a result of the Berlin Conference in 1884/1885, Africa was divided between the European nations and the area which today includes Kenya became British (see e.g. Ajala, 1983, pp. 179–80; Leifer, 1977, p. 139; Skandera, 2003, p. 10).

Despite the increasing number of British settlers, English did not spread easily among the indigenous population. When English reached this part of Africa, there was no need for a lingua franca among the people that suddenly found themselves united under the British Crown, as they already shared Kiswahili (Abdulaziz, 1982, p. 97; Hancock & Angogo, 1986, p. 309). Furthermore, speaking English was regarded as a prestige rather than a necessity – only very few Africans were taught English in order to work in administration, while the vast majority was intentionally kept away from the settlers' language (Abdulaziz, 1991, pp. 394–5; Mazrui & Mazrui, 1996, p. 272; Skandera, 2003, p. 11). It was not until Africans were sent to fight for Britain in both World Wars that this view was challenged by the indigenous population, and English began to spread.

When Britain lost its most valuable colony, India, in 1947, the Empire faced an increasingly weak position in Africa as well. With more and more colonies successfully fighting for independence, Britain finally introduced English as an educational language in Kenya in order to ensure close bonds for a potential postcolonial phase (E. W. Schneider, 2007, p. 192; Skandera, 2003, pp. 12–13). At the same time, many British settlers left Africa in the face of what might happen, thus dramatically reducing the British speakers of English while simultaneously increasing the number of African speakers. It is therefore at this time, at the end of the colonial area, that many scholars (e.g. E. W. Schneider, 2007, p. 193; Skandera, 2003, p. 13) see the start of

Kenyan English, with a characteristic context and typical linguistic features of its own.

Kenya finally gained national independence in 1963 (see e.g. Fishman, 1996, p. 6), and being fluent in English became the only language requirement for anyone wishing to be elected into parliament. This law was challenged and also changed numerous times in subsequent years; in 1974, the constitution was altered to name Kiswahili as the only parliamentary language, excluding English. Only a year later, it was declared that Kiswahili would remain the only language spoken in parliament, but English was to be used for everything fixed in writing. In 1979, English was reintroduced as a language for parliamentary debate, alongside Kiswahili, and both have been required from potential candidates ever since (Abdulaziz, 1982, p. 99; Heine, 1977, pp. 266-7; Mazrui & Mazrui, 1996, pp. 287-9; Skandera, 2003, pp. 14-15; Zuengler, 1983, p. 114). Possibly due to these fast changes, there is considerable disagreement as to the exact status of English in the literature. Since the Kenyan constitution defines it as an official language, it will be referred to as that in this book.

Considering this historical framework, it is not surprising that Kenya's linguistic landscape is still diverse today. English might be omnipresent and multifunctional in Kenya, but its way to this status was a long and winding one. Schmied (1991a, p. 27) claims that "calling African nations anglophone is obviously a gross exaggeration, because all of them – including the nations with a sizeable number of English mother tongue speakers – are primarily 'afrophone'". This is no doubt true, as many African countries are making more or less ambitious efforts to promote and support local languages, or at least save them from extinction (Schmied, 1991a, 24, 35; Skandera, 2003, p. 14). Nonetheless, to discuss English in Africa blurs the boundaries between what is happening in individual countries.

This is reflected in the research in this field, too. Kenyan English is rarely analyzed as a separate variety. More often, as described earlier, studies refer to East African English (e.g. Abdulaziz, 1991; Bobda, 2003; Hancock & Angogo, 1986; Hänsel & Deuber, 2013; Rooy et al., 2010; Schmied, 1989a) or use Kenyan English in comparative approaches to other African countries (e.g. Kanyoro, 1991; Mazrui & Mazrui, 1996). The shared background of colonial history justifies such analyses; however, African countries have been moving in very different directions (Kanyoro, 1991, p. 402; E. W. Schneider, 2007, p. 189) after gaining independence, and treating them as one entity neglects the changes that have happened since.

Among those studies which focus on Kenya alone, a clear sociolinguistic focus is recognizable. Topics such as speaker identities (e.g. Schmied, 1989b;

1991b), attitudes towards English (e.g. Abdulaziz, 1991; Sure, 1989) and differences in language use between regions (Abdulaziz, 1982; Michieka, 2009) and social contexts (Michieka, 2005; Zuengler, 1983) are dominant. If concrete linguistic features are analyzed, the fields of phonology and grammar are the ones most extensively covered, although, as Schmied (1991a, p. 90) and Skandera (1999, pp. 220–21; 2003, p. 61) rightly criticize, a lot of the work is impressionistic rather than based on systematically collected data.

The most thorough analyses of the linguistic shape of Kenyan English are Skandera's (2003) and Budohoska's (2014) studies, both of which combine a corpus analysis based on the ICE with a survey. Furthermore, Buregeya (2006) offers a paper which, with the help of a questionnaire, aims at determining grammatical features that are typical for the variety, as well as a larger qualitative analysis (Buregeya, 2019) of several text samples. These studies do not compare Kenyan English to other varieties, but their results are a sound basis for the inclusion and interpretation of Kenyan English in this book.

2.3.2   Hong Kong English

Hong Kong, too, has been shaped by a history heavily influenced by colonialism. Today, it is nearly a hundred times more densely populated than Kenya, and also has two official languages, Chinese and English (Hong Kong Department of Justice, 2015, p. 3).

English was brought to China by British trading ships landing in Macau and Canton (today called Guangzhou) in the early 17th century; and, throughout the next two centuries, a pidgin English developed as trade with this part of the world became more frequent and important for the British Empire (Bolton, 2000, p. 267; E. W. Schneider, 2007, p. 133). But while demand for Chinese goods was high in Europe, European products were hardly needed in China, which resulted in a trade imbalance between the two regions and eventually led to the First Opium War (Ford, 2010, pp. 121–6; Gray, 2002, pp. 39–40). After the British military had occupied Canton and Shanghai, the war ended in 1842 and the Treaty of Nanjing was signed to define, among other things, the surrender of Hong Kong to British rule, starting its colonial history (Bolton, 2000, p. 267; Moise, 1986, p. 30).

Once in charge of Hong Kong, the British took a different approach concerning the spread of English to that employed in Kenya. Instead of making it an exquisite good provided to only a selected few, mission schools were established in Hong Kong which used English as a teaching medium. In 1911, the English-speaking University of Hong Kong was established (Bolton, 2000, p. 267; Sweeting & Vickers, 2005, p. 117). Although these institutions were very elitist, education levels began to rise on the whole and, in the 1920s and 1930s, numerous Chinese-speaking schools were opened in addition to the English-speaking mission schools (Bolton, 2000, p. 268; So, 1992, p. 72). In the decades to come, Hong Kong turned into a "wealthy commercial and entrepreneurial powerhouse" (Bolton, 2000, p. 268).

This status was boosted by the China trade embargo established by the USA and the UN throughout the 1950s and 1960s (Huang, 2001) – while China was isolated economically as well as politically, Hong Kong remained under British rule and open to the West. Nevertheless, despite the rising worldwide tension between communist and capitalist countries culminating in the Korean War and the Cold War, Hong Kong took some small steps towards their Chinese neighbors; in 1963, the Chinese University of Hong Kong was established (So, 1992, p. 75) and, ten years later, the colonial administration in Hong Kong published a proposal that opened up the possibility of installing Chinese as the major language in education, but suggested that every school should decide for itself (Bolton, 2000, p. 271; E. Chan, 2002, p. 271; Pennington & Yue, 1994, p. 2). This indecisiveness proved characteristic of the colonial government throughout the years to come, as no real language policy was put in place; in 1974, at least, Chinese was finally recognized as a co-official language beside English (So, 1992, p. 76).

At this time, whether or not English was the medium of education was still only a concern of very few. In the late 1970s, however, primary and secondary school education became compulsory, and Hong Kong saw a huge rise in immigration rates (Bolton, 2000, p. 268; Hong Kong Census and Statistics Department, 1982, p. 90). This meant that more people were exposed to English in schools, and the language spread widely. In 1984, Hong Kong's independence from Britain was negotiated and planned for 1997. With this step ahead, learning English became a priority for many to ensure a safe position for the future (So, 1992, p. 86).

More speakers of course also meant more linguistic variety, but this diversity was scowled upon. The ensuing debate found a lot of resonance in newspapers like the *South China Morning Post* (*SCMP*, 1989), which claimed that "the decline in the standard of spoken and written English in recent decades is obvious and measurable". Although these arguments did not appear much in academic literature, the *SCMP* made an obvious point when writing that "English is pre-eminently the language of international trade, which is, and for the foreseeable future will remain, Hongkong's *raison d'etre*" (*SCMP*, 1986). International standards of English were therefore taken as a norm, and any variation from them was considered counterproductive.

This line of argument brought the issue of nationalism and national identity into focus. Should and could English be treated as nothing more than a means for trade? Or had it necessarily entered the national self-conception by being so prominent, for instance in education?

Early studies (e.g. Bond, 1985; Pierson & Bond, 1982; Sin & Roebuck, 1996) found that the major language in everyday life and "the language of the home and intimacy" (Hyland, 1997, p. 191) in Hong Kong was Cantonese. English, on the other hand, was seen as a necessity but also as a status symbol, as being proficient in English usually went hand in hand with financial success and social prestige (Hyland, 1997, p. 193; Platt, 1986, p. 384). With Hong Kong being a center for trade and business, English was desirable and often omnipresent, but apart from professional ambitions, the main emotion towards English was found to be indifference; speakers did not connect it to the Chinese culture or fear any influence on it, and did not feel particularly close to the Western culture either (Axler, Yang, & Stevens, 1998; Evans & Green, 2001; Hyland, 1997; Pennington & Yue, 1994).

Maybe it was because of this very pragmatic and detached view of English that scholars have remarked that the variety of Hong Kong English seems to have received more attention and support from outside of Hong Kong than from within (Bolton, 2000, p. 265). The status of English as an official language is not in doubt so far; however, there is an ongoing debate on the actual degree of autonomy and the uniqueness of Hong Kong English. Before the end of colonial rule in 1997, the notion of a specific Hong Kong English was mainly rejected, not least because it was argued that if English was desired mainly for business purposes, particular Hong Kong characteristics would be of little help. Luke and Richards (1982, p. 55) come to the conclusion that English in Hong Kong follows external standards rather than develop its own, a view which is supported by Tay (1991, p. 327) and R. K. Johnson (1994, p. 182). Other scholars observed that some localized varieties of English, influenced by Cantonese, had begun to emerge (e.g. Bolton & Kwok, 1990; Pennington, 1995). In more recent literature, Hong Kong is consistently listed as a region with a New English (e.g. Gut, 2011, pp. 113–14; E. W. Schneider, 2007, pp. 133–9), and Jim Chan (2013) found that tolerance for potential deviations from the British standard is also increasing within Hong Kong.

The research into Hong Kong English has since shifted to the description of the variety and attempts to categorize it in the terms of Kachru's concentric circles as well as Schneider's Dynamic Model and, especially concerning empirical analyses, Hong Kong has been examined more closely than Kenya. One major methodological advantage for the study of Hong Kong English certainly is the availability of a Hong Kong section in the ICE (see Bolt &

Bolton, 1996), which means that empirical data is readily available. Several linguistic aspects such as the usage of verbs (e.g. J. F. K. Lee & Collins, 2004), pronunciation (e.g. Deterding, Wong, & Kirkpatrick, 2008; Sewell & Chan, 2010), syntactic characteristics (e.g. Gisborne, 2002, 2009) and lexical variation (e.g. Benson, 2002; Bobda, 2009; Cummings & Wolf, 2011) have been analyzed using both quantitative and qualitative methods. Apart from this, the phenomena of code-mixing and code-switching have received a lot of attention, mainly due to the highly contextual uses of English and Cantonese (e.g. B. H.-S. Chan, 2009; Li, 2000; Luke, 1998; Pennington, 1998a, 1998b).

2.4   English varieties in this book

In this book, we will look in more detail at the English varieties from five regions: the UK, the USA, Australia, Kenya and Hong Kong. The UK holds a special position as the "origin" of English, and Australia and the USA are home to dominantly native varieties. Together, they represent three native standards which are spread across the globe and have varying degrees of influence on the many L2 varieties, through their presence in popular culture, historical connections and geographical location.

The varieties from Kenya and Hong Kong contribute the L2 perspective. Looking at their historical frameworks, it can be said that while they share certain aspects, especially the colonial rule by the British, they have differed greatly in matters of language policy and identity. Today, English still plays an important part in both areas, but the differences are pronounced.

In both cases, there are primary and secondary schools that use English as the main medium of instruction instead of Kiswahili or Cantonese respectively (for Hong Kong see Evans, 2009, p. 291; Sin & Roebuck, 1996, p. 252; for Kenya see Kanyoro, 1991, p. 403; Lewis et al., 2015, p. 33). In both cases, too, this has led to debates about language priorities. In Hong Kong, English is welcome as a means to success in a later career – yet, for many children in early education, it is hard to follow classes if they are held completely in English, which leads to the question whether it is worth putting a child's education at risk in order to ensure proficiency in English (Llewellyn, Hancock, Kirst, & Roeloffs, 1982, p. 30; Poon, 2009, pp. 23–4). Similar perspectives have emerged in Kenya; while the sense of English as a business necessity is less prominent, the original British idea that English is a privilege has not yet entirely died out (Kanyoro, 1991, p. 404; Nabea, 2009, pp. 135–6). Furthermore, it is feared that the language diversity of the country is endangered if children are not taught in their mother tongues in a school context (Begi, 2014, p. 48).

In Kenya, especially, it is difficult to determine just how many people speak and use English at all; Crystal (2003, p. 63) lists 24,300 native and 2.7 million L2 speakers, which is roughly 6% of the total population. In Hong Kong, 4.3% of all people older than 5 name English as their "usual language", and another 48.9% use it as an additional language (Population by-census Office, 2016).

Despite these differences, both Englishes are categorized as outer-circle varieties in Kachru's terms, and as being in phase 3 in Schneider's model. This discrepancy shows very clearly that it is necessary that research into these varieties looks at different facets and details of the language and the respective societies as well as keep in mind their overall structure and history. The Kenya and Hong Kong varieties were chosen for this study because the differences regarding how English is used in combination with an almost identical categorization in terms of linguistic models demonstrate precisely the need for this kind of research based on multiple factors.

3 The role of news and its language

A. Bell (1991, p. 1) writes that "people in western countries probably hear more language from the media than they do directly from the lips of their fellow humans in conversation". It has been found that the language used in media is likely to have an influence on the way it is used by the readers (Bednarek & Caple, 2012b, p. 6; Fowler, 1991, p. 7), but journalists, too, have to follow certain rules and standards and are influenced by their environment in turn, which makes the connection more complex. In addition, media is not the same everywhere, but depends on economic, political and sociological factors, among others.

This chapter will look at the context from which media language originates. We will discuss linguistic norms that are generally recommended and taught for journalistic writing, and then examine the idea of press freedom and its implications. Since the analysis is based on newspaper language, we will put the focus of this chapter on this format, too.

3.1 Journalistic norms and styles

As we said above, media language has been found to be highly influential on its recipients, but this is only one side of the story. Journalists, too, are subject to influences and are not entirely free in their linguistic choices. Rather, journalists learn certain rules and guidelines during their professional training. The respective textbooks and manuals are often fairly prescriptive in their approach; nevertheless, their content is valuable to a linguistic analysis, as they are in themselves a source of linguistic particularities of media language.

The number of volumes that have been published to this end is nearly infinite. Most of the works in question specialize in one particular type of mass media, because the individual requirements are very different. For TV journalism, it is essential to keep images and text in a balance, whereas radio broadcast has to rely on audio alone. Both share the non-permanence of their content; a hearer or viewer only gets the information once, and the speed for the succession of items is controlled by the producers, not the recipients (Katzenberger, 1999, p. 91). Whilst both media nowadays often feature online streams, podcasts or, in the case of TV, video on demand, both still mainly have to cater for a target group which listens or watches live (Boyd, Stewart, & Alexander, 2008, p. 71). This is a challenge, because recipients are easily distracted or switch between channels.

The language has to adapt to this, and the guidelines offer very clear suggestions. Sentences should be shorter than in written language, with less complex syntactic structures. Any kind of ambiguity is to be avoided, as are technical terms or rare expressions (Boyd et al., 2008, pp. 71-7). In general, writers are advised never to use a long word when a shorter one is available and to leave out redundant words (Boyd et al., 2008, p. 93). Features like figures, acronyms and homonyms have to be treated with care as they require more time to be processed by the audience and can lead to confusion (Boyd et al., 2008, pp. 94-104; Kolodzy, 2006, p. 135).

The situation is slightly different for newspapers. An average newspaper consists of actual news to a greater degree than most TV or radio programs, which contain talk shows, live broadcasts, sitcoms, movies and magazine shows, to name but a few. News is one fixed element out of many, while in newspapers, in contrast to magazines as another print medium, it is the main part. Also, reading a paper is not something that can be done alongside another activity, as it demands more attention. Newspapers do not have to consider any time restrictions concerning broadcast schedules either, but at least the print versions are limited in space (Fest, 2015b, pp. 54-5).

These external characteristics of course influence the language. The syntax used in newspaper items can be more complicated than on radio or TV, because readers can read a sentence again or jump back and forth in the article as needed. Generally speaking, the recipients of newspapers have more control over the speed with which they wish to receive and process new information. Nonetheless, a reader will give up when a text is too tedious to read and understand, which puts limits on the linguistic complexity (Fest, 2015b, p. 55; Harcup, 2005, pp. 107-8; Kolodzy, 2006, p. 157).

On the levels of lexis and syntax, many similarities can be found with what is recommended for TV and radio writing, namely the avoidance of unfamiliar abbreviations or too much technical terminology. In newspapers, too, active voice is to be preferred over passive, and the language is to be simple and to the point. In contrast to TV or radio broadcast, newspaper articles often work with puns, as it is less problematic that the audience might need more processing time (Keeble, 2006, pp. 96-7; Pape & Featherstone, 2005, pp. 49-56).

On a structural level, the dominant assumption is that a newspaper reader wants to be informed as quickly as possible. The headline and the first paragraph of an article should contain the most vital bits of information on the story. The rest of the article then gives more detail and provides the background, resulting in the so-called "inverted triangle" of information density (Harcup, 2005, pp. 108–13; Randall, 2000, p. 147). As a rule, a reader should be able to stop reading at any point and still get the essence of the story; even the headline should function as a news bulletin when taken on its own (Burger, 2005, p. 114). Throughout the article, the questions *Who?*, *What?*, *When?*, *Why?*, *Where?* and *How?* should be answered if possible (Keeble, 2006, p. 111).

When we look at such recommendations, we have to keep in mind that the language in mass media has long been characterized by the entirely one-sided nature of its communication. Any reaction from the recipients' side to what was heard or read could only be shared with other recipients, but did not reach the producers (Bonfadelli, 2004, p. 12; Luhmann, 2000, p. 2). In more recent years, this relationship has changed and become more complex, as media outlets have begun to make use of online platforms and websites to distribute their content.

The production of news items still lies with the journalists alone, but once they have been published, recipients can react within seconds. These reactions can take place on the same platform (e.g. in comment sections) or be taken to a different platform if the content is shared on social media. These developments have influenced the language in media, too, and have brought about new dimensions especially for newspapers.

Traditionally, daily newspapers were doomed to cover news from the day before as they were printed during the night to be out in the morning. The printed versions of newspapers still have this restriction, but on the online platforms that almost all papers have now established, numerous articles can be published at any time and with a negligible delay between production and publication. This primarily affects the component of recency of news, as newspapers can now react to events as fast as radio programs, for instance. This can be expected to change the temporal scope still counting as "recent" and thereby altering the story's newsworthiness in this respect (cf. Bednarek & Caple, 2014; Potts, Bednarek, & Caple, 2015).

Other changes are even more evident. Headlines are often structured to function as clickbait, displaying a syntactic structure which withholds information to make users click on the link to the full article. This stands in direct contrast to the recommendation mentioned above, that a headline alone should provide enough information to work as a news bulletin. Clickbait has been found to be closely linked to false news and rather less credible news sources, though (Chen, Conroy, & Rubin, 2015; Munger, Luca, Nagler, & Tucker, 2020) professional and high-quality news outlets can be assumed to make less use of this mechanism.

Other features made possible by online journalism have brought about entirely new linguistic characteristics. For example, web articles often contain hyperlinks or embedded content from other sources, which would make no sense in actual print. Animated content, too, can be implemented, so that articles are enriched with multimodal elements like video, audio and interactive maps or diagrams.

The influence such technological innovations have is undisputed but, when we discuss such features, it should be kept in mind that their theoretical possibility does not mean that they appear everywhere. Their availability depends on several factors, like the financial means of the media outlet, the technical infrastructure and the expertise of the staff. The newspapers included in this study vary greatly in these respects – some make use of a vast range of possibilities, whereas the websites of others contain no more than a print newspaper, namely text and pictures. This variation does not allow for any comparisons between the regions, newspapers or domains. Interactive features, including comment sections, will therefore not be covered explicitly in the analysis, but we will consider their potential influence when interpreting the results.

Also, none of these rules or tendencies are entirely universal. Their applicability may vary depending on the story, the news domain or the paper, but they reflect basic assumptions about the function of newspapers and the demands of readers. Finding these suggestions realized in the language should therefore be traced back, to a considerable degree, to their origin in prescriptive guidebooks for journalists and the purpose of newspapers. In contrast, deviances from these norms, especially if they turn out to be characteristic of any particular grouping (such as a particular paper, country or topic), can offer insights into varying standards or purposes within the field of newspaper language.

3.2   Freedom of press

Apart from journalistic norms for language use and matters of technological availability and accessibility, one major influence on mass media is the political and legal framework in which they are situated. Freedom of press is a vital element for a democratic society, and several institutions have created instruments to measure press freedom. These indices do not work the same way though – both their methods and the countries they evaluate vary.

On the one hand, several smaller rankings exist that look at selected countries and often put their focus on one particular aspect of press freedom. One example is the UNESCO (2019) index *Media Development Indicators*, which covers 12 countries and evaluates them in terms of five categories, being explicitly qualitative in its approach and method. A greater overview with a more defined method is provided by the *Media Sustainability Index* (IREX, 2020), which concentrates on economic sustainability and independence of media in about 80 countries.

The two largest rankings are the *Freedom of the Press Index* by Freedom House (2021) and the *Press Freedom Index* compiled by Reporters without Borders (2020). The first analyzes about 200 regions, and has been compiled annually since 1980. It works exclusively with a survey, but no details of the method or questionnaire are published. The institution is a non-partisan organization based in the USA (Freedom House, 2021). Since, in the past, it has received funding from governmental sources and included several politicians on its board, it has been accused of a lack of transparency (Dinmore, 2006; Herman & Chomsky, 1988).

The second large-scale ranking, the Press Freedom Index, covers about 180 countries (the exact number having changed slightly over the years) and has been published annually since 2002. It relies on a combination of a survey for journalists and in-depth analyses of individual regions by the organization's staff. The organization behind this ranking, Reporters Without Borders, has been accused of bias, too (e.g. Rosenthal, 2007a, 2007b); however, its directorial board is elected democratically and it is explicitly a non-profit organization (NPO) and a public-interest entity (RSF, 2020).

Other measurements to capture press freedom have been suggested (e.g. the *Media for Democracy Monitor* by Trappel & Maniglio, 2009), but were often unsuccessful due to limited resources and scope. The existing rankings, although they managed to establish themselves, have often been questioned and critically evaluated. Several studies compare different indices (Banda, 2010; Banda & Berger, 2008; Becker, Vlad, & Nusser, 2007; Burgess, 2010; contributions in Price, Abbott, & Morgan, 2011), while others put their focus on only one (e.g. Le Pelley, 2013). The subjects of these reviews vary from methodological concerns to issues of representativeness, but there are no studies with a linguistic perspective on the topic.

This is curious, since the language of news is so obviously a window to its producers and writers. In many cases, especially in non-democratic societies, restrictions of press freedom are explicitly fixed in law and supported by governments, which makes them easily recognizable and undeniable. But it is not always that simple – pressure on journalists can be exerted more subtly, which often leads to self-censorship (C.-C. Lee, 1998; F. L. Lee & Lin, 2006). This is not easily traceable in official documents and statutes, and indicates that the government of the respective region will not admit freely that it aims to control media. The questionnaires used by some of the press freedom rankings described above as well as several studies (e.g. J. M. Chan & Lee, 2011; C.-C. Lee, 1998) cover self-censorship to a certain degree, as they address journalists directly, but they cannot reach those who are scared to put their concerns into words or to participate in a survey in the first place.

It is these cases for which a linguistic analysis can be of enormous value. We assume that articles that are written in an atmosphere in which journalists feel the need to censor their own writing will mirror that in their linguistic realization. They are effectively produced in a different situational context from articles in a country with a free press. This tense (or even fearful) environment must be institutionalized in order to function as a mechanism for self-censorship, which means the language will adapt to this particular context and display characteristics that set it apart from news items written without these restrictions. Seeing that journalists are not always free to express their concerns, language must be the means of choice to identify these safely.

Since there are no previous linguistic studies to draw on for this concrete aspect and the existing press freedom measurements are partly critical, this book will provide only a first insight into language as an indicator of press freedom. For this, we will rely on the *Press Freedom Index* by Reporters Without Borders, as its method is most transparent and it contains data to cover all regions included in our corpus. It has ranked all five of them ever since its first publication in 2002, which makes it the best choice for the present study. Figure 1 gives an overview of the development of press freedom in the regions and already shows a very diverse picture.

Australia, the UK and even more so the USA have undergone some variation regarding their press freedom ranks, but move within the first 50 places at all times. The media in the two L2 varieties on the other hand is more restricted – and particularly Hong Kong, which was characterized by a fairly positive score throughout the first decade, has gone into a steady decline since 2012. Our corpus contains data published until 2013 (see Chapter 6), and the respective figures will be taken up during the analysis and interpretation.

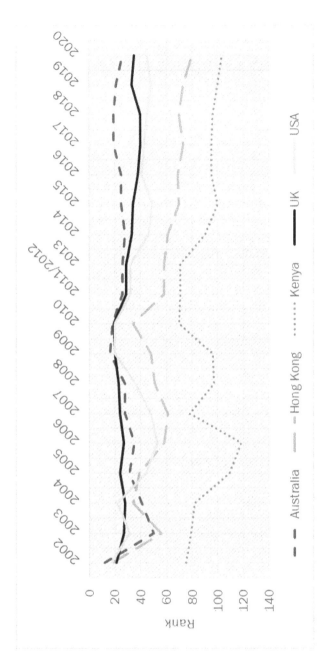

Figure 1 Ranks of press freedom based on the index by RSF (2020)

4 A functional approach to variation in English

It has been argued in the previous chapters that existing models of development of English varieties neglect functional perspectives, that is, how the language is really used in a society. We argued that situation types that occur frequently get institutionalized, and so does the language connected to them. These situation-specific registers are recognizable and have linguistic particularities that make them the best choice for the respective context. It follows that these registers can be found when linguistic parameters are analyzed, and that a language is more widely spread in a society the more registers it has developed.

It is the purpose of this section to look into these claims more closely and to trace the line of argument that led to them. Again, we will meet an accumulation of terminology that is not always clear-cut, and define what is relevant for this study as we move along. In order not to lose sight of the core topic of this book – varieties and variation with a focus on newspaper language – we will briefly discuss the origins of the register concept, and then limit ourselves to functional approaches in these fields.

4.1 The concept of register

In systemic functional linguistics (SFL), the concept of register goes back to the assumption that speakers adapt their language to the situation in which they find themselves. The concrete notion was introduced by Halliday (e.g. 1974; Halliday & Hasan, 1985), but goes back to the observation made by Malinowski (1935, p. 8) that "speech is meaningless without the context of the activity in which it is enveloped". This means that there are always two sides to a communicative event, and a clear definition of the context helps to disentangle them for a better understanding: "Context is an interlevel […] since it relates language to something that is not language; it is an interlevel because it is not with the non-language activity itself that linguistics is concerned but with the relation of this to language form" (Halliday, 1961, p. 269).

The non-language aspect is reflected in situations we as speakers encounter in our lives. The central message is that context adds meaning to language and, as was said above, potential contexts are institutionalized and can be grouped: "Looking at how people actually use language in daily life, we find that the apparently infinite number of different possible situations represents in reality a very much smaller number of general *types* of situation" (Halliday, 1974, p. 29; emphasis in original). Since the context is vital to the meaning, we need to define it as clearly as possible in order to analyze language, and creating categories of types makes a theoretical grasp of *context* possible.

A first framework for this purpose was suggested by Firth (1950, p. 43), who identifies the context of speech to be defined by relevant features of the participants, relevant objects and the effect of the discourse. This was refined by Halliday (1975, pp. 130–31) who formulates the following parameters:

- *field of discourse* (representing the ongoing activity),
- *tenor of discourse* (representing the participants and their relationships) and
- *mode of discourse* (representing the part language plays in the interaction).

These variables are more abstract than Firth's categories, but can also be analyzed separately. The respective shapes they take in any given situation can, through the numerous possible constellations, describe every register of a language by determining its contextual configuration (Butt & Wegener, 2007, p. 590; Halliday, 1974, p. 50; Halliday & Hasan, 1985, pp. 55–6; Halliday & Matthiessen, 1999, p. 321). Eventually, since context directly influences the language, the three parameters can be found to be reflected linguistically: "The linguistic features which are typically associated with a configuration of situational features – with particular values of the field, mode and tenor – constitute a REGISTER" (Halliday & Hasan, 1976, p. 22; emphasis in original).

This definition of *register* is quite straightforward, but the term has been used differently in other contexts. In particular, it often appears seemingly synonymously with the terms *genre* and *text type* (for more detailed discussions, see Fest, 2016; D. Lee, 2001). For this volume, we will work with Halliday's definition as described above, as it offers the most structured access to what we are interested in – social and political influence on language. Because the three parameters are distinguishable and cover separate facets of the situational context, a linguistic analysis reveals more than just characteristics and particularities; instead, it can be enhanced by linking the results back to field, mode or tenor, so that their origin can be more clearly identified. In other words, it allows us to determine on which level the potential influence is mainly reflected.

This means that we need to link field, mode and tenor to the actual, observable language. This operationalization is crucial, because it determines the conclusions we can draw in the end. The three variables are very abstract, though. Too abstract to clearly outline the linguistic features linking back to them on the language level. For an analysis, especially for an automatized, quantitative approach, the variables of register need to be more clearly defined so that very concrete linguistic characteristics can be connected to them. Various subdimensions for the three parameters have been suggested that work as an intermediate step between the abstract variable and the actual linguistic representation. Not all of them are relevant for the language type analyzed in this book; which ones are used and why, as well as their linguistic operationalization, will be the subject of Chapter 5. Before we move on to this methodological part, however, we will review how the functional approach has previously been applied to the research fields relevant to our study.

4.2   Functional perspectives on media language

As registers are seen as reflections of different situation types, the functional approach of course lends itself to analyses that aim to describe a particular register or to compare several of them. Just like the number of registers themselves, the quantity of studies is nearly infinite. Due to its central role in societies, media language has received extensive attention, too, with research covering various angles and methods and presenting foci ranging from individual aspects of context to broad descriptions of many of its dimensions.

On the one hand, samples of media language, especially texts from newspapers, have served as comparative values in larger studies (e.g. Biber & Conrad, 2009; Biber, Johansson, Leech, Conrad, & Finegan, 1999). For this purpose, media language is regarded as one of the most widespread examples of public written language, and although these studies do not explicitly focus on media, they are immensely valuable as they help place newspaper language within the overall language system and filter out characteristic linguistic features.

On the other hand, we can find numerous studies that concentrate on newspapers alone and do not only take language into account, but also consider, for instance, implications and use of multimodality (e.g. Bateman, Delin, & Henschel, 2007; Caple, 2010; Knox, 2009a, 2009b; K. Schneider, 2000), or connect to the field of media studies by examining dimensions like "audience design" (A. Bell, 1984, 1991) and target group construction (Conboy, 2006; Crawford, 2009).

Studies with a predominantly linguistic focus take very different approaches. One perspective we find frequently is based on discourse analysis, which is useful, for instance, for analyzing the linguistic representation of news values (Bednarek & Caple, 2012a; Caple & Bednarek, 2015; Potts et al., 2015). It is linked to the more clearly defined field of Critical Discourse Analysis, which provides a framework for analyzing relations and construction of power and is often applied to sociological news topics, like the portrayal of protesters, racism or refugees (e.g. KhosraviNik, 2009; Stamou, 2001; Teo, 2000).

The systemic functional approach is another angle to take, and several studies have applied individual aspects of it to newspaper language. One important focus is outlined by the Appraisal framework, which looks at evaluative effects of language (Martin & White, 2005). "The events reported in newspapers should of course be both new and true, but they should also appear to be true" (Vestergaard, 1999, p. 89) – meaning that the language in which news is presented can make all the difference. The impression it leaves can hinge on evaluation and attitudes that are implied in what is being said, and a number of studies have analyzed this in more detail (e.g. Bednarek, 2006, 2008; White, 2004, 2006, 2012).

Apart from this aspect, which is often dealt with on its own rather than in connection to other dimensions, a register- or genre-based approach to newspaper language has frequently been adopted. On this basis, individual domains of news have been described in detail and certain categories have emerged. A very common one is sports (e.g. Dreyfus & Jones, 2010; Fest, 2017; Ghadessy, 1988a), which is easily identified, as it can be found in separate sections in almost all major newspapers and sports news items are clearly recognizable. Editorials (or opinion pieces) have also been analyzed thoroughly (e.g. Fest, 2021; Liu, 2018), whereas lifestyle articles, though also clearly labelled, have not received as much attention in research (Welch, Fenwick, & Roberts, 1997).

Other thematic domains are less clear-cut. In particularly the category of hard news has proven difficult to grasp. It is often defined in contrast to soft news (e.g. Reinemann, Stanyer, Scherr, & Legnante, 2012), but the labels are not used consistently and the differences are blurry. Despite this, hard news as a domain has been analyzed (e.g. Dijk, 1985; Mahlberg & O'Donnell, 2008; Thompson, White, & Kitley, 2008; White, 1997), and the results from these studies make finding a workable definition a lot easier. Whether other thematic fields – e.g. politics, economy, international and national news – are defined at all and, if so, to what degree, depends heavily on the individual newspapers. In this book, we will include five domains: economy, hard news, lifestyle, politics and sports. Chapter 6 will describe in more detail why these were chosen and how they are defined for the purpose of this book.

With all these – and many more – studies already completed, we need to ask which insights and values we can still add. In other words, why do we need another analysis of newspaper language? Newspaper language has been analyzed between countries and across domains, but as was said before, the two perspectives are hardly ever combined. So far, research has either focused on a functional-level comparison between news domains, not taking into account differences between (varieties of) languages, or on regional-level comparisons between languages without the element of variation in news topics. Yet the close connection between news and their target societies calls for such a cross-dimensional perspective: it is not just newspaper language in general that is of interest, but also the degree of differentiation between the individual topics that reflects the relevance attributed to them.

4.3   Functional perspectives on regional variation

In contrast to functional variation, regional variation seems less evident as a field for a functional approach but, due to its focus on the way language is really used, it is a good instrument for studying linguistic variation of any kind. Regional and functional variation are often distinguished theoretically, but in reality they are closely intertwined. Geo- and sociopolitical factors have a huge influence on the situation types that develop in a speech community, and thus also on the registers that appear. Which registers are typical and shared can in turn blur regional differences or sharpen them. Furthermore, as we argued above, the extent to which registers of a certain language have formed reflects the degree to which that language is rooted in the society. A combination of regional and functional variation seems logical under these assumptions, but studies with a functional approach that consider regional differences are surprisingly rare.

We saw in Chapter 2 that, in theory, the importance of functional variation when discussing English as a worldwide language has been recognized. Kachru (1996, p. 135; emphasis added) writes that "[the term] 'Englishes' symbolizes variation in form *and* function", and *English for Specific Purposes* became the label covering functional varieties as opposed to regional ones. That registers depend on the language status was also agreed on fairly early – both B. B. Kachru (1983d, p. 38) and Schmied (1991a, p. 36) explain that ENL (English as a native language) and ESL (English as a second language) varieties usually contain more functional diversity than ESL ones. Nevertheless, the focus of research into regional varieties has mainly been a sociolinguistic one.

A lot of emphasis has been put on attitudes towards English and the influence language has on shaping identities (e.g. Hiraga, 2005; Yoshikawa, 2005). The methods in use vary from qualitative approaches (e.g. Aguilar-Sánchez, 2005; Seargeant, 2005) to surveys (e.g. Coetzee-Van Rooy & Rooy, 2005; S. Richards, 1998), but all studies dealing with such topics do not work on the level of language itself, but rather examine the language environment and sociological context.

Linguistic properties of individual varieties have been another major focus in the field. Earlier studies (e.g. Holzknecht, 1989; Schmied, 1991a) still relied heavily on field work or manual analyses, but with technological advances in both data sampling and processing, quantitative studies became popular. A major impulse was the compilation of the International Corpus of English (Greenbaum, 1990), which to date offers comparable datasets of 14 varieties (ICE Project, 2016). It also includes a broad functional categorization of its texts, which creates a basis for further analyses.

Which role does a functional approach play in the research field of regional variation? The most basic distinction that can be made is that between written and spoken language, but this is too broad to allow any definite conclusions on the context of language production. Some (e.g. Louwerse, McCarthy, McNamara, & Graesser, 2004; Rooy et al., 2010; Xiao, 2009) make use of the individual categories the ICE offers, and follow Biber's (1985, 1988) multidimensional approach, which makes them corpus-driven rather than corpus-based. This means that they do not aim to link differences on the language level to concrete aspects of the context predefined by a theory such as SFL.

Of those studies that adopt a theory for their analyses, several focus on individual registers (e.g. contributions in Ghadessy, 1988b) or compare registers within one variety (e.g. Guz, 2009; Taguchi, 2002). A few studies combine several varieties and registers, but concentrate on one dimension of the register framework or on a few linguistic features only (see e.g. Fest, 2017; Neumann, 2012; Neumann & Fest, 2016). A functional approach has also been used to analyze translations (e.g. Diwersy, Evert, & Neumann, 2014; F.-A. Haase, 2013; Neumann, 2013), covering not varieties, but separate languages.

All these studies offer valuable perspectives. The insights gained from them help complete the picture of individual varieties as well as of English as a global phenomenon. Yet few studies exist that examine functional and regional variation across all context variables with the goal of drawing conclusions about the context from which the language originated. Two notable exceptions are Neumann (2020), which uses the ICE to compare three varieties and 17 text categories, and Evert and Neumann (2021), which reproduces the approach with a refined method of multivariate analysis.

From a methodological point of view, too, the combination of regional and functional variation holds a clear advantage. If for instance a variety displays few differences between two particular news domains, this does not necessarily mean that it is typical for the regional variety. The similarity can be characteristic of the two domains in general, which would make the difference in one variety not striking at all. By analyzing both the regional and functional dimension, we can avoid such false conclusions and use them to test for assumptions in either direction.

Combining registers and varieties almost inevitably leads to large amounts of data and a quantitative approach; although more susceptible to generalizations, it can rely on more language samples and find differences "no observer would have expected [...] to exist" (E. W. Schneider, 2007, p. 87). Of course, a qualitative analysis is not impossible, but the goal to have enough data to accurately represent both dimensions renders it fairly impractical. Instead, qualitative elements can often be found to complement quantitative analyses by adding in-depth perspectives of individual characteristics and layers.

This book will follow a similar strategy, but fill the gap of a large-scale study with a systemic functional foundation. The five regions and their varieties included here – Australia, Hong Kong, Kenya, the UK and the USA – reflect the axis of regional variation, and the newspapers and their domains provide a functional distinction. Most parts of the analysis are quantitative, but whenever necessary or helpful, qualitative aspects will be included.

The second part of this book is going to present both the dataset and the methodology in more detail. Most importantly, it will also describe the process of the operationalization of the register dimensions field, mode and tenor.

PART II: METHODOLOGY

5 Defining register for a quantitative analysis

In Chapter 4.1, the systemic functional concept of register was described and we came to the conclusion that for a quantitative analysis, the dimensions field, mode and tenor are too abstract to be linked directly to features on the lexico-grammatical level. Before we can start the corpus work, we need to get a more exact idea of what they really mean, and the best way to approach this is via an intermediate step. For every dimension, subdimensions have been suggested and discussed that are on a lower level of abstraction and can be operationalized more easily and with less risk of ambiguity.

There is no final agreement on any particular set of subdimensions; rather, this is an ongoing debate which reflects different perspectives on and expectations of the theoretical framework. In the following sections, we will briefly review these suggestions and define which ones are relevant for our study. For these, we will explain the operationalization: that is, we will define which linguistic features will be used to represent them in the analysis.

5.1 Field of discourse

The field of discourse has been defined as "the nature of the social action" or, in more colloquial words, "the general sense of what it is on about" (Halliday & Hasan, 1985, 12, 24; cf. also Wegener, 2011, p. 104). More specifically, this includes the topic and the goal of an interaction, and we can find these aspects reflected in the suggested subdimensions.

The topic, or subject matter, is covered in the dimension of the experiential domain. It is complemented by the second aspect, the goal or purpose the activity has from the sender's perspective. Halliday and Matthiessen (2014, p. 37) call this "the nature of the social and semiotic activity", which, however, is a bit confusing as the wording overlaps with the overall definition of *field*. What it implies refers to a lower level; the authors distinguish between "doing" and "meaning" as the general functions language can have, and formulate seven more detailed ways of "meaning" which essentially mirror the authors' potential intentions. This subdimension has therefore also been termed "goal orientation" (e.g. Neumann, 2013) or "oriental goal" (e.g. Steiner, 2004), which are more precise labels and reduce the risk of misunderstandings. In this book, both the experiential domain and the goal orientation will be included.

5.1.1 Experiential domain

The essence of this subdimension, the experiential domain, is "to elicit the subject matter of the register" (Neumann, 2013, p. 49; cf. Halliday & Matthiessen, 2014, p. 33). In other words, its purpose is to reflect the topic of an interaction.

Several linguistic markers have been suggested to trace the experiential domain on the language level. Steiner (2004, p. 15) works with lexical fields, terminology, cohesive lexical chains, aspects of reference, headings and titles, paragraphing, transitivity, expressions of time, perspective and *aktionsart*. Neumann (2013, p. 49) also includes the first four of these and adds lexical density, but summarizes terminology and lexical fields under "vocabulary" (see also Halliday & Hasan, 1985, p. 24).

The **VOCABULARY**, of course, is a crucial and direct way of determining what a text is about, and we will include it by analyzing keywords both of the individual domains and the varieties. It will be complemented by **LEXICAL DENSITY**, which puts function words and lexical words into relation and reflects the complexity that is constructed around a given topic. Not all of the other features are easily analyzed on a lexico-grammatical level, and some are problematic in a quantitative study with automatized corpus queries. Perspective, for instance, is too abstract to be queried, and the categories of verbs defining transitivity, although highly valuable for understanding the social background of texts, are too ambiguous and overlapping to be a reliable basis for an automatized analysis. To avoid increased subjectivity and keep the results as comparable as possible, these features will be left out.

In contrast, the aspect of the temporal scope mentioned by Steiner (2004) is of great interest to us. We saw in Chapter 3 that the rise of online news has further narrowed what counts as "recent". Nonetheless, what is still relevant and for how long also depends on the topic. Articles covering accidents and crime, and also sports match reports and political decisions are usually of interest soon after the event itself, and lose their relevance quickly. Items dealing with travel reports or health topics, for instance, can be relevant for much longer, and do not lose their value if they are not read soon after their publication. Apart from this, it is not only the coverage of what has happened that is presented in news; for some topics, outlooks are given and speculations are voiced. Big political summits, announcements of events, and also transfers of sports players are often subjects of future references.

Through such mechanisms, the temporal scope that is given in news items is linked to the experiential domain. Since news, however, is by definition not old, we must expect differences to occur on a very fine-grained level. To distinguish among them, we will analyze the **USE OF TENSES** along with a variety of **EXPRESSIONS OF TIME** that refer to past, present and future and cover time spans of different lengths.

The analysis of the subdimension of the experiential domain is most directly affected by the difference between corpus-based and corpus-driven approaches. This is because texts are most likely predefined with regard to the topic. When examining the experiential domain, we can either start from an external categorization and sort the texts into this pattern, or we can do our analysis first and then create categories based on the linguistic similarities that emerge. The corpus-driven approach has the advantage that we can analyze texts without any bias from a non-linguistic level. The corpus-based approach offers the possibility of considering texts not only in relation to each other, but also in the context of the bigger picture, which can include the fact that the author of a text categorized it in a certain way.

In our study, the five newspaper domains that are included in the corpus are an externally predefined categorization. The texts will be treated as instances of the category in which they were published; but, as given by the operationalization, we will not rely on predefined word lists or category-specific characteristics. Within the domains, the analysis will be open, which will allow us to observe any degree of variation within them. Instead of re-sorting the texts based on the results, however, we will draw conclusions regarding the context of their production.

5.1.2 Goal orientation

The second subdimension that we will examine for the field of discourse deals with the goal of the interaction. This is a difficult category – on the one hand, goals can be explicit or implicit, obvious or indirect (Grice, 1979), oriented towards the field or the tenor (Halliday & Matthiessen, 2014, p. 41), and these characteristics do not exclude each other, but can be present in a text to varying degrees. On the other hand, speakers are not always fully aware of their own intentions (Hasan, 1999, p. 234), which makes it even more likely that a text contains more than one goal.

When focusing only on written texts, like we do in this study, the picture becomes a little simpler. The communication of newspaper articles is one-sided, which means that only the author expresses goals at all. The addressees, in this case the readers, can be assumed to have goals, too, but there is no possibility of tracing them linguistically because they do not directly contribute to the texts in question. This reduces the focus to one participant of the interaction.

Since producing a written text requires more awareness of one's intentions and means that the authors have time to organize their thoughts, the likelihood of goals being included unintentionally also decreases. In the case of journalistic texts, this control is taken even further by the editing that articles go through and the numerous people involved in the process.

Several suggestions have been made for taxonomies of goal types. Engel (1988, pp. 118–19; my translation) presents a model of six potential functions: to inform, induce, convince/persuade, teach/correct, maintain contacts, and reduce emphasis. Brinker, Cölfen & Pappert (2014, pp. 60–80, 101–21; my translation) mention five functions, namely: information, contact, declaration, obligation and appeal, and four types of underlying text structures (descriptive, narrative, argumentative, explanatory). Neumann (2013, pp. 55–56) works with four functions: narration, argumentation, exposition and instruction. These different categories show that the concept is not treated alike by everybody; the ones by Brinker and Engel describe desired outcomes of texts (see also Halliday & Matthiessen, 2014, p. 41), whereas Neumann's categorization is more closely linked to the way these outcomes are achieved.

Another model, presented by Lüger (1995), specifically aims at classifying media texts. Based on the main intention of a news text, it can be identified as informative, evaluative, appellative, instructive or contact-oriented (Lüger, 1995, pp. 66–74; my translation). Although this model offers a discourse-specific perspective, it also unveils a problem with the concept of goal: when all texts in an analysis come from the same discourse area, such as newspaper language, the differences are small and, based on Lüger's taxonomy, practically all texts from our corpus would have to be labelled *informative*. Specialized text samples are less compatible with models with broad categories. As we said above, since texts are likely to have more than one intention, an analysis would have to take place on the level of sentences or phrases to pick up any differences at all and come to meaningful results with regard to a taxonomy of goals.

Our corpus does not contain mark-up for syntactic functions or parsing, which makes an analysis within the texts difficult, but goal orientation will still be included in our study in a simplified manner. One main purpose of news is to inform, which means that newspaper articles can be expected to be informative in their style (Fest, 2015b, p. 54) – we can assume this goal to be present in all texts in our corpus to varying degrees. How dominant it appears depends on a number of factors, including the topic, the intended audience, the newspaper and the degree of press freedom. Although it is of course only one aspect of the subdimension of goal orientation, the intensity of informativeness can therefore be seen as a good reflection of this part of the context.

With the focus on one goal, the operationalization becomes more straightforward. Brinker et al. (2014) and Engel (1988) agree that on the language level, a factual style is connected to informativeness. Neumann (2013) connects this to her category of exposition, which in turn draws on the definition of descriptive texts by Beaugrande and Dressler (1981, p. 190), who name "objects and situations" as the core of this text type. Based on these descriptions, we can say that the language that characterizes an informative goal is factual in the sense that it is rather impersonal and content-oriented.

What does this mean for the lexico-grammatical level? Which linguistic features can we rely on to represent this kind of language? Neumann (2013) and Biber (1995) mention the use of **DECLARATIVE MOOD** as one indicator, because in contrast to interrogatives and imperatives, it puts a clear emphasis on information. Also, the **TYPE/TOKEN RATIO** (TTR) is suggested because it signals a wider focus of content. Both features will be included in our analysis.

Other indicators suggested in previous studies do not apply to news language. Neumann (2013) links the use of present tense to an informative or expository style but, as we argued in the previous section, the use of tenses is influenced by many factors in newspaper language. Articles can report on what has already happened or include outlooks, but whichever tenses are used do not imply that the information density is lower; rather, they reflect the news values which are constructed for a given story. If an article is written in the present tense, this can simply mean that timeliness is less relevant for the topic it deals with. The distribution of tenses cannot be linked to the degree of informativeness without the risk of drawing false conclusions, and will not be used as an indicator in this study.

Another suggested feature, that of **PRONOMINAL USE**, will be included, but in a slightly modified way. Neumann (2013, p. 58) argues that out of all personal pronouns, the singular 3rd person *it* stands out as being more factual than the others and referring to facts more than to people. This means that *it* can be expected to occur much more frequently than other personal pronouns in informative texts, whereas personal references are rare. In newspaper language, however, people themselves can be the dominant news value of a story (Bednarek & Caple, 2014; Potts et al., 2015). This makes them an important, if not the most important, piece of information to refer to. In such a case, personal pronouns must be expected just as much as *it*, without changing the information value.

Still, we face a problem with the use of pronouns, because in text books for journalistic writing (e.g. Keeble, 2006, p. 113; Papper, 2013, pp. 49–56), it is sometimes recommended to replace pronouns with other bits of information:

[1]   **Heather Watson** is hoping glandular fever will not rule her out of next month's French Open. […] **The 20-year-old** has not picked up a racket since her diagnosis three weeks ago (…). (Hart, 2013, the *Daily Telegraph*; emphasis added)

This strategy means that we cannot expect 3rd person pronouns to appear frequently in general terms. Instead, in order to capture their meaning for an informative style, they have to be put into relation to other pronouns that are used, as 1st and 2nd person pronouns reflect a more interpersonal dimension, and we will use this relation as a measurement.

5.2   Tenor of discourse

The second dimension to define the context of a communicative situation is the tenor of discourse. Broadly speaking, it deals with all interpersonal aspects that can have an influence on the way the participants use language. In the literature dealing with register, we can find different suggestions both for the subdimensions of tenor and the related terminology, but three aspects are mentioned most frequently: the agentive roles the discourse participants take, the power relations between them and the social distance that underlies the interaction (Halliday & Hasan, 1985, p. 57; Hasan, 1999, p. 233; Lukin, 2010, pp. 100–101; Lukin, Moore, Herke, Wegener, & Wu, 2011, pp. 199–201; Neumann, 2013, pp. 61–2; Poynton, 1989, pp. 76–7; Steiner, 2004, p. 17). A fourth dimension that is sometimes added is that of affect or appraisal (cf. e.g. Martin, 1992, pp. 533–7; Neumann, 2013, p. 61).

The concept of agentive roles draws on the assumption that in every interaction, certain parts need to be played. These parts are not arbitrary, but which ones are needed depends on the situation itself. When we buy bread in a bakery, the participants take the roles of buyer and seller, during a lecture, we have a lecturer and an audience. In some settings, roles can shift between participants in the course of an interaction, for instance when someone from the audience asks a question and is, for a short period of time, the main speaker.

For newspapers, the roles taken are very static. The author's role is given and cannot be shifted to the reader for any period of time. Also, the author is the only participant whose language is visible to us, so the readers and the roles they take are unknown. For these reasons, we will not include this subdimension in our analysis, but some parts of it influence the subdimension dealing with the power relations, as we will see below.

Another critical aspect is appraisal. News items are often claimed to be objective, but evaluation can take place on various levels, and not all of these are easily detected. Martin (1992) and Martin and White (2005) formulate taxonomies for evaluation in language, but because it can lie in such small details, a meaningful analysis needs to look at the immediate context of a potentially evaluative utterance to avoid misinterpretation. In other words, a qualitative analysis would be required, because the exact linguistic features for evaluative language are hard to operationalize in more general terms.

This makes an in-depth examination of appraisal difficult for our corpus. However, the expression of evaluation has often been found to be closely connected to the construction of solidarity (e.g. Drasovean & Tagg, 2015; Martin, 2004), which in turn is related to the subdimension of social distance (Halliday & Matthiessen, 2014, p. 35; Martin, 1992, p. 525). Although we will not use any taxonomy to distinguish between different types of evaluation, we will at least look at obvious instances, like the frequency of boosters and minimizers, in this context.

As we can see, the subdimensions of the tenor are a little less clear-cut than the ones for field. We will work with two: the social distance and the social role relationship. In the next two sections, we will define what exactly we understand by these categories, and how they are represented in our analysis.

5.2.1 Social role relationship

The first subdimension we will consider is the one dealing with all aspects of power between communicative partners. We can find different names for this concept. It is often referred to as "social hierarchy" (e.g. Bowcher, 1999; Halliday & Hasan, 1985; Hasan, 2009b, 2009a; Scott, 2011; Steiner, 2004), but, as Neumann (2013, p. 64) argues, this is problematic when looking at written texts, because the term *hierarchy* defines a relationship between two points that are known. Another name for this subdimension is "status" (Martin, 1992), which can easily be applied to only one party of an interaction, but does not reflect the idea of relating the participants, which is the essence of the parameter of tenor. The term "social role relationship" (Neumann, 2013; Steiner, 2004) covers this, and suggests a less absolute or given nature of power than hierarchy.

Like we said above, we cannot know anything about the roles the readers have in mind for themselves – we can only treat them as the addressees of the text produced by a journalist. We cannot define any hierarchical structures. What we can see, however, is the role the journalists have in mind for their audience. In other words, we have to consider a constructed role for the addressees, and the term "social role relationship" covers this concept best.

Whichever term is used, the question remains how power is reflected in language. Power relations can be influenced by various aspects of both natural and artificial origin. On the one hand, characteristics like age, gender or race can contribute to the hierarchical structures between people. These are beyond our control and are often called "ascribed roles" (H. M. Johnson, 1966, p. 140). On the other hand, we take on "achieved roles", which are aspects we can influence, such as education, profession and expertise. These two types condition each other, depending on the society within which we move, but for most of the authors of the texts we are analyzing, the ascribed roles are not known. The achieved ones, too, are largely unknown, but we can work with some basic assumptions.

Halliday and Hasan (1985, p. 57) argue that "the degree of control (or power) one participant is able to exercise over the other(s)" is mainly predefined by the agentive roles they hold. In our case, this means that readers read a newspaper to get information from the journalists, and that already implies that in terms of expertise and authority, these journalists have to be superior. They know something the reader does not, and are in a position to pass on the information. We said above that the agentive roles in a newspaper setting are static, and we can define them as "expert/information giver" on the one and "reader/information seeker" on the other end. It is exclusively the journalists who control to what degree they construct their superiority in terms of knowledge; the output can vary immensely and influence the image of the journalists' own role as experts as well as the presumed role of the readers.

Of course, the only tool a journalist has to work with regarding this mechanism is language; and again we move to the lexico-grammatical level to trace it. Poynton (1989, pp. 8, 75, 81) names three linguistic features: mood, modality and reciprocity. The last one is relevant for spoken discourse, but can be left aside in a one-sided, written communication. **MODALITY** is quite straightforward. The use of modal verbs relates to weakening a statement, making it less definite (Fest, 2021, p. 283; Poynton, 1989, pp. 71, 79) or signaling uncertainty about a topic or piece of information (Neumann, 2013, p. 66). This reduces the constructed expertise of the author and is an important feature to include in our analysis.

Regarding **MOOD**, we can say that imperatives, especially, are a clear indicator of being in control. Interrogatives can be interpreted in different ways, either as signaling equality by asking for somebody else's opinion, or as an implicit imperative, which might be preferable, for instance for subordinate speakers (Neumann, 2013, p. 65; Poynton, 1989, p. 71). In the case of newspaper writing, both are possible, but due to the one-sided character of the situation and the difference in time and space between text production and reception, it is unlikely that an interrogative is really meant to trigger an answer. Instead, interrogatives can be used to make the readers think about and possibly challenge their beliefs and opinions, somewhat resembling the function they have in literature (Fest, 2015b, p. 59; Krings, 2003, p. 151; Wenzel, 2015, p. 28). Another purpose questions can have is to introduce a new topic or to lead over to a new piece of information. Whether they increase or reduce authority and superiority is difficult to generalize and depends on the individual cases. Since questions are rare in newspaper writing, we will include qualitative spot checks in our analysis of mood to define this feature more closely.

Another linguistic marker that has been linked to the construction of expertise is the use of technical terminology (Neumann, 2013, p. 66), because by definition this requires knowledge of a topic. Journalists are advised to use this as little as possible to make news accessible to a large audience (e.g. Keeble, 2006, p. 99; Pape & Featherstone, 2005, p. 27), so for the purpose of our study, we will need to modify this operationalization. Every news domain is set apart by certain keywords which are more relevant in that domain than in others: like *match* and *season* in sports news or *bank* and *stocks* in economy. This does not necessarily mark them as technical terms in a general sense, but the more words are key for a domain, the more that domain displays what we can call language for specific purposes. So instead of determining whether individual terms are technical or not – a decision which would be highly subjective and influenced by the researchers' own expertise in a field – we will look at the **AMOUNT OF KEYWORDS** that set the categories apart.

5.2.2 Social distance

Social distance, as part of tenor, is the subdimension for which we can find most suggestions regarding its linguistic representation. It describes "the frequency and the range of previous interaction" (Hasan, 1978, p. 231) – in other words, how often and for how long the participants have been in touch before. As Lukin (2010, p. 101) points out, when the addressee is imaginary, as in newspaper discourse, we must assume the social distance in this sense to be maximal, because we simply cannot know if the participants have ever met, let alone where and how often.

This aspect of this subdimension is reflected in the term "contact", which some scholars (e.g. Martin, 1992; Poynton, 1989) use instead of "distance". The subdimension includes another perspective, however, which is independent of direct personal contact. People can share backgrounds, for instance by coming from the same country or town, having attended the same school, being supporters of the same sports club or having the same profession, which connects them without ever having spoken to each other. This is reflected in the term "solidarity", which is used by R. Brown and Gilman

(1960) and has been connected to the abstract idea of social distance in SFL (e.g. Halliday & Matthiessen, 2014, p. 35; Martin, 1992, pp. 523–5; Martin & White, 2005, pp. 30, 35). Steiner (2004, p. 18) offers a definition which covers both sides and describes social distance as "the degree to which the contextual space is shared by participants". It is this definition that we will rely on for our study.

For the previous subdimension, the social role relationship, we saw that the one-sided character of the discourse means that the control over this variable lies with the journalist alone. This is the case for social distance, too. Journalists cannot know whether they have anything in common with their readers, i.e. share any bit of background with them, but they can make assumptions based on the fact that readers choose to read a specific article. If, for instance, a reader decides to read a report on a sports match, it is a safe guess that they are interested in sports. If somebody picks a news item on health, books or the stock exchange, this most likely reflects their priorities and interests as well. Because the reading of newspapers is a deliberately chosen action, newspaper journalists can work with the idea that they have an audience that actively selects topics that are of interest to them, which provides a basic common ground.

This process takes place before the actual reading of the article has even begun and is located on a personal level which cannot easily be influenced by the author. But there are other mechanisms that can be used to create (the image of) a shared background in the text itself. A good example of this is the construction and prominence of certain news values; readers feel more concerned by events happening in places that are geographically or culturally near to them (Bednarek & Caple, 2014, pp. 155–6; Fowler, 1991, pp. 13–14; Harcup, 2005, p. 30; Kolodzy, 2006, pp. 60–61), so creating the impression of proximity increases the sense of closeness. In contrast to selecting news of interest, this effect of regulating the social distance unfolds within the text and is perfectly under the control of the author, who can use linguistic strategies to employ it.

If we speak of distance and closeness in terms of shared backgrounds, this leads us to the question of how to measure it. Backgrounds cannot simply be counted, there is no inherent scale to this concept. Martin (1992, p. 531) contrasts involved and uninvolved contact, but refers mainly to spoken interaction. Poynton (1989) distinguishes between task-oriented and person-oriented texts. This links back to the idea of goal orientation but, as we saw above, the difference is not clear in news writing, where a person, e.g. a celebrity or politician, can themselves be the topic of interest. Neumann (2013) suggests a taxonomy of neutral, casual and consultative style to reflect differences in distance. For our purposes, the first two are of particular interest, yet should be seen not as absolute categories, but rather as a continuum along which texts can move. We will therefore work with the concept of a scale ranging from casual to formal style.

There are many suggestions for a potential operationalization. Casual style reflects a low social distance and a tendency to be reader-oriented, and a formal style is characterized by a more neutral, less personal language use. In more concrete terms, this can be mirrored in **PLACE REFERENCES** as markers of closeness, frequent use of **1ST AND 2ND PERSON PRONOUNS** to involve the reader, a focus on active rather than passive **VOICE** to include an actor, and the use of **NOMINALIZATIONS** (Bartsch, 2009, p. 112; Biber, 1988, pp. 73–75; Neumann, 2012, p. 86; 2013, pp. 67–71; Steiner, 2004, p. 18). All of these markers can be traced on the lexico-grammatical level, and will be included in our analysis.

Also, as we said when introducing tenor of discourse, evaluative language plays a role in constructing closeness. Some scholars (e.g. Martin & White, 2005, p. 30) associate evaluation with the dimension of social role relationship on the basis that it implies "who can express feelings and who can't". In a one-sided communicative situation, though, this does not reflect hierarchy or control – the journalists are the only ones who can express emotions, simply because they are the only ones who express anything at all. Nevertheless, the journalists are not entirely free in their judgment, but have to keep in mind that they must not lose their audience. Rather than expressing a particular opinion in an unfiltered way, evaluative language is a means to seek or increase approval and build solidarity. In our case, evaluative language therefore fits into this subdimension

As it cannot be analyzed reliably in an automatized way, we will include only one linguistic feature to trace it, namely that of **BOOSTERS AND MINIMIZERS**. Different studies (e.g. Benamara, Cesarano, Picariello, Reforgiato, & Subrahmanian, 2007, p. 2; Biber et al., 1999, pp. 564–7; Eggins & Martin, 1997, pp. 231–2; Matsumoto, Hwang, & Sandoval, 2015, p. 232) provide lists of adverbs that fulfil these functions. For our analysis, we will work with the following:

- **Boosters:** *absolutely, completely, entirely, exceedingly, extremely, fully, immensely, more, most, really, thoroughly, totally, utterly, very*
- **Minimizers:** *barely, fairly, hardly, just, merely, nearly, only, pretty, quite, relatively, scarcely, simply, slightly*

Of course, there are many other adverbs that can have a similar effect; the precise meaning often depends on the exact context in which the word is used. We decided on the ones above because their meanings have been found to vary very little, and they can be analyzed quantitatively without the risk of including too many false hits in the results.

5.3   Mode of discourse

The last variable that defines the situational context is the mode of discourse. It asks "what part the language is playing, what it is that the participants are expecting the language to do for them in that situation" (Halliday & Hasan, 1985, p. 12).

To capture this, Halliday and Matthiessen (2014, pp. 33–4) name six aspects of mode. Two deal with the degree to which individual linguistic, social and semiotic activities play a role in a situation, while the other four cover the orientation towards the variables of field and tenor, the text structure, the medium and the channel. Neumann (2013) and Steiner (2004) also work with medium and channel, but summarize the other concepts under the heading of language role.

Language role defines how central language is in order to successfully complete an interaction. To achieve a desired outcome, we can use different techniques, and language is just one option. We can also use gestures or draw pictures or rely on the institutionalization of a situation. If, for instance, pupils always stand up at the beginning of a lesson when their teacher enters, the mere action of entering will convey the message to the pupils and trigger the desired reaction. This means that language can play an ancillary role, where it plays a minor, supportive part, or a constitutive role, where it is the dominant vehicle for a successful interaction (Halliday & Hasan, 1985; Hasan, 1999; Neumann, 2013; Steiner, 2004).

In newspaper writing, the case is pretty clear – without language, there is no article. Although multimodal elements like videos or pictures contribute to the overall communication, we focus only on text. We will therefore treat language as constitutive and not include language role in our analysis in more detail.

The subdimension of channel is a similar case. It describes "the physical conditions of the communication" (Neumann, 2013, p. 75) and is defined as either graphic or phonic (Halliday & Hasan, 1985, p. 58; Halliday & Matthiessen, 2014, p. 33; Hasan, 1999, p. 282), meaning that it is perceived by the addressee either visually or acoustically. In the present study, all articles were taken from the newspapers' websites and are brought to the reader in the form of (digitally) printed text. There is no variation in this aspect between the articles – the channel is always graphic, and the subdimension plays no further part in our analysis. This leaves us with the third subdimension, medium, which we will look at in more detail now.

5.3.1 Medium

For the concept of medium, we distinguish between spoken and written, but it is located on a more linguistic level than the difference between phonic and graphic channel (Halliday & Hasan, 1985, p. 58; Halliday & Matthiessen, 2014, p. 33; Neumann, 2013, pp. 75–6). Rather than the physical properties of a text, the medium can be said to capture its style, and the categories "spoken" and "written" work as end points of a scale.

Why is this relevant for newspaper writing? Journalistic writing is a very conscious process, and articles undergo several cycles of editing by various people before being published. Tendencies towards either end of the spoken–written scale are not random, but contribute to and influence the whole text and reflect the context of its production. Nonetheless, we need to be a bit more specific.

The differences between spoken and written language, which underlie the assumptions of typical styles of the two categories, are located on various linguistic levels. Some can be found on the overall structure of an interaction; spoken language, especially when it is dialogic, contains turn-taking and interruptions, which are not present in written language. Also, the entire range of phonological properties, such as speed, paratones and intonation, is exclusive to spoken discourse. These aspects do not need to be considered further in our study because, for a compilation of written texts only, there can be no variation on these levels. But there are differences on the lexico-grammatical level which are of interest to us.

The focus lies on the lexis: spoken language has been found to contain more **CONTRACTIONS** and **SENTENCE-INITIAL COORDINATORS** than written language. In addition, we can find more **PRONOUNS** of all types in spoken discourse, whereas a written style is characterized by a frequent use of **NOUNS AND NOMINALIZATIONS** (Biber et al., 1999, pp. 81–92, 33; Eggins, 1994, pp. 56–7; Neumann, 2012, p. 78; 2013, pp. 75–8; Steiner, 2004, p. 20).

These markers will be examined in our analysis, and are of course reflected in the **LEXICAL DENSITY** – more pronouns and coordinators in contrast to more nouns automatically create a density gap between the categories of spoken and written. We will include this summarizing feature, but make it more meaningful by combining it with a more detailed examination of the distribution of individual **WORD CLASSES**.

5.4 Summary of the operationalization

All in all, we will work with five subdimensions to represent the variables of field, mode and tenor of discourse, and analyze twenty linguistic features on the level of lexico-grammar. Some of these features overlap; pronouns, lexical density, mood and nominalizations occur under different subdimensions. This is simply due to the fact that linguistic choices hardly ever have just one effect, but originate from and reflect different aspects of the production context. Assigning a feature to more than one dimension is unavoidable, but, as we saw in the previous sections, what part of a feature is relevant for the respective category can vary. The analysis will, for instance, not always contain all pronouns, but be more specific. Table 1 summarizes all linguistic markers included in our study.

Table 1 Operationalization – Overview

Parameter	Subdimension	Linguistic indicators
Field of Discourse	Experiential Domain	Vocabulary Tense Lexical density Expressions of time
	Goal Orientation	Type / token ratio (TTR) Declarative mood 3rd person pronouns
Tenor of Discourse	Social Role Relationship	Interrogative and imperative mood Modality Number of keywords
	Social Distance	Boosters and minimizers 1st and 2nd person pronouns Place references Voice Nominalizations
Mode of Discourse	Medium	Pronominal use Sentence-initial coordinators Contractions Nominalizations Lexical density / Distribution of word classes

6 Corpus Design

Throughout the previous chapters of this book, the corpus for this study has been mentioned several times. In total, the set contains 4,000 articles and ~2.4 million tokens. It is the aim of this chapter to describe the data set in more detail and explain what is included and why.

Biber (1993, p. 243) criticizes the fact that many studies that work with corpora are not careful or precise enough when defining what their collection is supposed to represent. In the worst case, this means that the corpus does not fit the research questions that are being asked, and that the interpretations drawn from the results are not valid. To avoid this, he suggests an exact definition of the target group, in other words, a clear-cut description of what the corpus is supposed to represent, then basing the actual sampling on this foundation. For our corpus, many decisions had to be made and limitations had to be overcome, which made such a structured approach even more crucial. In the following sections, we will trace this path as suggested by Biber, from target population to sampling frame to the final sampling technique and completion.

6.1 Target population

The target population is the starting point when we set out to compile a new data set. To define it as precisely as possible, Biber (1993, p. 243) names two variables: "(1) the boundaries of the population – what texts are included and excluded from the population; (2) hierarchical organization within the population – what text categories are included in the population, and what are their definitions".

Our research aim itself – a combination of comparisons of functional and regional variation in newspaper writing – points the way to define the boundaries of the population. To serve the purpose, the corpus has to represent different varieties of native and L2 origin as well as a range of thematic domains. Since we focus on a synchronic perspective, the texts are to be recent, and of course come from the discourse area of newspaper journalism.

Within these broad categories, hierarchical structures were implemented, but we work with only two levels. On the higher level, thematic domains and regional varieties provide the two axes along which we can move. Each text in the corpus is assigned a value corresponding to its position respective to each axis, i.e. the thematic domain and regional variety it comes from. On the lower level, other aspects of meta-information were added to allow for further distinctions so that, for every text, we can determine the author, newspaper, year of publication and newspaper type. These elements will not constitute crucial variables for the analysis itself, but they further specify the target population and help to find an adequate sampling frame.

6.2 Sampling and representativeness

The sampling frame is the next step on the way to the final data set and can be seen as an operationalization of the target population. What we defined above is very general, and cannot be sampled in its entirety. It is the job of the sampling frame to narrow this down to a level where we can really decide on specific texts to collect. For this, we look at every aspect of the target population and translate it to concrete variables.

6.2.1 Varieties

The first variable is that of regional variation. We chose to include native and L2 varieties, and there are plenty of both. To make sure that we will not come to wrong generalizations and always have a control group ready, every category should be represented by at least two specimens.

In the case of the L2 varieties, some restrictions were encountered simply by the availability of newspaper articles or the existence of newspapers published in English. Of the ones where sampling was possible to a sufficient degree, Kenya and Hong Kong were picked because of their diverse historical developments. As we saw in Chapter 2, English was introduced in these regions with very different intentions. Also, Hong Kong saw a fairly peaceful, but late handover from British rule, whereas Kenya faced a violent transition several decades earlier. Despite the differences, both English varieties show signs of nativization in terms of Schneider's (2007) model and are categorized as phase three varieties. This means that they provide contrasts as well as resemblances, which makes them an ideal choice to represent L2 varieties in our corpus.

Regarding the native varieties, there were fewer restrictions in terms of available newspapers, and of course fewer varieties to choose from. British English was set as the origin of the language in Hong Kong and Kenya, and US-American English was included due to its influence today. Especially in popular culture, the US-American variety of English is dominant, and in combination with the country's political and economic relevance, an influence on other speakers is very likely. Lastly, Australian English was included as a third native variety, because it is geographically closer to Hong Kong than the other two, and closer to Kenya than the USA. It is also connected to Britain via the Commonwealth of Nations. From the point of view of news values, Australia should therefore play a role in the news in these regions, and is of course also a potential source of linguistic influence on the L2 varieties.

6.2.2 Domains

The second main category that is represented in the corpus is the one reflecting the functional variation in the form of thematic domains. To keep the varieties comparable, the data set contains only those domains that could be found in all newspapers. In concrete terms this means sports news, hard news, lifestyle, economy and politics.

We mentioned in Chapter 3 that not all of these labels are self-explanatory, and we will briefly define how we understand them in the analysis to come. The most clearly defined domain is that of sports news, because the topic is specific and precise, and most newspapers, both in print and online, have separate sections for it. The domain is diverse in that it deals with various sports, but patterns can be found when articles deal with teams or individual athletes, or match days or tournaments. The sampling of the articles from this domain did not stratify in terms of sports in any way, but was purely random in this regard.

The second domain to be examined here, that of lifestyle, is much more diverse in its content, but easily distinguishable, too. In newspapers, the respective sections are usually called either "Lifestyle" or "Life & Style", and the range of topics is as broad as the label itself. In this category, we can find articles about health, beauty, wellness, fashion and social issues, to name but a few (Harcup, 2005, p. 119); but, despite this diversity, this domain shows a pattern in that it foregrounds particular news values. Often, the topics covered are not as directly bound to being recent as those in other domains, because they remain relevant independent of any particular event or happening. Instead, personal involvement plays a major role and articles are often centered around people or characters and their stories.

The three remaining domains in the corpus, economy, politics and hard news, are not as clear-cut as the other two. For hard news, especially, an exact definition is hard to find. Shoemaker and Cohen (2006) distinguish it from other news on the basis of timeliness, and Curran, Iyengar, Brink Lund, and Salovaara-Moring (2009) use the perspective of the story as the main characteristic that sets it apart. Others use the topic as an indicator (e.g. Granato, 2002; K. Schneider, 1999). In all cases, articles about politics or economy for instance are included in this category, but most newspapers analyzed here had separate labels for these fields.

This of course is natural, as many topics simply fall into two or more categories. Political and economic news, especially, often overlap; and even sports news can contain financial aspects or elements of crime. In turn, athletes or clubs – but also politicians – can be a focus in the lifestyle section. So as not to confuse the domains in our study, we will work with the categorizations given by the newspapers themselves. Articles were sampled from the respective areas on the websites, which was clear for sports, lifestyle, politics and economy. Hard news, as the fuzziest category, contains items that were labelled "news", but not sorted into any of these four domains.

6.2.3 Newspapers

We defined for the target population that the functional and regional variations, reflected in the five varieties and five domains, are the highest hierarchical level in the data set, and that the other criteria are subordinate. For the sampling, the question of which newspapers to include is a very relevant one, however, because it directly influences the representativeness of the whole data set.

If only one newspaper is used to represent an entire variety, results are not generalizable, so more newspapers are of course desirable. The papers for this study were chosen on the basis of three criteria, namely that they were (1) published in English; (2) published online (exclusively or in addition to print versions); and (3) published nation-wide to avoid strong influences of regional dialects and accents. In addition, we aimed to represent both quality and popular press by balancing the different newspaper types. Because a definition of these two concepts is very difficult and varies greatly between the regions, this categorization has to be treated with caution; it serves as a basis to ensure more diversity in the corpus, but conclusions to this end will only be drawn in the case of very clear and well-researched newspapers.

Within these boundaries, the number of newspapers to include was set to four per region, because this was the maximum that could be sampled from Kenya, which is represented by the *Star*, the *People*, the *Daily Nation*, and the *Standard*. In the other regions, if more newspapers were available that met the criteria, papers with high circulation numbers were preferred. For Hong Kong, this simply resulted in the four biggest papers: *China Daily HK Edition*, the *Standard*, *South China Morning Post*, and the *Wall Street Journal Asia*.

For the native regions, some further considerations were necessary. In Australia, the additional aspect of ownership was taken into account; at the time of sampling, six of the ten biggest daily newspapers were owned by News Ltd, another three were held by Fairfax Media, and only one, the *West Australian*, was separate (Audit Bureau of Circulations, 2013, pp. 1–2). Articles are sometimes shared between newspapers from the same owner, especially if they come from the same part of the country, which decreases the data diversity. So, in addition to the *West Australian*, the corpus includes the *Sydney Morning Herald* (Fairfax Media) and two News Ltd papers from different regions: the *Herald Sun* (Victoria) and the *Courier Mail* (Queensland).

When we look at the other dimension of comparison, that of regional variation, a difference between the native and the L2 varieties becomes very evident. In all five cases, we can find keywords that relate to the region itself – names of cities, states and politicians – which confirms the assumption that proximity is a frequent news value. In the UK and the USA however, the keyness values are much smaller, which means that the respective terms occur in the news in other regions, too. In contrast, Hong Kong and Kenya hardly feature in the news in the other regions, presumably because they are less influential and present in political and economic terms.

For newspapers representing the UK, the two biggest papers, the *Sun* and the *Daily Mail*, were included. Both of them are generally categorized as popular press (Bednarek, 2007, section 4.1; Conboy, 2006, pp. 7–9; UK Audit Bureau of Circulations, 2015, p. 2). Quality papers have slightly lower circulation numbers, but to ensure a broader range of news types, the *Daily Telegraph* and the *Guardian* were included instead of other larger, but also popular papers.

Finally, the selection for the USA followed a similar pattern. The two biggest national papers, the *Wall Street Journal* and *USA Today* (Alliance for Audited Media, 2013; The State of the News Media, 2012), are usually categorized as quality papers (Boykoff & Boykoff, 2004, p. 127; 2007, p. 1194; Carpenter, 2007, p. 766; Kleinnijenhuis, Schultz, Utz, & Oegema, 2015, p. 7) and were included. The popular category is represented by the *Daily News* and the *New York Post*. Although they are not the next biggest papers in line, they were preferred over other, larger papers tending towards the quality end.

6.2.4 Other specifications

The main parameters of data sampling are set with the definitions described above, but two more specifications were decided on for the sake of representativeness and precision. On the one hand, the target population defined "present-day English". For the sampling, this was interpreted as published between 2000 and 2013. Within this scope, the corpus is not balanced, because a diachronic approach is not our focus.

The second restriction for the sampling frame was defined with regard to the authors involved. Particularly in specialized domains like sports, journalists are often experts in their field and contribute large parts of the articles published in a paper. To prevent bias and overly strong influences of individual styles, no more than three articles from the same author were sampled. This was applied to the whole collection with one exception, the sports domain from *the Standard* (Hong Kong). In this case, only ten articles could be sampled which gave the authors' names, while others simply give news agencies as their sources. Because no other articles were available, these were included to complete the category.

6.3 Annotation and mark-up

The last aspect to discuss regarding the corpus design is the annotation. The data was annotated on a structural and a linguistic level to allow computational analyses.

First of all, every article was given a header in XML format which includes meta-information on its title, author(s), newspaper, newspaper type, region, domain, and year of publication. In a second step, the headline was annotated with XML tags. This annotation covers several layers. Every article has a clearly distinguishable headline, which is set apart visually and functions as the title. This headline was tagged as *h1*, but many articles contain other elements which are located in between the title and actual article. In some cases, the format or positioning of these elements indicate that they have a special function which resembles that of a headline; they can be separated from the main body of the text by a line, or have the same color as the headline. Often, they are also in larger font than the rest of the text, but smaller than the main title. In other cases, they are set apart, but not as clearly, for instance when the whole first paragraph is printed in bold.

Most newspapers follow their own styles in this respect, so that it was not always easy to decide what is a headline and what is not. To make the mark-up as systematic as possible, common features defined for headlines were used as a basis. Subheadlines have been found to have a different syntactic structure from the main text, because they are often elliptic and written in present tense, and tend to contain single quotation marks rather than double ones (Bednarek & Caple, 2012b, p. 101; Burger, 2005, pp. 115–20; Conboy, 2007, pp. 13–16). In contrast to this, we can sometimes find the element of an intro, which dives right into the topic and answers the first questions relevant to the story. In many articles, intros start with a place name, often printed in capital letters (Bednarek & Caple, 2012b, pp. 96–100; Burger, 2005, pp. 121–3). Last but not least, a (sub)headline can be followed by an intro, but not the other way round. Occurrences of subheadlines and intros were marked *h2* and *bold* respectively, based on these common characteristics.

For the linguistic annotation, lemmatization and part of speech-tagging were added to the data using the TreeTagger (Schmid, 1994, 1995). Originally, the tagset contained 43 tags (Santorini, 1991), but three further tags were added to improve the reliability of the results for lexical density. The feature measures the relation between content and function words, but especially for adverbs, this distinction is not always clear and it is difficult to call the whole word class either functional or lexical. To separate the items in this word class, all adverbs were subjected to an annotation software which assigns not one, but all parts of speech which a given word has been observed to take and the probabilities of these options (Brysbaert, New, & Keuleers, 2012).

For our purpose, all adverbs with <90% likelihood or being a content word were classified as function words. Some lemmata were not sorted at all, which was due either to variation in spelling or to rarity of the words. These cases, which amounted to 146 in total, were sorted manually. All adverbs defined as function words received a new tag based on the old one – RB (adverb) became RBF, RBR (comparative adverb) became RBRF and RBS (superlative adverb) was changed to RBSF.

6.4 Size and proportions

In summary, the corpus contains texts from five varieties, five domains and 20 newspapers, and is annotated with a tagset consisting of 46 tags. The collection of the texts is not proportional – that, according to Biber (1993), would mean that the distribution of articles across the domains would have to be the same for every newspaper as it is in real life. That is not only impossible to determine, but would also not serve our purpose to make the individual parts comparable.

Instead, every part is represented by an equal number of articles. Within the boundaries of the target population and the sampling frame, this resulted in 4,000 articles in total – 160 for every variety–domain combination, containing 40 from every newspaper from the region. Because the number of articles was taken as a unit for balancing, the parts vary in their amounts of words and tokens. In the analysis, this will be accounted for by working with relative frequencies.

Table 2 Corpus size (articles, words and tokens)[1]

	Economy	Hard News	Lifestyle	Politics	Sports	Σ
Australia	160	160	160	160	160	800
	71,066	54,782	101,356	76,612	80,170	383,986
	78,975	61,217	115,117	85,370	89,768	430,447
Hong Kong	160	160	160	160	160	800
	81,964	64,952	117,602	82,300	86,364	433,182
	91,658	72,583	134,499	91,790	97,237	487,767
Kenya	160	160	160	160	160	800
	65,698	58,354	126,416	74,983	64,736	390,187
	72,391	64,103	141,928	82,535	72,217	433,174
UK	160	160	160	160	160	800
	84,546	82,584	114,133	88,545	99,894	469,702
	94,622	93,582	130,119	99,407	112,298	530,028
USA	160	160	160	160	160	800
	85,238	85,297	117,630	89,072	97,703	474,940
	96,140	97,429	136,926	101,070	111,797	543,362
Σ articles	800	800	800	800	800	4,000
Σ words	388,512	345,969	577,137	411,512	428,867	2,151,997
Σ tokens	433,786	388,914	658,588	460,172	483,317	2,424,777

---

[1] In future tables and figures, the regions and domains will be abbreviated as AUS, HK, KEY, UK and USA, and ECO, HN, LIFE, POL and SPO whenever necessary to ensure readability.

PART III: RESULTS AND WHAT TO LEARN FROM THEM

7 Field of discourse

The following chapters will present the analyses of the individual operationalizations defined in Chapter 5. We will follow the structure of the theoretical framework there and first look at the parameters of field, tenor and mode as well as their respective subdimensions separately.

7.1 Experiential domain

The experiential domain was defined as describing the topic of a text. We operationalized it via the vocabulary, use of tenses, expressions of time and lexical density. Since the vocabulary, analyzed in terms of keywords, is not only valuable in itself, but also points to details that are part of other analyses, we will use this feature as a starting point.

7.1.1 Vocabulary

The vocabulary used in a text is a direct reflection of its main content. In this section, we will work with keyword analyses both across and within the domains and varieties. On the highest level, categories were contrasted with each other, and on the lower level, they were compared within these sections:

- For keywords of individual varieties, the other four varieties combined were used as a reference corpus, e.g. Australia vs UK, USA, Hong Kong and Kenya.
- For keywords of individual domains, the other four domains were used as a reference corpus, e.g. economy vs hard news, politics, sports and lifestyle.
- For keywords of individual domains within one variety, either
  (1) the same domains from the other varieties were used as a reference corpus, e.g. lifestyle from Kenya vs lifestyle from the UK, the USA, Hong Kong and Australia (domain-internal comparison); or

(2) the other domains from the same variety were used as a reference corpus, e.g. lifestyle from Kenya vs the other four domains from Kenya (variety-internal comparison).[1]

Regarding the domains, the lexical patterns that can be seen in the keywords are very clear for economy, politics, sports and hard news. They reflect topics which we expected to be relevant for the respective areas. Apart from these obvious trends, however, there are some differences which indicate characteristics of the domains.

In all domains except lifestyle, most keywords are content words. In lifestyle, on the other hand, pronouns dominate the keyword list. This somewhat contradicts the guideline for journalistic writing to avoid pronouns and use the slots in the text for more information. A reason for this might be that the actors in lifestyle articles are often portrayed as "people like you and me", and less information on them is available or known. Since *you* and *your* are the most prominent pronouns among the keywords, constructing the reader as an actor in the story seems to be common, too. Moreover, these references cannot be replaced easily.

Within the focus on human activity indicated by the pronouns, lifestyle displays another particularity in its emphasis on female actors. *She* and *women* are both key in this domain, but neither word is very frequent in absolute terms, meaning that they are practically non-existent in the other domains.

Looking at the lexical word classes that are represented in the keyword lists, we can see differences, especially with regard to verbs. Economy and politics feature no verbs in their top ten keywords, lifestyle contains *says* and the modal *can*. For hard news, on the other hand, *was* and *were* as forms of *to be*, *said*, *arrested* and *killed* are key, giving the stories in this domain a very active character. Sports news features *win* and *play*, which of course also imply action, but in contrast to the verbs frequent in hard news, locate the events in the present or future rather than the past.

On the level of the keyness values themselves, we can also find differences between the domains. Hard news displays a very high keyness level for *police*, whereas the other keywords, even items like *crime* and *murder*, are fairly moderate in their keyness. This suggests that the involvement of the police is in itself a decisive factor to assign the news story to this domain and makes the story newsworthy, because it increases the news values of impact and relevance (Bednarek & Caple, 2014, p. 156). Lifestyle on the other hand has

---

[1] A detailed overview of the keywords in all 25 cells can be found in appendix 1. All keywords were calculated using AntConc (Anthony 2019). Words with a keyness value of 15.13 (p < 0.0001) or more were considered key.

Table 3 Top ten keywords per domain

Economy

No.	Word	Freq.	Keyness	No.	Word	Freq.	Keyness
1	market	1,294	2,718	6	its	1,866	1,565
2	per	1,471	2,058	7	shares	528	1,512
3	cent	1,291	2,026	8	investors	575	1,444
4	billion	1,000	1,998	9	stock	510	1,427
5	bank	833	1,732	10	growth	645	1,292

Hard News

No.	Word	Freq.	Keyness	No.	Word	Freq.	Keyness
1	police	2,118	5,681	6	were	1,878	1,071
2	was	4,382	1,439	7	court	773	1,029
3	murder	422	1,249	8	said	4,040	972
4	crime	434	1,124	9	arrested	359	955
5	officers	405	1,094	10	killed	382	912

Lifestyle

No.	Word	Freq.	Keyness	No.	Word	Freq.	Keyness
1	you	3,126	2,258	6	she	2,196	773
2	says	2,271	2,073	7	can	1,965	736
3	your	1,376	1,918	8	or	2,101	701
4	I	4,327	924	9	women	781	652
5	my	1,389	824	10	hair	306	587

Politics

No.	Word	Freq.	Keyness	No.	Word	Freq.	Keyness
1	election	1,061	2,871	6	president	887	1,311
2	minister	1,031	2,360	7	political	645	1,274
3	party	1,086	2,309	8	prime	574	1,270
4	Mr	2,343	1,993	9	coalition	363	950
5	government	1,480	1,520	10	labor	410	929

Sports

No.	Word	Freq.	Keyness	No.	Word	Freq.	Keyness
1	team	1,339	2,749	6	coach	563	1,530
2	game	1,034	2,417	7	win	760	1,414
3	players	827	2,001	8	cup	514	1,356
4	season	843	1,910	9	play	681	1,231
5	league	665	1,604	10	match	497	1,105

Table 4 Top ten keywords per variety

Australia

No.	Word	Freq.	Keyness	No.	Word	Freq.	Keyness
1	Australia	724	1,555	6	Abbott	255	687
2	Australian	633	1,482	7	WA	242	673
3	Queensland	234	806	8	Perth	197	641
4	Sydney	284	772	9	Brisbane	180	591
5	labor	359	704	10	Melbourne	246	589

Hong Kong

No.	Word	Freq.	Keyness	No.	Word	Freq.	Keyness
1	China	1,660	3,605	6	Yuan	355	1,085
2	Hong	841	2,233	7	Beijing	407	1,025
3	Kong	840	2,202	8	Li	288	763
4	Chinese	791	1,675	9	mainland	264	740
5	HK	447	1,369	10	percent	427	642

Kenya

No.	Word	Freq.	Keyness	No.	Word	Freq.	Keyness
1	Kenya	1,443	4,607	6	Kenyan	234	697
2	Sh	980	3,268	7	Mombasa	200	683
3	Nairobi	477	1,536	8	Kenyatta	235	657
4	county	590	1,284	9	Uhuru	193	638
5	Ruto	224	734	10	Kenyans	185	588

UK

No.	Word	Freq.	Keyness	No.	Word	Freq.	Keyness
1	Britain	434	846	6	I	3,272	448
2	UK	402	734	7	bn	172	440
3	England	353	489	8	London	363	392
4	labour	261	457	9	Blair	148	385
5	British	364	449	10	Cameron	189	268

USA

No.	Word	Freq.	Keyness	No.	Word	Freq.	Keyness
1	s	6,930	612	6	t	1,805	348
2	u	575	577	7	Berlusconi	148	270
3	York	365	502	8	Knicks	95	269
4	Boston	228	425	9	Weiner	79	239
5	Obama	308	367	10	center	218	230

the lowest keyness values on average, which reflects the broad range of topics covered in this domain.

Of course, keyword analyses only elicit the differences between texts. It should not be forgotten that news across all thematic areas shares similarities which characterize this particular discourse. In our corpus, there are not many such features, but a notable one is that in all domains analyzed here, the verb *say* is the most frequent lexical item. This clearly points at the reporting nature of the texts and the focus on sources and human actors.

When we look at the other dimension of comparison, that of regional variation, a difference between the native and the L2 varieties becomes very evident. In all five cases, we can find keywords that relate to the region itself – names of cities, states and politicians – which confirms the assumption that proximity is a frequent news value. In the UK and the USA however, the keyness values are much smaller, which means that the respective terms occur in the news in other regions, too. In contrast, Hong Kong and Kenya hardly feature in the news in the other regions, presumably because they are less influential and present in political and economic terms.

These trends become clearer when we compare the varieties with a focus on individual domains (see appendix 1). In particular, the USA stands out in terms of regional references; the national reference *US* (split into the keywords *U* and *S* because of its spelling *U.S.*) is key only in the economy domain, whereas in the other domains, more local points, like cities, are key. In sports news, US newspapers refer to teams such as Knicks or Giants instead of places, showing that the readers are assumed to know both the city and the sport the team belongs to (Fest, 2017). This is a strategy unique among the varieties analyzed here; in UK sports news we can find names of individual athletes, but apart from that, the types of sport are more dominant as keywords.

As we said above, the analysis of keywords is a reflection of the most characteristic topics of texts, but also unveils many trends that will be analyzed further in the other analyses, like the use of pronouns, time and place references and word classes. In the next step, we will move away from concrete content to the time span that is relevant in articles.

7.1.2 Tense

The use of tenses is an interesting indicator, because in combination with what we have learned from the keywords about the thematic focus, it shows us within which temporal scope the articles are moving.

Generally speaking, news stories are about something that has already happened (Harcup, 2005, p. 107), and we would assume that descriptions are

72 NEWS ACROSS FIVE CONTINENTS

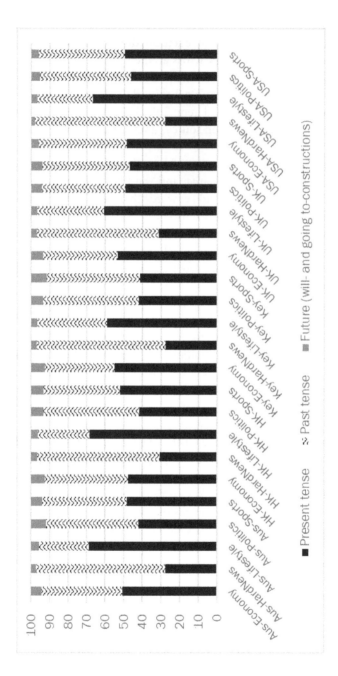

Figure 2 Distribution of tenses

therefore in the past tense, but a look at the distribution of the tenses proves that it is not quite that simple. The past tense is the most frequent tense in use, but present tense verbs are common as well, and most importantly, the domains show very different tendencies, so that there is no generalization for news as such. Instead, we can see similar patterns across all varieties.

In all five regions, hard news articles contain the highest amount of past tense constructions. The domains of economy, politics and sports are close together in their use of tenses, whereas lifestyle contains more present tense than past tense verbs across the board. This confirms what we already assumed looking at the keywords, namely that the topics in lifestyle articles are more diverse and less dependent on recency. The dominance of personal pronouns, which we discussed in the last section, strengthens this assumption. Topics in this domain appear to be aimed more at the readers than at passing on current information, and can be formulated in the present tense because their content does not become outdated very quickly. In contrast to that, hard news, which deals with crimes, disasters and court happenings, is usually focused on reporting past events.

Although all varieties have this distribution of the domains in common, we can see noteworthy differences in the degree to which this variation is expressed. This difference is created mainly by the lifestyle articles, whereas hard news displays similar values for use of tenses in all five regions. The discrepancy between hard news as one end of the scale and lifestyle as the other is narrowest in newspapers from Kenya and the UK. Here, the two domains differ by 31.35 and 29.73 percentage points respectively for their use of past tense. In the other varieties, the differences are greater: in Hong Kong we observe 37.77 percentage points, in the USA 40.1, and for Australia the difference amounts to 42.64. These three varieties can therefore be said to include much more internal variation between the domains than Kenya and the UK.

Of course, different structural elements that appear in newspaper articles can have varying influences on the distribution of tenses. Our dataset is not annotated for an in-depth analysis of direct quotes, but it is likely that these contain present tense verbs to a considerable degree. The same holds true for headlines, for which present tense has been identified as a characteristic, as we saw in Chapter 6. In the headlines in our corpus, present tense verbs make up 78.9% of all finite verbs. These of course influence the temporal scope defined in an article, but since their length is limited, this influence is restricted, too.

Apart from past and present tense, we can observe a small number of future structures in our data. *Going to*-constructions are nearly non-existent, the median value for every category is 0. *Will*-constructions occur more frequently, but the highest amount, found in Kenyan sports articles, is still only at 8.18%. This might mean that future references are rare, but it could also be an indication that potential references are realized differently, for instance by adverbs of time. Before we draw any deeper conclusions, we will therefore look at expressions of temporal references in our next section.

7.1.3 Expressions of time

What we call "expressions of time" here is not a closed or narrowly defined word class. Temporal references can be expressed in many ways, and their meaning is dependent on the context in which they are used. A set list is difficult to define, but for the purpose of a quantitative analysis, we of course need a list of terminology to work with, and several suggestions can be found in the literature.

Many temporal references are constituted by adjectives and adverbs. Biber et al. (1999, pp. 552–3) distinguish four ways for an adverb to express meanings of time, in terms of position, frequency, duration, and relationship. For the investigation of the field of discourse, adverbs that refer to a position in time are most relevant, because they define the concrete times to which an article refers and determine the scope of the news story. Of the adverbs listed by Biber et al. (1999, p. 561) as the most frequent ones, *now*, *today*, *ago* and *yesterday* are of most interest to us. To this list we will add *tomorrow*, *last*, *previous* and *next*.

These expressions differ from each other in two important aspects. First, some – namely *yesterday*, *now*, *today* and *tomorrow* – carry their meaning alone, whereas the others only unfold it in combination with their collocates. For this second group, collocation lists were used before the analysis to distinguish the relevant temporal uses from other constructions. Based on these, the relevant collocates were defined, and our analysis will include the following combinations:

- *last* + [year|week|month|night|season]
- *next* + [year|week|month|season]
- *previous* + [year|month|week]
- [year|week|month|decade|day] + *ago*

The second major difference between these expressions is the scope they cover. *Now* and *today* are closest to the time at which the article is presumably read. *Yesterday*, *tomorrow* and the singular *day* followed by *ago* move within one day of the article. *Week*, *month*, *year* and even *decade* refer to ever larger time frames, either in the past or the future. To adequately capture these differences, we will look both at the temporal orientation and the time span covered.

Of course, all of these constructions can be used in different ways: they can rely on the time of the article as a reference point, which is what we are interested in here, but also draw on some other point in time previously defined in the article. *Previous year*, for instance, can refer to the year previous to now, but also previous to some other reference point that can be further in the past, or also in the future, depending on how the journalist structures the article in question. Since an analysis of these differences would require a manual examination of every instance of these terms, for the purpose of this investigation they will be generalized as references to the past, present or future respectively.

To begin with, we will take a look at temporal references with a narrow scope of the day of the article and the one before and after. The combination *day ago* does not occur in our dataset. Figure 3 shows the distribution of *today*, *yesterday* and *tomorrow*.

Again, we can see much more variation based on function than on region. The past and present are the dominant references, but with regard to the domains, lifestyle again stands out as containing fewer references in total than the other domains. Within lifestyle, *today* is most frequently used, but because recency was so far found not to play a major role in this category, it stands to reason that *today* in these articles has a broader meaning in the sense of "nowadays" or "in our time".

Sports news, too, includes *today* as the most frequent reference point. In this domain, *tomorrow* is also more frequent than elsewhere, which indicates that in this case, we really look at a temporal scope rather than a broader meaning. The dominance of *today* can be traced back to match reports, which are often brief but published right after a match. The future orientation hints at the particularity that in sports news, future events (like upcoming tournaments, matches, seasons etc.) are often scheduled far ahead and can easily be announced, in contrast to crimes or stock exchange developments, for instance.

The other domains show less consistent results across the regions. In hard news articles, references to the past dominate, which shows that the temporal dimension is highly relevant in this domain. Stories under this headline are reported directly on the next day, and since hard news also contains most references in absolute numbers, a general assignment of times to happenings appears crucial. Nonetheless, there are differences in hard news depending on where it comes from: the trend towards the past day is particularly strong in Kenya and Hong Kong, whereas in Australia, the present is equally represented.

This regional characteristic can be observed in political news, too, but might be influenced by factors outside the immediate context of language production. A better internet infrastructure within the country allows articles to be put online faster, i.e. on the same day. The fact addressed in Chapter 6,

76 NEWS ACROSS FIVE CONTINENTS

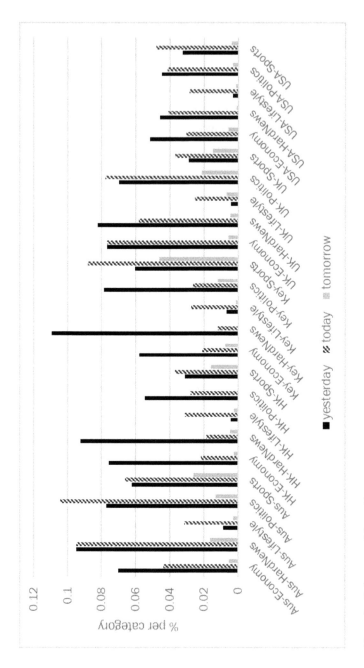

Figure 3 References of time – Narrow scope

that many news outlets share articles because they are owned by the same corporation, is another potential impact on the publication speed. Since Australia did not stand out much in terms of tense, we can assume references to be to events earlier the same day.

In contrast to these narrow scopes, we have the units *week*, *month* and *year* representing points further away in time. Figure 4 shows the frequencies of these items as a collocate of next, previous, last or ago, to exclude meanings of absolute duration, like "the suspect was sentenced to six years in jail".

With the exception of two domains in Kenya – hard news and politics – the lemma *year* appears most frequently. Since it already occurred in the keyword lists, this is not a surprise, but it shows that journalists often contextualize news by referring to previous, but related events.

The precise scopes that the three items most often describe vary slightly. *One* is the most frequent amount for all three. In addition, *year* sometimes refers to two or three years, but also to round numbers like 10, 50 or 100. *Week* is often combined with *two*, whereas *month* often describes a time frame of six months, and in a few cases 12 months as an alternative formulation to *year*.

In terms of variation, we can see that the domain of economy diverges in its use of *year*. This is no coincidence, but originates to some degree from the set terms *fiscal year* and *financial year*. In Hong Kong, this is particularly frequent, which shows the importance of the relation between the use of English and the field of economy.

One lexical combination which has not yet been mentioned is *this* + [year|month|week]. Regarding the scope, it depends on the item following it, but in most cases refers to the year/month/week in which the article was written. Defining its temporal direction is very difficult, which is probably the strongest reason for its use in news writing. The construction puts the emphasis on the relation to the present time, and not on how far away something is, making whatever is being reported much more relevant to readers. *This week* for instance is not preferable to a reference with a narrow scope, like *yesterday*, but contributes to the news value of recency much more effectively than *six days ago* does. It is therefore not surprising that *this* occurs most frequently with *year*; a story that happened several months ago sounds old and decreases in relevance, and something that will happen in half a year is still very far away, but the inclusion of *this* puts both frames into perspective to the current time.

How are the categories oriented in time in overarching terms, independent of the scope? If we combine all results and sort them by past, present and future references, we get the summarized distribution shown in Figure 5.

78 NEWS ACROSS FIVE CONTINENTS

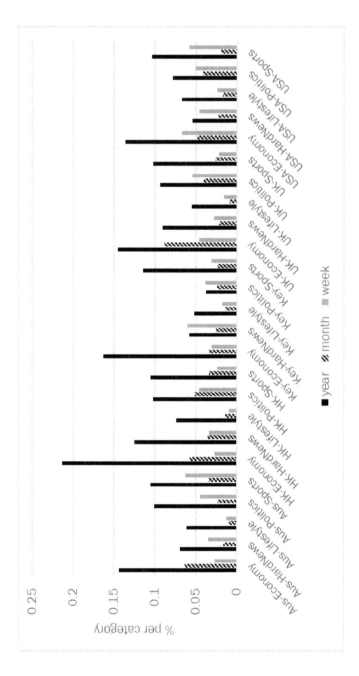

Figure 4 References of time – Wider scope

FIELD OF DISCOURSE 79

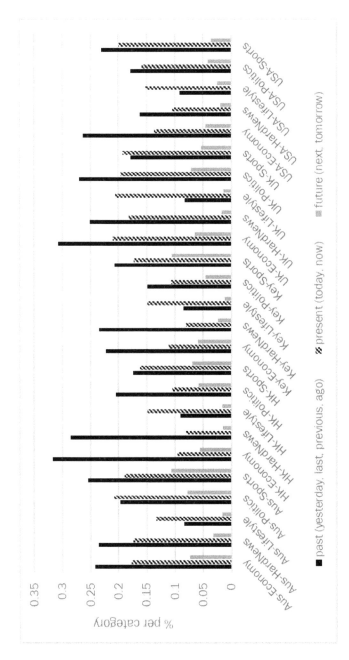

Figure 5 References of time – General

For lifestyle and hard news articles, the tendency towards present and past references respectively is confirmed. Hard news no longer contains the highest overall number of temporal references, however; they make up 1.94% of all word tokens in this domain, whereas for economy, they amount to 2.1%. Economic news also displays a clear orientation towards the past in this bigger picture, and political and sports news follow this trend, although not as clearly.

For sports news, the references to the future also increase when *next* is included in the count. This is due to collocations with *season*, which is exclusively used in this domain and has a very specific meaning in many areas of sports, defining as concrete a time span as the other items *year*, *month* and *week*.

The regions, as was said above, show less variation overall than the domains, yet we can see some patterns in the internal distribution. The domains show similar trends in Kenya and Hong Kong and are closest to that observable for the USA. These three varieties also display the lowest total values of references with 1.61%, 1.8% and 1.87% respectively, whereas Australia and the UK have 2.1% and 2.3%.

7.1.4   Lexical density

The last operationalization of the experiential domain is lexical density. In contrast to the previous linguistic markers, this is more general and does not reflect the precise content in detail. Instead, it gives insight into the amount of information that is contained in an article by defining the proportions taken by function and content words. To adequately interpret lexical density, it should be kept in mind that the value is dependent to some degree on the length of a text. Shorter texts tend towards high lexical density, because repetitions are rarer and some function words, like pronouns, are therefore less frequent and necessary. For the current dataset, a Pearson's correlation test reveals a correlation of $r = -0.28$ between article length and lexical density.

Looking at the distribution of lexical density, the domains of economy, hard news and politics have the most constant values across the five regions, with average numbers of content words of 61.7%, 60.69% and 61.17% respectively. Lifestyle and sports are close together, too, with averages of 59.44% and 58.91%, but once again stand out because they show a lot more internal variation.

Within lifestyle, news from Kenya shows the lowest median for the density value, and is also responsible for the biggest range between highest and lowest density in this domain. Here, as well as for lifestyle articles in general, we can see that in contrast to news items from other domains, they show hardly any outliers and also feature fairly centrally positioned medians. The density values therefore are widespread, but evenly distributed. If we take into

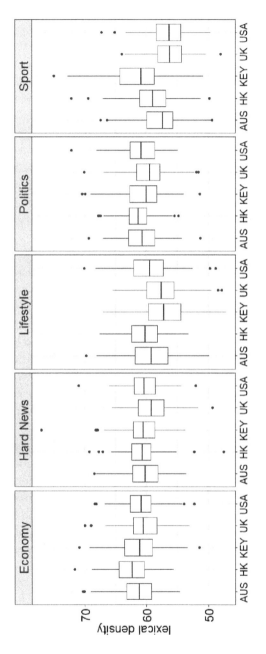

Figure 6 Lexical density – Distribution

consideration what we learned from the keyword analysis, this is interesting because pronouns, which were significantly frequent in lifestyle articles, would of course lower the lexical density value. Based on the pattern visible here, it appears that they are not overly frequent in all articles, but that depending on the exact topic, content words are more dominant. Once again, this hints at the diversity of topics in this domain, which clearly sets it apart.

The most divergent domain in terms of lexical density however is sports, and it is in this category where the regions are most clearly distinguished. The USA and the UK are very close with median values of 57.4 (range: 16.6) and 56.8 (range: 15.6), and Australia is only slightly higher (58), although it shows a wider range (17.1). The L2 varieties on the other hand have higher medians (59.5 for Hong Kong and 61.2 for Kenya), but most of all display a much higher internal range. In the case of Hong Kong, this is due to the three outliers – without them, the range is just 15. For Kenya, the one outlier does not change much, and the range is still the highest with 21.4.

Like we said above, lexical density is a fairly general measurement that does not work on the level of the content itself, but a number of conclusions can be drawn nonetheless. First of all, we can summarize that Kenyan news articles are set apart from news from the other regions in terms of lexical density, because they show very few outliers and high ranges in all domains. The only exception to this is observable for hard news, but is caused by one very short article of just 48 words which, due to the correlation of lexical density and text length mentioned above, reaches maximum density levels and raises the average of the whole category. Not counting this extreme outlier, it is safe to say that Kenya is the variety with the highest internal variation across the domains.

Regarding functional variation, the low values for lifestyle and sports articles across the board first of all mean that we have lower information density in these domains, but it can also suggest that these articles are more centered around one topic or person. If few actors appear in a story, personal or pronominal references can be included more frequently because the risk of ambiguity is lower and fewer participants have to be introduced to the reader. The same holds true for place references or team names – the fewer entities we have in a story, the more an author can work with pronouns without risking mix-ups.

In addition, the keyword analysis showed a personal dimension directed towards the reader for lifestyle articles, reflected in the use of 1st and 2nd person pronouns. Such pronouns do not lend themselves to the strategy of replacing personal pronouns with pieces of information, which was addressed in Chapter 5.1. If the reader is addressed directly, or the author speaks about themselves, this is a consciously applied mechanism to create closeness. A substitution would decrease the personal involvement. If at all, additional information is added to the pronoun, as in the following example:

[2] Why is there sugar in all these things? Partly, it's because **we, the consumers**, want it. (Leith, 2012, the *Daily Telegraph*; emphasis added)

Leaving out the pronoun *we* in such a statement would turn it into a 3rd person reference to consumers in general. The use of *we* ensures that both readers and authors are included. For such purposes, the pronoun is necessary, and no pieces of information or proper names can replace it without decreasing the interpersonal meaning.

Texts that aim at more personal dimensions are therefore likely to tend towards a lower lexical density, which is confirmed in the case of lifestyle by the pronominal keywords. For sports news, pronouns are among the top ten keywords in Australia, the UK and the USA (see appendix 1), although they are, by far, not as dominant as in lifestyle articles. Since this is already within the range of social relationships between the discourse participants, we will postpone a closer look at 1st and 2nd person pronouns until chapter 8.2 on social distance.

7.2   Goal orientation

The second subdimension of the field of discourse is the goal orientation, which we defined in terms of the orientation towards the goal of informing. The analyses above, most of all that of lexical density, has already provided some insights regarding information in the texts. Here, we will look at the type/token ratio, declarative mood and 3rd person pronouns.

7.2.1   Type/token ratio

The type/token ratio is a measurement of the variation in the vocabulary that is used in a text. It is applied here to examine how wide or narrow the focus of the content in the articles is. Since this refers to stylistic differences, we will use lemma as a base for type in the TTR (cf. e.g. Francis & Kučera, 1982). As with lexical density, there is a correlation between the TTR and the article length – for our dataset, this correlation is $r = -0.76$, i.e. the longer the article, the lower the TTR. The absolute length of articles varies greatly throughout the corpus, but within the individual categories, the range is smaller, so that an average on this level is most useful in terms of type-token-measurement.

Table 5. Average type/token ratios

	AUS	HK	KEY	UK	USA	whole domain	range
Economy	44.40	42.30	43.13	43.92	42.55	3.19	2.1
Hard News	46.49	45.77	45.39	42.47	43.06	3.67	4.02
Lifestyle	40.98	40.26	37.69	40.19	39.46	3.33	3.29
Politics	42.88	43.19	41.87	43.98	45.16	3.22	3.29
Sports	42.61	42.79	43.39	41.65	39.08	3.15	4.31
whole variety	3.66	3.56	3.18	3.42	3.56	1.47	
range	5.51	5.51	7.7	3.79	6.08		8.8

Regarding the domains, the first observation we can make is that lifestyle again stands out. It has the lowest average TTR in every variety except the USA, where sports news is slightly lower. In Kenya, in particular, the low TTR of the lifestyle domain is responsible for the comparatively wide range in the variety, even though its highest value, that of hard news, is not above the highest values of other regions.

Hard news holds the highest value in terms of the total average. One explanation for this is that hard news articles are on average the shortest, but the relevance of places and people in these stories also contributes to the high TTR, as names are usually not repeated often, leading to more variation. The keyword analysis showed that the strikingly dominant actor in hard news stories is the police, which indicates that topics consist of accidents and crimes to a large degree. In these contexts, the six W-questions that guide a reporter – *Why? What? When? Where? Who? How?* – are of particular interest and constantly require new elements in the vocabulary. The substitution of pronouns by bits of information occurs frequently in such stories, too, which additionally increases the TTR, because pronouns per se have less potential for variation.

With regard to the varieties, it can be seen that the UK displays the most compact picture. With a range of just 3.79% the TTR is relatively constant across the domains. Kenya and the USA are to be found on the other end of this scale, with comparatively large internal ranges. The values for informativeness point towards more diversity amongst the domains than amongst the varieties, which is in line with the results of the previous analyses.

7.2.2 Declarative mood

Mood as an operationalization is included twice in this study, for goal orientation and social role relationship, but will work with different foci. For the parameter of tenor, imperative and interrogative mood are of particular interest. Here, as a measurement for the degree of informativeness, we will concentrate on the frequencies with which declarative mood is used in the texts.

First of all, it can be said that declarative statements are by far the most frequent ones in news. This is not surprising, because to inform is of course a key function of news. Yet we can see differences between both the regions and the domains in the degree to which declaratives are used.

Looking at the regions, we can see that Australia, the USA and Kenya are fairly similar in terms of overall averages, with values of 97.7%, 97.6% and 98.1% respectively. Hong Kong has the highest average of 98.8% of all sentences being declaratives, whereas the UK has the lowest with 97.1%. The L2 varieties have the smallest ranges, though – in both Kenya and Hong Kong, lifestyle has the lowest average values and economy the highest, but the difference between the two is only 3.8% in Kenya and 2.5% in Hong Kong. In the native varieties, the internal variation is higher with 5.4% in Australia, 4.9% in the UK and 4.4% in the USA.

All in all, the differences between the regions are significant at $\chi^2=141.63$ (df=4, p<0.000). This is mainly due to the high amount of declaratives in Hong Kong and the comparatively low amount in the UK. Similar to the other features analyzed above, the domains show more variation than the regions: the differences here are significant at $\chi^2=1176.4$ (df=4, p<0.000). Sports and, even more so, economy, hard news and politics are very constant across the regions however, which means that once again, lifestyle is the most divergent domain. This is confirmed when we take a look at the more detailed distributions of declaratives, shown in Figure 8.

Many texts do not include any imperatives or interrogatives at all, which raises the median values for declarative mood in most categories to nearly 0. In hard news, all medians equal 100% – the few articles in this domain which contain any imperatives or interrogatives are outliers. In economy, the comparatively low value from the UK data in terms of averages is shown to be not just the product of one or two extreme values, but depicts a slightly broader variation despite numerous outliers. For politics and sports, news items from the USA share this trend. In sports, the regions produce few outliers, indicating a more even distribution of the values. The wide range of lifestyle of course means that here, imperatives and interrogatives are more common,

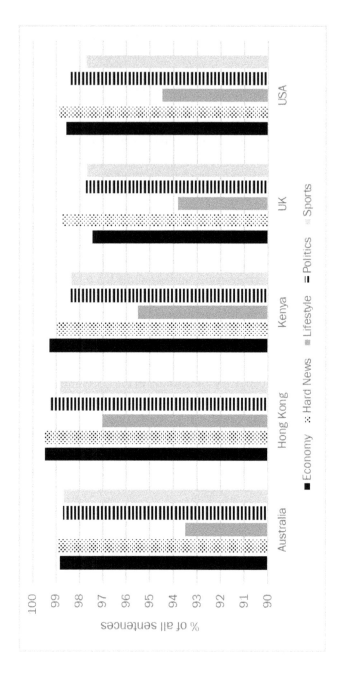

Figure 7 Declarative mood – Relative frequencies

FIELD OF DISCOURSE 87

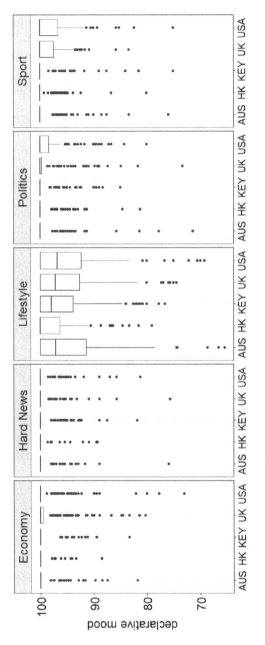

Figure 8 Declarative mood – Distribution

which will be analyzed in more detail for the sub-dimension of social role relationship.

In terms of the degree of informativeness, we can assume that there is little variation between the domains of hard news, economy and politics, and that even sports, which stood out slightly in the other analyses, is more closely related to these three domains than to news from lifestyle. The values for lifestyle news, in contrast, further confirm the assumption that these topics have an interpersonal focus.

7.2.3   3rd person pronouns

An analysis of 3rd person pronouns was defined as the last indicator for the subdimension of goal orientation. As was argued in the chapter on the operationalization (5.1.2), informativeness in news language in terms of pronominal use cannot be restricted to the 3rd person singular *it*. It has to include references to persons as well since their involvement alone can be the dominant topic and the element that makes a story worthy of being news. For this reason, all 3rd person pronouns will be counted and all their forms included:

- *he, his, him, himself*
- *she, her, herself*
- *it, its, itself*
- *they, their, them, themselves*

The trend that became evident during the other analyses, that differences are larger between the domains than between the varieties, is observable for this linguistic feature, too, but it is not expressed as strongly. Table 6 lists the relative frequencies of the 3rd person pronouns, all pronouns, and the percentages of 3rd person in relation to all pronouns.

Looking only at 3rd person pronouns, the lowest average among the varieties is that for news from Hong Kong, and the UK part contains the highest. In Hong Kong news the domain of economy stands out especially, containing the fewest pronouns across the whole dataset; the trend for this domain to be at the lower end is constant across all varieties however, and it shows little internal variation. The same holds true for politics, which takes different values within the individual varieties, but contains a small range of percentages in itself.

The other three domains are subject to wider variation. Hard news contributes the highest values in the UK and the USA, whereas they are less extreme in the other varieties. The most dominant pronoun in this domain is

Table 6 3rd p. pronouns – Relative frequencies

		AUS	HK	KEY	UK	USA	domain	range
ECO	3rd p. pron.	2.57	2.03	2.04	2.81	2.49	2.4	0.78
	All pron.	3.43	2.37	2.76	3.61	3.13	3.07	1.24
	3rd p./all	74.93	85.65	73.91	77.84	79.55	78.18	11.74
HN	3rd p. pron.	4.18	2.78	3.92	5.2	3.98	4.07	2.42
	All pron.	5.17	3.17	4.71	6.53	4.95	4.99	3.36
	3rd p./all	80.85	87.70	83.23	79.63	80.40	81.56	8.07
LIFE	3rd p. pron.	3.62	3.27	4.4	4.22	3.44	3.8	1.13
	All pron.	6.74	4.92	7.06	7.42	5.72	6.37	2.5
	3rd p./all	53.71	66.46	62.32	56.87	60.14	59.65	12.75
POL	3rd p. pron.	3.2	2.81	3.29	3.78	3.39	3.3	0.97
	All pron.	4.41	3.31	4.17	5.15	4.35	4.29	1.84
	3rd p./all	72.56	84.89	78.90	73.40	77.93	76.92	12.33
SPO	3rd p. pron.	4.19	3.49	3.17	4.67	4.36	4.04	1.5
	All pron.	6.61	4.94	4.77	7.25	6.49	6.12	2.48
	3rd p./all	63.39	70.65	66.46	64.41	67.18	66.01	7.26
variety	3rd p. pron.	3.54	2.92	3.51	4.15	3.55	3.54	
	All pron.	5.41	3.87	5.05	6.11	5.02	5.11	
	3rd p./all	65.43	75.45	69.50	67.92	70.72	69.44	
range	3rd p. pron.	1.62	1.46	2.36	2.39	1.87		3.17
	All pron.	3.31	2.57	4.3	3.81	3.36		5.05
	3rd p./all	27.14	21.24	20.91	22.76	20.26		33.99

the singular *he* and all its forms (6,471 occurrences, 1.87%), followed by *they* (2,918 occurrences, 0.84%). This is similar to sports news, where the dominance of *he* is even slightly stronger with 8,463 occurrences (1.97% of sports news in total, 48.76% of 3rd person pronouns in sports news). This aspect sets the two domains apart from the area of lifestyle, where *it* is most dominant (6,546; 1.13%) before *they* (6,052; 1.05%) and *he* (5,321; 0.92%).

At a first glance, these results seem to contradict the assumptions made above that lifestyle articles focus on people and aspects of human interest more than hard news does; however, a look at all pronouns puts the 3rd person frequencies into perspective. Hard news only contains 4.99% pronouns in general, of which 3rd person pronouns are the largest group with 4.07%. Lifestyle articles in contrast contain 6.37% in total, only 3.8% of which are 3rd person pronouns. This observation on the level of domains across varieties holds true also within the regions; the smallest discrepancies between all pronouns and 3rd person forms are to be found in the domains of economy, politics and hard news, while lifestyle and sports articles display the largest differences.

From this perspective, the results tend to confirm the assumption that sports news and lifestyle news have a more expressed interpersonal dimension than the other domains, because they contain larger shares of 1st and 2nd person pronouns. In contrast, economy, hard news and politics show a clear focus on informativeness due to their preference for 3rd person pronouns. Among the varieties, Hong Kong is clearly set apart – across all domains it has the highest averages of 3rd person pronouns, and its total average is 4.73 percentage points above that of the USA, which is second.

7.3 Summary

Summing up the results for the parameter of field, it can be said that, in general, there are more differences with regard to functional than to regional variation. The keywords clearly represent the topics that are dominant in the respective domains, which was to be expected, because the topic is an external criterion for the news outlets to categorize the articles. This is especially evident for hard news and the keyness of the lexical item *police*. Lifestyle and sports articles present strong keyness values for verbs and pronouns, indicating that the thematic scope of these domains is slightly different from the rest.

The regions are distinguished mainly by their inclusion of references to places and important actors. This, too, is not surprising, but the keyness values of the reference points allow us to draw conclusions on how relevant the individual regions are relative to the others. Most notably, spatial references from the US are much less key than their counterparts from Kenya, which shows that the USA is present in news in all five regions, whereas Kenya is not as relevant in the other countries.

With regard to temporal orientation and scope, a general tendency can be observed to refer to the past, but at the same time stress the recency of the news story. Lifestyle articles display the fewest temporal references of all domains, which indicates that they do not deal much with topics that need to be located on a temporal scale to be relevant. Instead, articles from this domain tend to concentrate on the present, which ensures that the article sounds up to date even when read long after it was written.

The results are similar for sports news, but since news here is more dependent on current developments, we have to assume that the present references have a different effect. Quotes from players or coaches are a likely source for present tense verbs, and the item *today* is often used when sports events are reported on later the same day. In addition to the present, sports articles also refer to the future frequently, giving outlooks and reporting on rumors. The opposite is reflected in hard news. The dominant reference point here is the past, with a strong focus on the day before the article.

The different foci of the domains are also reflected in the lexical density. Sports and lifestyle news display broader internal ranges as well as few outliers, indicating an even distribution across the individual texts. From that we can conclude that variation in terms of density is common in these two domains. In economy, politics and hard news, on the other hand, there is a clear standard that allows less variation and is disregarded only by the few texts with statistically outlying values.

In terms of goal orientation, this lower degree of standardization of sports and lifestyle is confirmed in individual features; sports news produces a very wide internal variation regarding the TTR, whereas lifestyle articles vary most in terms of the use of declarative mood. For the overall degree of informativeness, we can say that lifestyle articles are least focused on the function of informing. Sports news, too, emphasizes other functions, but not as strongly. The other three domains are quite focused on the dominant purpose to inform their readers.

Looking at the five regions, the picture is more mixed. Only the UK and Hong Kong show trends with some consistency. The UK contains fewest declaratives and relatively low values for 3rd person pronouns and the TTR. Hong Kong, on the other hand, contains most pronouns and declaratives, and the second-to-highest TTR. Based on these results, it appears that news from the UK focuses least on the informative function, and articles from Hong Kong emphasize this most strongly.

8 Tenor of discourse

The second parameter to define the situational context is that of the interpersonal relations between the participants. As we said in Chapter 5, the subdimension of agentive roles is not relevant for this study; instead, the tenor will be analyzed in terms of the social role relationship and the social distance.

8.1 Social role relationship

The social role relationship deals with the power structures that are at work between the participants of a communicative situation (Neumann, 2013, p. 63; Steiner, 2004, p. 17). For our analysis, it has been operationalized via interrogative and imperative mood, modality, the amount of keywords and mean word length. These linguistic features contribute to the definition of this parameter in different ways: modality and mood reflect differences in authority between the participants, whereas mean word length and the amount of keywords are more general indicators of the use of technical language and signal expertise for both author and reader.

8.1.1 Interrogative and imperative mood

The linguistic feature of mood has already been discussed as part of the subdimension of goal orientation, but here, interrogatives and imperatives are the focus, because they reflect the interpersonal factor of the discourse.

In general, these two types of mood are relatively rare in the texts analyzed here. Of the 4,000 articles, 2,979 (74.48%) contain neither interrogatives nor imperatives. Of the remaining 1,021 texts, 119 are from the domain of economy, 105 from hard news, 152 from politics, 205 from sports and 440 from lifestyle. Table 7 lists the frequencies for both types of mood.

Of the two types, imperatives are the ones with many fewer instances in the corpus. Regarding the overall frequencies of the domains, the variation in terms of imperatives is significant (χ^2=604.71, df=4, p<0.000). This mainly originates from the relatively high numbers in lifestyle articles. These are reflected in the individual varieties as well; in every region, this domain is clearly set apart from the others. The other four domains behave differently

Table 7 Frequencies of imperatives and interrogatives

		AUS	HK	KEY	UK	USA	Σ % of domain	range
ECO	Imp.	17	10	7	28	29	91	22
	% of all	0.56	0.29	0.25	0.68	0.73	0.53	0.48
	Int.	18	8	13	78	28	145	70
	% of all	0.6	0.23	0.47	1.9	0.7	0.84	1.67
HN	Imp.	21	3	20	12	12	68	18
	% of all	0.81	0.1	0.74	0.28	0.28	0.4	0.71
	Int.	7	13	8	45	36	109	37
	% of all	0.27	0.44	0.29	1.05	0.85	0.65	0.78
LIFE	Imp.	195	82	125	100	135	637	113
	% of all	3.67	1.37	1.95	1.58	2.11	2.1	2.3
	Int.	150	97	163	290	218	918	193
	% of all	2.83	1.62	2.54	4.59	3.4	3.02	2.97
POL	Imp.	19	3	14	17	16	69	16
	% of all	0.59	0.09	0.45	0.41	0.38	0.38	0.5
	Int.	23	23	35	76	50	207	53
	% of all	0.71	0.69	1.12	1.85	1.2	1.15	1.16
SPO	Imp.	16	15	23	23	39	116	24
	% of all	0.43	0.4	0.78	0.45	0.75	0.56	0.38
	Int.	33	29	26	97	81	266	71
	% of all	0.89	0.77	0.88	1.88	1.56	1.28	1.11
Σ % of variety	Imp.	268 / 1.5	113 / 0.58	189 / 1.05	180 / 0.75	231 / 0.96	981 / 0.95	
	Int.	231 / 1.29	170 / 0.87	245 / 1.36	586 / 2.44	413 / 1.72	1,645 / 1.59	
range	Imp.	179 / 3.24	79 / 1.28	118 / 1.7	88 / 1.3	123 / 1.82		192 / 3.58
	Int.	143 / 2.56	89 / 1.39	155 / 2.25	245 / 3.54	190 / 2.7		283 / 4.36

depending on their origin: economy articles show by far the lowest amount of imperatives in Kenya, whereas this form of mood is comparatively frequent in the UK and the USA. Hard news, on the other hand, exhibits high values in Kenya and Australia, but contains few imperatives in the other varieties.

Most of these values can be traced back to clusters in individual texts, however. In all regions, the median value for imperatives is 0 in all domains except lifestyle and, from a statistical perspective, texts that contain imperatives are outliers. This means that we can only draw tentative conclusions, but a close-up look at the instances shows that imperatives can be used in news writing to fulfil different functions.

One factor that influences the meaning of imperatives is whether or not they are part of a quotation. The percentage of imperatives that are at the beginning of a direct quote are much higher in politics (29%, 20 instances), sports (31.03%, 36) and hard news (32.35%, 22) than in economy (19.8%, 18) and lifestyle (13.19%, 84). This means that they reflect a news actor, not the journalist, and the intended purpose of including an imperative depends on the speaker. In sports news, an imperative, positioned at the beginning of a quote, is often used to introduce a statement and weaken it, or ask for understanding or consent, as in the following example:

> [3] [...] "**Look**, I'm not going to comment on that," Schumer said of his former aide on ABC's "This Week." (Edelman, 2013, *Daily News*; emphasis added)

In the domain of lifestyle, on the other hand, imperatives are least often at the beginning of a quote; instead, they seem to fulfil an advisory function which strengthens the constructed expertise of the author on a particular topic:

> [4] Solo female travel tips
> **Understand** the cultural norms
> **Read** about your upcoming destination, **email** local expats or locals who blog; **figure** out the geopolitics and religions [...]
> **Involve** others in your safety
> **Find** ways to involve the people in this new place in your safety [...] **Tell** your hotel you're travelling alone [...]
> **Carry** a doorstop and safety whistle [...]
> **Stay** aware [...]
> **Stay** sober [...]
> **Carry** travel insurance [...]
> **Pay** for your safety [...]
> (O'Donnell, 2013, *the Courier Mail*; emphasis added)

For topics such as this, imperatives seem appropriate because they involve the readers as well as inform them. This is reflected also in the verbs which are most frequently used to form imperatives. In news from politics, economy and sports, *let* occurs most frequently (often in combination with *us*), in hard news, *look* is dominant, but in lifestyle, *try* and *get* are used most often, both reflecting material action to be taken by the reader. Since lifestyle articles, especially in Australia, Kenya and the USA, are the only ones that show any distribution beyond a median of 0, this can be seen as another indicator of the interpersonal focus of this domain.

This focus is again confirmed when we look at the second type of mood we are interested in here, namely interrogatives. With a total of 1,645 occurrences in the corpus, they are generally more frequent than imperatives, and the results are more diverse. At the minimum end of the scale we find the news from Hong Kong, which contains fewest instances of both interrogatives and imperatives. At the other end there is the UK, most notably its lifestyle articles. Although the domain once again stands out in all categories as being particularly reader-oriented and including many questions, the UK part has a total average of 2.44% of interrogatives – 0.72% more than the USA, which has the second highest value. The variation between the regions is significant at χ^2=194.49 (df=4, p<0.000), and the differences on the functional axis are even more pronounced at χ^2=587.83 (df=4, p<0.000). However, both values are influenced heavily by the UK lifestyle data.

What makes this particular data stand out? One answer to this is: headlines. Here, 20 (6.9%) instances of interrogatives occur in headlines – more than in any other category. And in this prominent position, they fulfil a function that is also characteristic of UK media in general, namely word plays:

[5] What's got interim? Neuropsychologist analyses short-term Chelsea boss Rafa Benitez (Weeks, 2013, the *Sun*)
[6] The sexual politics of hair – are all cuts created equally? (Adewunmi, 2013, the *Guardian*)

Such constructions can trigger the interest of a reader, and frame a given topic as being less serious and more entertaining in nature. Another purpose that is observable in headlines is where syntactic structures work as teasers and, in an online surrounding, could function as click-baits:

[7] Bitcoins explained: A viable future currency, or an accident waiting to happen? (Meade, 2013, the *Daily Mail*)

Within the texts, questions sometimes show a similar function when positioned at the end of a paragraph to lead over to the next. In many such cases, the questions are either answered right away or are phrased more personally so that they take the form of a rhetorical question:

> [8] For instance, how many people do you know still use an alarm clock? (Barnett, 2012, the *Daily Telegraph*)

In these cases, the interrogative does not require an actual answer, either from the reader or from the text itself. It is an alternative way to phrase content which would otherwise have been another declarative, and it is a means to make the text more geared towards the audience, thereby strengthening the interpersonal dimension. These different ways of using interrogatives can be found in the lifestyle domains from the other regions as well, with the exception of puns, which hardly ever occur outside the UK. In the UK variety, however, it occurs in all domains, especially in headlines.

Apart from this British particularity, the domains and varieties show little variation beyond the mere frequencies; interrogatives are used either as more audience-oriented substitutes for declaratives or as teasers for the article itself, and often as a combination of both. Particularly in headlines, they open up the topic to the reader and summarize the major issue, stimulating the curiosity of the readers. In none of these functions, however, are interrogatives used as indirect imperatives, nor do they signal a difference in authority; rather, rhetorical questions, especially, connect the discourse participants by showing that they share attitudes and experiences. With regard to the social role relationship they seem to create equality, and in this way also contribute to the subdimension of social distance, as they construct closeness and emphasize similarities.

8.1.2 Modality

The linguistic feature of modality was defined as the second operationalization of the social role relationship, because the use of modals is seen as a mechanism to weaken a statement or signal insecurity about a topic or piece of information. This means that a high frequency of modals lowers the levels of authority and expertise constructed in a text, although not all modals have this effect to the same degree. In our analysis, we consider 12 modal verbs: *can, could, do, may, might, must, need, ought, shall, should, will* and *would*.

First of all, we can see that the modals differ greatly in their overall frequencies across the whole corpus. *Shall, ought, must, need* and *do* (in their

TENOR OF DISCOURSE 97

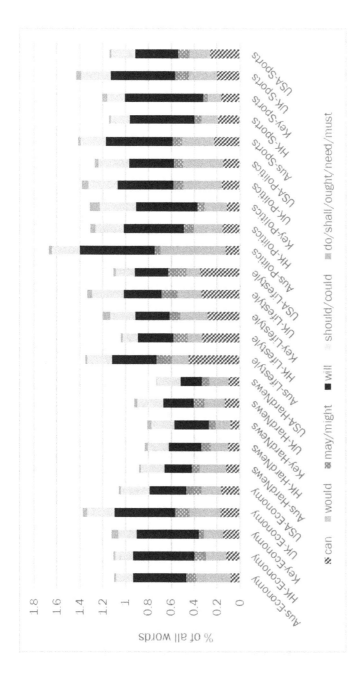

Figure 9 Modal verbs – Relative frequencies

modal functions) are used very little, together making up only 0.03% of the dataset. *May* and *might* reach 0.06% and 0.03% respectively, and *should* (0.08%) and *could* (0.13%) are slightly above that. To be visible at all, these groups were summarized in Figure 9. The most frequent modals are *will* (0.43%), *would* (0.22%) and *can* (0.19%). The exact distribution shows that the dominance of *will* applies to every category, whereas *would* and *can* change ranks in some cases. In politics, economy and hard news, *would* is more frequent but in lifestyle articles, *can* outweighs it, and this pattern is visible in all regions.

Some other particularities regarding the domains also stand out. Hard news contains fewest modals in all regions, which confirms the previous results that these articles are focused on facts and do not require relativizations of statements as much as news from other domains does. It appears that speculations are left out and articles are restricted to what is known for certain, so that the domain can be said to clearly tend towards informativeness.

Among the other domains, economy appears very constant with the exception of texts from the UK. Lifestyle and sports are more diverse internally, although it can be seen in both domains that Australia and the UK are very similar and produce higher values than the other regions. The domain with the highest overall frequencies of modals is politics, and this is manifested in the use of individual modal verbs, too. *Should*, which is nearly irrelevant in the other domains, reaches an average of 1.31% in political news, and *will*, too, has a higher average use here (0.52%) than in the collection in total. Both modals can be used to project ideas for the future, which means that political news seems to tend towards promises and an avoidance of commitment rather than present facts. Additionally, as we can see from the distribution in Figure 10, the domain also produces fewest outliers, indicating that this trend is not caused by individual texts but holds true for the majority of articles. The differences between the domains in their overall use of modals are statistically significant at $\chi^2=538.83$ (df=4, p<0.000).

Looking at the regional variation, the differences are less pronounced ($\chi^2=196.39$, df=4, p<0.000) and the values are more evenly distributed. Australian news contains the most modals (1.31%), followed by the UK (1.3%), Kenya (1.15%), Hong Kong (1.09%) and the USA (1.07%). What can be said is that the tendency shown for interrogatives and imperatives, especially regarding the low use of these features in Hong Kong news, is not confirmed here. Interrogatives were analyzed as markers of a more equal social role relationship, and Hong Kong appeared the most unequal variety in these terms. Regarding modal verbs as a means to lower authority, however, the region is in line with the others. This is true for the USA as well, which contains a relatively high number of interrogatives but the fewest modals of all regions.

TENOR OF DISCOURSE 99

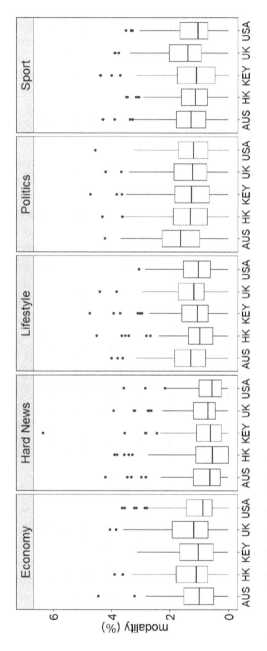

Figure 10 Distribution of modal verbs

8.1.3 Amount of keywords

In contrast to the factors of mood and modality, the next two operationalizations are more general measures which are meant to complement the overall analysis of social role relationship. One of these is the amount of keywords. In Chapter 7.1, we took a rather detailed look at the keywords on a lexical level, but the amount of significant words is an indicator of the specialization of the vocabulary and, as such, reflects the authority and expertise of the author and shows what kind of knowledge is assumed in the reader. For all categories, the keywords were counted in both domain- and variety-internal comparisons, and Table 8 summarizes the overall amounts of keywords as well as the percentages which their cumulative frequencies comprise in relation to the whole category.

These numbers allow several conclusions, but they should be put into perspective based on what we learned from the keyword analysis in Chapter 7.1. Kenya, for instance, is prominent as it has the most keywords in all domains, and they make up most of the total word count in every category, too. Like the news from all regions, Kenyan articles refer to place names and locally popular or important people quite often; but that these terms are key is not only due to them being included often, but also to the fact that they are relatively rare elsewhere.

Although this has an influence on Kenya's rank in Table 8, it should be noted that place names, too, imply specialization. *Kenya* and *Nairobi* for instance are not technical terms as such, and they are most likely familiar to most people; yet detailed knowledge on these places is less common and the reader needs some expertise to put information on them into context. This becomes more relevant as the place references become more local, whereas – especially in the USA and Australia data – several bigger cities are prominent worldwide and feature in news internationally.

Another aspect that becomes visible from the results is that, in lifestyle articles, the percentages of keyword types are generally lowest and the differences between the varieties smallest. In terms of the domain-internal comparison, that means that articles from the different regions are most similar in this domain. In contrast to that, the largest differences can be found in sports news. These articles are very specialized within their region, which is not surprising seeing that different sports are popular in these societies and the national leagues are usually dominant (Fest, 2017). A high degree of specialization is also displayed in political news, where internal political matters and national politicians and parties are key.

Table 8 Amount of keywords – Domains

Domain-internal dimension					
Economy	AUS	HK	KEY	UK	USA
Keywords (% of all word types)	239 (3.13)	328 (4.15)	361 (4.96)	224 (2.57)	287 (3.29)
Σ keyword freq. in % of all words	12.13	17.49	30.64	11.48	15.08
Hard News	AUS	HK	KEY	UK	USA
Keywords (% of all word types)	249 (3.55)	351 (4.34)	367 (5.04)	260 (2.88)	339 (3.75)
Σ keyword freq. in % of all words	13.83	16.25	27.23	15.51	14.54
Lifestyle	AUS	HK	KEY	UK	USA
Keywords (% of all word types)	246 (2.05)	393 (2.82)	468 (3.54)	249 (1.9)	357 (2.47)
Σ keyword freq. in % of all words	11.62	16.63	26.58	12.22	11.23
Politics	AUS	HK	KEY	UK	USA
Keywords (% of all word types)	306 (3.86)	360 (4.19)	482 (6.11)	230 (2.43)	310 (3.22)
Σ keyword freq. in % of all words	19.16	17.85	29.73	14.63	14.84
Sports	AUS	HK	KEY	UK	USA
Keywords (% of all word types)	316 (3.84)	345 (3.79)	591 (7.35)	224 (2.28)	361 (3.96)
Σ keyword freq. in % of all words	14.53	24.95	29.83	14.87	18.30

Looking at the distribution of keywords from the other, variety-internal angle, many of these results are mirrored (see Table 9).

The figures show that, within every variety, lifestyle articles produce the lowest numbers of keywords, although in Hong Kong their cumulative frequencies make up a larger portion of the category in total than in hard news. The differences between the domains are statistically significant in every region, but are most explicit in Kenya, which means that we can find most internal variation in this variety of English – between economy, which appears very specialized, to lifestyle, which contains fewest keywords, there is a difference of 3.77%.

The other regions are less diverse internally, but they do show differences between them. News from the USA, which displays the highest average of keywords with 6.08%, seems to be particularly specialized. The lowest degree of specialization occurs in news from the UK.

Tracing these results back to their meaning for the social role relationship, we can summarize that lifestyle articles seem to be written in a way

Table 9 Amount of keywords – Regions

Variety-internal dimension					
Australia	ECO	HN	LIFE	POL	SPO
Keywords (% of all word types)	481 (6.29)	508 (7.24)	462 (3.86)	364 (4.59)	566 (6.89)
∑ keyword freq. in % of all words	32.32	29.89	26.60	32.01	28.13
Hong Kong	ECO	HN	LIFE	POL	SPO
Keywords (% of all word types)	508 (6.43)	470 (5.81)	581 (4.17)	416 (4.85)	463 (5.08)
∑ keyword freq. in % of all words	31.78	20.75	25.11	27.84	29.79
Kenya	ECO	HN	LIFE	POL	SPO
Keywords (% of all word types)	513 (7.04)	437 (6)	433 (3.27)	415 (5.26)	547 (6.8)
∑ keyword freq. in % of all words	31.04	33.37	28.76	33.23	27.81
UK	ECO	HN	LIFE	POL	SPO
Keywords (% of all word types)	515 (5.91)	515 (5.7)	432 (3.3)	408 (4.31)	573 (5.84)
∑ keyword freq. in % of all words	34.53	29.52	23.98	27.34	27.12
USA	ECO	HN	LIFE	POL	SPO
Keywords (% of all word types)	618 (7.09)	649 (7.19)	556 (3.85)	474 (4.93)	667 (7.32)
∑ keyword freq. in % of all words	30.90	29.80	25.42	25.20	38.69

that reflects very low degrees of authority and expertise. This matches what we found for interrogative mood, but the frequent use of imperatives demonstrated that authors do indeed construct expertise. The domain does not require the use of technical terminology though – instead, the topics are broad and meant to be easily accessible to a wide audience. Sports news, on the other hand, requires expert knowledge from the reader and the author, although this is relevant on the level of individual types of sport rather than on that of the whole domain.

Due to the dominance in the keyword lists of place names and persons, the conclusions we can draw regarding the varieties are not as clear. One category that becomes increasingly noteworthy, though, is that of Kenyan lifestyle articles, which are the main source for Kenya's wide internal range in terms of keywords.

8.2 Social distance

Along with the relationship between the social roles of the participants, the tenor of discourse is concerned with the distance or closeness created between the speakers. This aspect is reflected in the subdimension of social distance, which we will look at more closely in the next sections.

We stated in Chapter 5 that social distance will be operationalized in terms of place references, voice, 1st and 2nd person pronouns and the inclusion of boosters and minimizers as well as nominalizations. The last parameter implies a certain degree of subjectivity, because it does not form a given word class or has a special part of speech tag. To make sure that our analysis remains transparent, we will work with frequent examples in this section and start the discussion of social distance with this feature, so that the results can be put into perspective when looking at the other linguistic markers.

8.2.1 Boosters and minimizers

Boosters and minimizers have been included as an operationalization for social distance because frequent use of these items has been found to indicate casual style, which in turn lowers the distance between the participants (cf. Eggins & Martin, 1997, p. 232). Also, they increase the degree of evaluation in a text because they modify the meaning of the boosted or minimized concept. For our investigation, 27 lexical items are included, 14 of which have been defined as boosters, and 13 as minimizers.

The overall frequencies of these words in the dataset vary immensely: of the boosters, only three items have more than a thousand hits, *more* (5,263), *most* (2,110) and *very* (1,514). Another four – *completely* (139), *extremely* (120), *fully* (153) and *really* (786) – have more than one hundred each, but the other seven items are so rare that, together, they only have 215 hits. All in all, we can find 10,300 boosters in the corpus, which equals 0.48% of all words.

Among the minimizers, *just* (2,531) and *only* (2,151) occur more than a thousand times, *nearly* (397), *pretty* (226), *quite* (259), *relatively* (137), *simply* (213) and *slightly* (132) all yield more than one hundred hits, and the other five items only occur very infrequently with a sum of 252 instances. In total, there are 6,298 minimizing items in the corpus, which is 0.29%.

These numbers do not include instances where the respective lexical item co-occurs with a negation, because the effect on the word's function was found to differ, so that these constructions could not automatically be sorted into boosting and minimizing ones. In some cases, the original meaning was indeed negated, like in example 9:

[9] A Google search for "fake nerds" will convince you that, **not only** are they a problem, they're an epidemic. (Mouton, 2013, *USA Today*; emphasis added)

The *not only* in this sentence introduces a step-up from a problem to an epidemic, which is clearly a boost. In other cases, it can simply mark the beginning of a list:

[10] People believe that those who wear glasses look **not only** more intelligent but more honest. (Black, 2011, *Daily News*; emphasis added)

Honest is not a development of *intelligent*, but describes a separate attribute, so the *not only* does not fulfil either a boosting or a minimizing function here. In total, the dataset contains 657 instances of negations co-occurring with one of the defined lexical items, predominately *only* (219) and *just* (209). In addition, we excluded the combination *any more* from our counts, which occurs 56 times.

When we look at the distribution of minimizers and boosters across the domains and varieties, differences can be found on both dimensions (Figure 11).

In every variety, lifestyle articles contain the highest cumulative numbers of the respective lexical items. In all regions, except Kenya, they are followed by sports articles. Hard news and politics generally produce the lowest values, but the two domains are further apart from each other in Australia (0.15 percentage points difference) and the USA (0.11) than in the UK (0.05), Hong Kong (0.03) and Kenya (0.01). Due to the large gap between lifestyle articles on the one and hard news on the other hand, the differences between the domains are significant at $\chi^2=734.1$ (df=4, p<0.000).

Of the five varieties, Kenya, with an average of 0.51%, contains by far the fewest instances of minimizing and boosting terminology. The other regions differ less: Hong Kong (0.73%), the USA (0.8%), Australia (0.81%) and the UK (0.83%) are only 0.1% apart. Although the variation between the varieties is statistically significant ($\chi^2=328.82$, df=4, p<0.000), this can mainly be traced back to Kenya's low values. News from this region therefore seems to create the highest distance between author and reader, whereas the other varieties make more use of evaluative language of this type.

The distribution across the domains and varieties reflects what was already suggested by the absolute numbers, namely that boosters are, by far, more common than minimizers. The only exceptions to this are hard news in

TENOR OF DISCOURSE 105

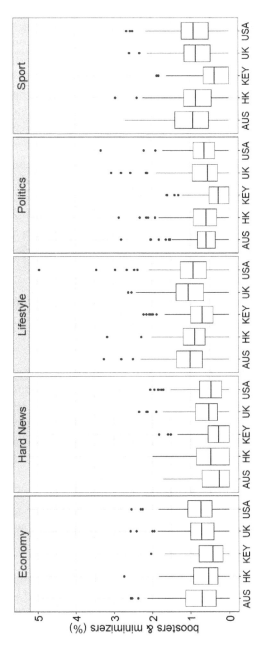

Figure 11 Distribution of boosting and minimizing lexis

Australia and sports news from Kenya, where minimizers are slightly more frequent (0.004% and 0.01% difference respectively).

These divergences in the use of these two lexical categories are quite interesting, because they reflect the respective domains and regions on different levels. The dominance of boosters can be explained by the construction of a news value based on superlativeness (Bednarek & Caple, 2014). Events and people with a maximum impact are more interesting than those with minimum relevance, and authors can create this impression by using boosting terminology. At the same time, such evaluative terms create closeness, because they construct an opinion that a reader can share.

Taking these factors into consideration, the interpersonal focus of lifestyle articles is once again confirmed very clearly. Including one's own opinion, and using a more evaluative style, seem appropriate in this domain, where the topics are of a more personal and therefore subjective nature anyway. The superlative aspect of newsworthiness is also present, but can be found to be emphasized in individual articles rather than used across the board, which can lead to clusters of boosting terminology:

> [11] Men obsessed with their muscles are **more** sexist, **more** likely to believe thin women are **more** attractive (Goldwert, 2012, *Daily News*; emphasis added)

In hard news, on the other hand, which was shown to focus on facts in the previous analyses, a subjective style of writing is less acceptable. Readers being informed about topics such as crimes, accidents or natural disasters are most likely more interested in concrete information than in anybody's personal opinion. In this domain, boosting or minimizing mainly happens in relation to countable or observable values, such as crime rates or degrees of destruction.

The other domains are less striking, but political news is characterized by the most even relation of boosters and minimizers. Neither are particularly frequent in this domain, but clusters of words illustrating how they are used can be found:

> [12] Collins took 4,648 votes, **nearly** 22 per cent of those cast [...] With **just** 451 votes, Mr Beckett was **just** 190 votes ahead [...] Mr McDonald, who won a share of **just** over 60% [...] (Rojas, 2012, the *Daily Telegraph*; emphasis added)

The concrete topic, election results, of course includes many numbers, which can be exhausting for a reader. It is not surprising that many of the

TENOR OF DISCOURSE 107

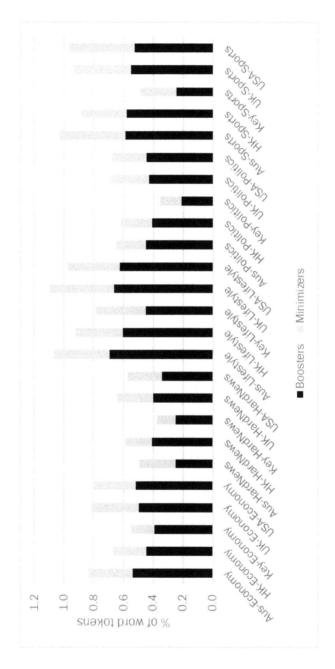

Figure 12 Boosters and minimizers – Frequencies

minimizing terms are used to work with round numbers instead of exact ones to enhance readability (*just over 60%*). Another function that can be observed here is helping the reader put the results into perspective: 451 votes might be a lot or very few – someone without prior knowledge would find that hard to decide. The *just* in front of it shows that it is not much, and at the same time raises tension and makes the decision seem more dramatic. Both functions ultimately aim at making the article more accessible and interesting, and in doing so lower the distance between author and reader.

8.2.2   1st and 2nd person pronouns

The second linguistic feature we will look at for the subdimension of social distance is pronominal use. In contrast to Chapter 7, where 3rd person pronouns were used as an indicator of goal orientation, our focus here will be on 1st and 2nd person pronouns, because they point at a constructed closeness between author and reader. Again, the relevant pronouns include all their forms:

- *I, me, my, mine, myself*
- *you, your, yours, yourself, yourselves*
- *we, us, our, ours, ourselves*

The distribution of pronouns across the corpus varieties is similar. In all regions, the 1st person singular pronouns are most common and the 2nd person pronouns least. Differences can be seen in the overall frequencies: Australia and the UK appear to address their readers directly most often, with average amounts of 1.93%% and 1.95% respectively. This confirms the results concerning interrogatives and imperatives, that the news articles from these regions construct a lower distance between authors and readers. Hong Kong and Kenya again move towards the more distant end. The USA produces very mixed results; comparatively high frequencies of interrogatives as well as minimizers and boosters indicated a strong reader orientation, yet regarding the use of 1st and 2nd person pronouns, it appears more similar to the varieties from Kenya and Hong Kong. Overall, the differences on the regional level are significant with $\chi^2=1914.13$ (df=4, p<0.000).

Among the domains, the results are more diverse, which is reflected in a higher statistical significance of the differences ($\chi^2=8070.24$, df=4, p<0.000). The 1st person singular pronoun is dominant in sports news across all regions. The 2nd person pronouns are most strongly represented in lifestyle articles. This is in line with our previous findings, especially for mood, that

TENOR OF DISCOURSE 109

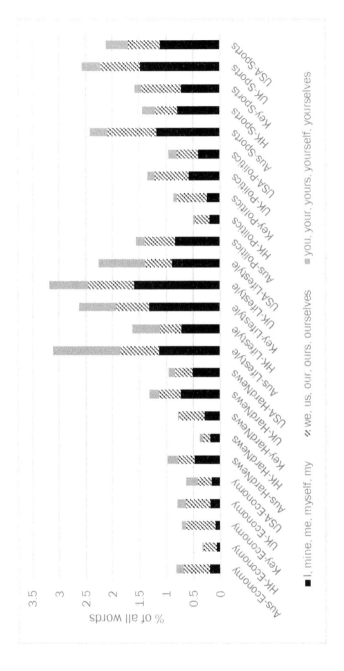

Figure 13 1st and 2nd person pronouns – Frequencies

these news items are more oriented towards the reader, and the interpersonal aspect is emphasized more strongly.

In economic and political news, on the other hand, the 1st person plural pronoun is used very extensively. This is very striking and clearly sets the two domains apart from the rest. In previous studies, the use of *we* and its forms has mainly been analyzed in connection to sports news and has been found to work as a mechanism for including fans and teams, often depending on the athletes' success (*we* after a victory, *they* after a defeat; Dunning, 1999, p. 5; Fest, 2011, pp. 52–3). In the fields of economy and politics, however, this competitive aspect is not relevant, so what function does this pronoun fulfil here? We can certainly assume that many instances originate from direct quotes. In these cases, it indicates that speakers refer to an entity – a company, employer or corporation – rather than to themselves, shifting from a personal to a professional identity (Fest, 2015a).

> [13] "**We**, as a coalition government, will come to [the next] summit with some bold ideas about how **we** can increase growth, increase competitiveness and increase employment. And – yes – **we** will stay until the end." (Cooper, 2011, *Daily Mail*; emphasis added)

In such contexts, the use of the 1st person plural pronoun creates the impression that the speaker is not alone in their opinion, but that there are others behind them, which makes the message more powerful. If the news is bad, the pronoun can be used to shift the gaze from the speaker to the entire group, making responsibility harder to grasp or blaming a non-personal entity, ensuring that individual people do not become immediate targets (Pyykkö, 2002, p. 246).

In other cases, the pronoun can be used to create solidarity with regard to critical topics or decisions, or in the face of difficult situations (Bull & Fetzer, 2006, p. 5; Pennycook, 1994, pp. 175–6).

> [14] Obama: "**We** are in a defining moment in our history. **Our** nation is involved in two wars and **we** are going through the worst financial crisis since the Great Depression." (E. Smith, 2008, the *Sun*; emphasis added)

Since such situations are most notably connected to political and economic contexts, for instance in election campaigns, company statements or with regard to relevant social topics like refugees and climate change, the frequent use of the 1st person plural pronouns in the two domains can be explained by these strategies. Although they work to construct closeness, the degree to which they do so varies, depending on who the scope of the pronoun includes.

8.2.3 Place references

Another way for journalists to create the impression of closeness to their readers is through a common environment. By using place names, their relevance is emphasized and the news value of proximity is constructed (Bednarek & Caple, 2014). In turn, we can assume that places that are mentioned often are perceived as geographically or culturally near and are of particular interest to the audience.

The role place names play in constructing closeness differs, though, because they work on different scales. On the one hand, shared backgrounds can be created on a local or regional level, when places within the country are the reference points. On the other hand, international references reflect closeness that is constructed between countries and cultures.

The regions that are under investigation here display very different scopes of reference. As we saw in the keyword lists analyzed in Chapter 7, every variety features place names from its own region very frequently. This tendency is most clearly visible in Australia and the USA – of the 20 most frequent place names, regional references make up 11 and 10 respectively (see appendix 2 for lists for all regions). This can be attributed to the size of the countries; the overall area that national news has to cover is so large that regional events and news are of more immediate relevance to the audience. Apart from the national references, both countries very rarely contain what could be labelled "continental references", that is, references to other countries on the same continent. In the case of Australia, this might be because of its isolated location – New Zealand is referred to 60 times, but all other place names have a clear international context.

In the case of the USA, the rare references to other American places contradicts what would be expected on the basis of closeness. *America* features 75 times in the US part, but only four of these refer to Latin America, and another two to South America. The only three frequent references to non-US places on the American continent are Toronto, Mexico and Canada. Instead, among the twenty most frequent items we can find seven references to places in Europe.

A curious case here is *Italy*, which reaches significantly more hits in the USA variety than in any other; a closer look reveals that this item occurs most frequently in hard news and politics and clusters in a few texts. In almost all cases, it is connected to law suits against Berlusconi, whose name also occurred in the US keyword lists. It can therefore not be said that there is a general relevance of this country for US news, but that its frequent mentioning is due to the political scandals happening at the time. Even without this oddity in the numbers, though, Europe seems a much stronger reference point for the USA than its immediate neighboring countries.

Of the other regions, the UK includes seven national place names among its top 20, which in this case can be related to its individual members – Scotland and Wales occur in the list – as well as to the overlapping frames of the UK and Britain. Hong Kong and Kenya on the other hand feature fewer national names with five each, counting Chinese place names as national for Hong Kong.

These trends are very telling as a reflection of the regions' general orientation, but it is important to consider that not all domains behave alike. We can see clear differences in the reference scopes and points between the five thematic areas. Table 10 lists the absolute frequencies of national and international hits per category. Because the numbers of national and international items differ within and also across the regions, percentages are not included; instead, the significance was tested within every category and the values which are lower than statistically expected are given in brackets

In hard news, national references are significantly more common than international ones in every variety, and the same holds true for lifestyle articles, with the exception of Kenya. In politics and economy, on the other hand, international references are more relevant, whereas sports news displays different tendencies across the corpus (Fest, 2017).

In politics, Australia's focus on internal matters is once more expressed in the significance of national references, which stands in contrast especially to the UK, the USA and Hong Kong. Kenya displays a less significant difference in this domain. In economic news, the Hong Kong variety stands out: national events appear much more relevant here than international ones. That the English-language press concentrates on the region especially in this domain reflects that Hong Kong is an important business hub and English has long been regarded as a gateway to professional success. In the other regions, news from economy tends towards international place names and, especially in the USA and the UK, Asian countries seem to be of interest. They hardly appear in other news articles, though, showing that the relevance is restricted to the field of business.

Table 10 Frequencies of national and international place references

		AUS	HK	KEY	UK	USA
ECO	national	(404)	947	(551)	460	(360)
	international	289	(503)	377	(402)	371
	χ²-value	140.42	55.37	30.88	0.11	52.13
	p-value	<0.000	<0.000	<0.000	0.739	<0.000
HN	national	268	326	293	267	450
	international	(27)	(208)	(22)	(79)	(58)
	χ²-value	41.78	3.83	108.66	91.47	200.51
	p-value	<0.000	0.05	<0.000	<0.000	<0.000
LIFE	national	381	560	(412)	193	326
	international	(97)	(327)	238	(111)	(97)
	χ²-value	5.59	15.99	3.91	15.12	55.93
	p-value	0.018	0.0001	0.048	0.0001	<0.000
POL	national	660	(725)	353	(356)	(349)
	international	(127)	617	(127)	603	588
	χ²-value	40.31	6.83	11.99	134.36	310.98
	p-value	<0.000	0.009	0.0005	<0.000	<0.000
SPO	national	(668)	(456)	(576)	479	336
	international	236	612	329	(369)	(70)
	χ²-value	1.59	112.93	5.1	5.95	96.54
	p-value	0.207	<0.000	0.024	0.0147	<0.000
Σ	national	2,381	3,014	2,185	1,755	1,821
	international	776	2,267	1,093	1,564	1,184

So what conclusions can we draw regarding the social distance that is constructed? Australian and US-American news items have a clear focus on internal matters and work on the level of states rather than the whole countries. With these references, target groups from the respective areas are addressed specifically, while in the other varieties the national level is more dominant. Regarding external references, geographical closeness is a decisive factor for all varieties except the USA, which appears closer to Europe than to other countries of the Americas. The distance towards Europe is thereby constructed as fairly low.

Looking at the domains, the display of national in-groups is particularly emphasized in hard news and lifestyle. In these domains, events within the countries are clearly more important than happenings elsewhere, and international relations are of little consequence. In economic and political news these dimensions are highly relevant, and readers are brought into contact with other countries and societies more frequently. Economic and political news articles require this wider focus for their topics, as international relations play a major role here and therefore automatically imply a greater distance than the other domains. This extended scope increases the closeness towards the respective regions abroad; but, since both domains projected little closeness in terms of pronouns and evaluation, we can assume that the relevance here is not on a personal level addressing or involving the reader directly, but kept on the level of the respective content.

8.2.4 Voice

The linguistic feature of voice is a very specific one in the analysis of news. In general, a high frequency of passive voice indicates a focus on events rather than actors, creating a higher distance (S. Lamb, 1991, pp. 255–6; Neumann, 2013, p. 127). But, in news language, we have to keep in mind that journalistic guidelines emphasize the use of active voice as a means to make the story more vital and easier to process for an audience who does not have much time (Harcup, 2005, pp. 107, 129; Keeble, 2006, p. 96; Pape & Featherstone, 2005, pp. 42, 51). This means that a dominance of active voice has to be expected, and is indeed reflected in the results.

What we can see from this distribution is that the USA stands out as containing the fewest instances of passive voice, and Kenya as featuring the most. These two regions contribute most to the significance of the differences (χ^2=545, df=4, p<0.000), whereas the other three varieties hardly differ at all with regard to their median values and only slightly regarding the range covered by their respective boxes and whiskers. The domains again differ more widely (χ^2=2187.03, df=4, p<0.000) – here, hard news and politics have the highest median values of passive voice and also display the widest ranges. Despite the evenness, some extreme outliers are observable – especially in hard news, and most prominently in Australia – and the content of these particular articles exemplifies some of the concrete functions passive voice can take in news. The most common themes in this domain are crimes and accidents, as was indicated by the keyword analysis; when dealing with these topics, some factors, like the identities of criminals, might be unknown or preferred to be kept back, which then makes the passive voice a handy choice for a report:

> [15] North Kuta Police chief Aldi Alfa said Mr Gill **was attacked** by two people attempting to rob the villa. (K. Lamb, 2013, the *Sydney Morning Herald*; emphasis added)

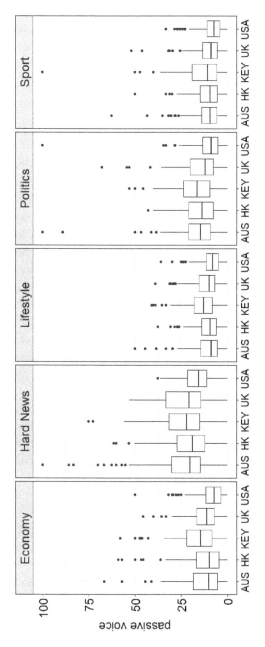

Figure 14 Frequencies of passive voice in % of all finite verbs

In other cases, the noun phrase that functions as the subject in an active construction is obvious or simply not important, and the passive is used to shift the focus to another party:

> [16] The victim **was rushed** to the Royal Brisbane and Women's Hospital [...] (Bochenski. 2013, the *Sydney Morning Herald*; emphasis added)

Even if a piece of information, for instance the identity of an attacker, is known, structuring the sentence in passive voice creates a different emphasis in a story. It foregrounds one news actor (in this case the victim) while hiding or backgrounding another (the attacker) (Fowler, 1991, pp. 77–8). This is related to a study by Bohner (2001), which found that, especially in crime news, the passive is frequently used to assign responsibility to the victim by omitting the assailant as an actor. An ideological construction of the roles of good and evil can thus be strengthened by a journalist's choice of voice.

Another strategy originating from Critical Discourse Analysis is described by van Dijk (1998, pp. 32–3; emphasis in original): "OUR people tend to appear primarily as actors when the acts are good, and THEIR people when the acts are bad, and vice versa: THEIR people will appear less as actors of good actions than do OUR people". This concentrates more on news with ideological dimensions, and in the present dataset respective examples can be found primarily in political news featuring violence or war:

> [17] Egypt's new military-backed government said its soldiers acted in self-defense during the altercation, in which soldiers **gunned** down at least 50 Islamists. One Egyptian soldier **was killed**. (Bradley, 2013, the *Wall Street Journal Asia*; emphasis added)

Here, the roles of good and bad are created by the verbs *gun down*, which is clearly attributed to an actor, and *killed*, which is phrased in passive voice, making it more laborious for the reader to identify the culprit. It is obvious which of the two involved parties the audience is supposed to feel close to, and towards which one the author increases the distance.

What we can see from these examples is that passive voice constructions are a powerful tool to distinguish groups in a text on moral grounds. Using the passive always implies a higher distance towards the backgrounded or omitted party. Active voice is more straightforward and brings the reader closer to the respective news actors, marking them as active members of the event. In this sense, the results show that hard news and political news work with a higher distance than the other domains, which makes sense as they also displayed high tendencies towards factual information and lower values for evaluative boosters and minimizers. What we can see for lifestyle and sports news is also in line with previous results – these domains contain the most active constructions, which once again underlines their interpersonal focus.

Among the varieties, articles from Kenya stand out as being more distant, which matches the impression gained so far. In contrast, US news appears most directly oriented towards its readers. Hong Kong is similar to the USA in most domains and shows surprisingly few passives, seeing that it appears to create distance rather than closeness in other respects.

8.2.5 Nominalizations

As a last operationalization of the social distance, we will examine the inclusion of nominalizations. The feature's frequency in itself is very helpful, but to put it into perspective, we will consider the overall amount of nouns (including nominalized forms), too. In the corpus query, nominalizations were defined as including all nouns that end on *-tion*, *-ness*, *-ity*, *-ism*, *-ment* or *-ing* in both plural and singular forms. Instances of *thing* and *things* were not counted (Table 11).

Table 11 Relative frequencies of nouns and nominalizations

		AUS	HK	KEY	UK	USA	Σ domain	range
ECO	Nomin.	2.8	3.09	3.89	2.25	2.3	2.82	1.64
	Nouns	24.15	25.33	24.66	23.83	24.36	24.46	1.5
HN	Nomin.	1.56	2.45	2.57	1.53	2.2	2.05	1.04
	Nouns	22.39	23.93	23.11	21.38	22.54	22.6	2.55
LIFE	Nomin.	1.76	2.01	2.29	1.48	1.62	1.84	0.81
	Nouns	22.25	23.88	22.05	21.38	22.69	22.46	2.5
POL	Nomin.	3.41	3.99	3.53	2.56	2.73	3.22	1.43
	Nouns	21.71	22.63	20.21	20.94	21.49	21.41	2.42
SPO	Nomin.	1.19	1.81	1.41	1.19	1.08	1.32	0.73
	Nouns	18.03	20.27	19.37	17.02	17.78	18.39	3.25
Σ variety	Nomin.	2.14	2.62	2.69	1.77	1.95	2.21	
	Nouns	21.36	23.2	21.85	20.81	21.73	21.83	
range	Nomin.	2.22	2.18	2.48	1.37	1.65		2.91
	Nouns	6.12	5.06	5.29	6.81	6.58		8.31

Again, the differences are larger between the domains than between the varieties. News from economy and politics produces the highest amounts of nominalizations, but in terms of all nouns, politics is more moderate and only economy is clearly set apart from the rest. Sports news on the other hand contains the fewest nominalized forms as well as the fewest nouns overall. The variation between the domains is almost equally significant in terms of nouns (χ^2=4844.17, df=4, p<0.000) and nominalizations (χ^2=4566.41, df=4, p<0.000) and, in both cases, the extremes of economy and sports news are the strongest factors.

Of the regions, the UK contains the fewest nominalizations in all domains except in sports news. The L2 varieties demonstrate a higher social distance, including the most nominalized forms, but have their peaks in different domains: in Kenya, articles from the economy, lifestyle and hard news sections contain the most nominalizations and, in Hong Kong, sports and politics are dominant in this respect.

What does this tell us about the texts and the regions they come from? We interpret nominalizations as a reflection of the social distance in this chapter, but the function of this linguistic feature goes a bit deeper.

> To understand this, reflect on how much information goes unexpressed in a derived nominal, compared with a full clause: compare, for example, "allegations" with the fully spelt-out proposition "X has alleged against Y that Y did A and that Y did B [etc.]". Deleted in the nominal form are the participants (who did what to whom?), any indication of time – because there is no verb to be tensed – and any indication of modality – the writer's views as the truth or the desirability of the proposition. (Fowler, 1991, p. 80)

Against this background, the frequent use of nominalizations in Hong Kong and especially Kenyan news can be interpreted as politically motivated. It decreases the evaluative stance of the text and suppresses the author's opinion, which is a useful tool for self-censorship.

It should be kept in mind, though, that the results here were not filtered by whether or not they appear in direct quotes. The omission of information caused by a nominalization might also originate from actors other than the journalist. To trace these instances, a qualitative analysis is required which looks at the nominalized expression and checks if the journalist fills the gaps created by the syntactic choice at another point in the article and, if so, how. In other cases, like the domains of sports and lifestyle, this function of nominalizations is not as relevant, because the topics treated here are less ideologically loaded.

8.3 Summary

For the tenor of discourse, we analyzed eight linguistic features, three to reflect the social role relationship and five to represent social distance. In summary, the results are very diverse for the individual linguistic markers, but some tendencies are seen which can be assumed to be characteristic of the respective domains and varieties. Again, we can find more variation on the functional level than on the regional one.

Looking at the domains, lifestyle news appears most characteristic. The articles published in this section contain the highest amounts of interrogatives and imperatives and are marked by a low specialization in terms of keyword amounts. These features make the news very accessible for a broad target group, because the readers do not need any particular knowledge. Additionally, they are faced with a social distance that is constructed at a very low level, via frequent 1st and 2nd person pronouns and rare use of passive voice and nominalizations. Lifestyle articles also hardly ever refer to places outside the country of their publication, so that local audiences are addressed strongly.

Lifestyle articles already stood out in the examination of the field of discourse, but showed parallels with sports news. For the tenor, we can see that the domains are again similar in terms of social distance, but for the social role relationship, sports news is much more specialized and definitely requires knowledge, or at least strong interest from its readers. The potential audience is therefore not as broad as for lifestyle news, although the stories are told in a similarly informal style.

Again, we can see hard news as the opposite to lifestyle and sports in most aspects. This domain contains the fewest modal verbs and boosters and minimizers, which shows a clear orientation towards neutral style and factual information unobscured by speculation or ambiguity. Hard news also stands out using many passive constructions, which further enhances the distance.

The other two domains, economy and politics, can be seen to be similar in many ways and can be considered between lifestyle and sports on the one and hard news on the other hand. One major difference between the two is that political news shows an interesting combination of frequent use of both nominalizations and modals. This constellation suggests that while these news items create a formal impression and atmosphere, they also include high degrees of vagueness and avoidance of clear statements.

Regarding the varieties, a rough distinction can be seen between the UK and Australia on the one and Hong Kong and Kenya on the other hand. News from Australia and the UK displays the highest amounts of non-declarative mood as well as the most modals. The UK demonstrates a very low degree of specialization, too. These indicators, which work to construct a low degree of hierarchy and a low distance between author and reader, are emphasized even further by the frequent use of boosters and minimizers, and 1st and 2nd person pronouns.

Hong Kong and Kenya often appear as opposites to this involved style, but some differences between the L2 varieties can be seen. Hong Kong is the most rigorous in terms of declarative mood and also contains fewest modals and 1st and 2nd person pronouns, whereas Kenya is firmly in the middle of the field for these indicators. Regarding boosters and minimizers and the use of passive voice, however, Kenya produces the extreme values indicating distance, always followed by Hong Kong. In terms of nominalizations, the two regions were similarly set apart from the rest. We can conclude from this that both regions emphasize a formal and distanced style, but realize it via different means.

Least clear in their tendencies are news items from the USA. On the one hand, they display the highest specialization of all regions, which means that readers are supposed to have background knowledge and the author constructs the image of expertise; on the other hand, they are not written in a more distanced way than the other news texts, with average values in most aspects and the fewest nominalizations. Most characteristic about news from the US is the way place references are used; it is the only region which does not put an emphasis on geographical nearness. Instead, it relates to European countries much more frequently than to its immediate neighboring places. Similar to Australia, it also shows a strong focus on regional and local events, which is to be attributed to the size of these two countries.

During the analyses, we found that the functions of the linguistic markers often vary and are not always consistent throughout all their occurrences. They were interpreted here as what they have been found to represent most strongly in previous studies, and what could be learned from spot checks into our data. Nonetheless, this diversity means that some fine-grained implications get lost in a quantitative study. As a conclusion, we can say that the parameter of tenor of discourse is reflected in some interesting clusters for both varieties and domains, which confirm some tendencies seen for the field of discourse and will be checked again in the analysis of mode.

9 Mode of discourse

The last of the three parameters that define the situational context of a discourse is the mode. It describes "the particular part that the language is playing in the interactive process" (Halliday & Hasan, 1985, p. 24). Usually, the subdimensions that characterize it are channel, language role and medium, but only the last one is relevant for our analysis.

9.1 Medium

The medium reflects the style of the language that is being used and determines whether it has more properties that are considered typical of spoken language, or whether it tends to be more similar to typical written discourse. We will examine it in terms of the use of contractions, sentence-initial coordinators, pronouns and nouns, and nominalizations, and take another look at the lexical density in combination with word class distribution. A frequent use of the first three indicates a more spoken style, which makes the discourse more colloquial and accessible. The use of frequent nouns and nominalizations on the other hand are characteristic of written language.

Like the other parameters and their subdimensions, medium is analyzed separately here, but should always be seen in the context of the whole analysis. Particularly the lexical density, which was examined for the field of discourse, reflects the medium to some degree, because the relation between pronouns on the one hand, and nouns and nominalizations on the other, has an influence on this measurement. Since medium is the only subdimension to represent the mode of discourse in our study, we will refer back to our previous findings frequently.

9.1.1 Pronominal use

The use of pronouns is the first linguistic feature we will look at in this section. Separate aspects of it have already been examined as representing goal orientation and social distance but, for medium, we are interested in the collective frequencies of the entire word class, rather than individual pronouns.

Across the domains, the differences regarding pronominal use are significant (χ^2=6709.18, df=4, p=0.000). Lifestyle and sports are similar and use relatively many pronouns, with overall percentages of 6.37 and 6.12. Hard news and politics contain fewer pronouns, but are also clustered together. News from economy stands apart, the texts contain by far the fewest pronouns across all regions. Looking at the varieties, we can see differences, too (significant at $\chi^2=2430.05$, df=4, p<0.000), most prominently in the case of Hong Kong. While the other four regions differ only within a range of 1.09 percentage points, the discrepancy of Hong Kong news towards the second lowest variety, the USA, is 1.15, and towards the UK with the highest value 2.24 percentage points.

These numbers are not surprising when we put them into the context of the previous analyses. Both lifestyle and sports news demonstrated trends towards low distance and informal style, and this is underlined by a spoken orientation of the medium. Economic news was found to create a higher degree of distance and more formality, which in turn is emphasized by a style more characteristic of written language. The same holds true for the variety of Hong Kong. For the UK and Australia, too, the tendencies that became visible before are confirmed: both regions construct more direct links between author and reader than the other varieties, and clearly display the strongest leaning towards the spoken medium in terms of pronominal use.

Table 12 Pronouns – Absolute and relative frequencies

	AUS	HK	KEY	UK	USA	Σ abs. freq. % of domain	range
Economy	2,440	1,943	1,816	3,056	2,664	11,919	1,240
	3.43%	2.37%	2.76%	3.61%	3.13%	3.07%	1.24
Hard News	2,832	2,062	2,754	5,399	4,223	17,270	3,337
	5.17%	3.17%	4.71%	6.53%	4.95%	4.99%	3.36
Lifestyle	6,837	5,786	8,936	8,471	6,727	36,757	3,150
	6.74%	4.92%	7.06%	7.42%	5.72%	6.37%	2.5
Politics	3,378	2,724	3,128	4,564	3,880	17,674	1,840
	4.41%	3.31%	4.17%	5.15%	4.36%	4.29%	1.84
Sports	5,306	4,270	3,090	7,238	6,342	23,246	4,148
	6.61%	4.94%	4.77%	7.25%	6.49%	6.12%	2.48
Σ abs. freq.	20,793	16,785	19,724	28,728	23,836	109,866	
% of variety	5.41%	3.87%	5.05%	6.11%	5.02%	5.12%	
range	4,397	3,843	7,120	5,415	4,063		7,120
	3.31	2.57	4.3	3.81	3.36		5.05

9.1.2 Sentence-initial coordinators

For conjunctions in general, an assignment to spoken or written discourse is not straightforward, because different findings on their frequencies have been reported. Coordinating conjunctions have been found to be more common in spoken language by Neumann and Fest (2016, pp. 210–11), but more characteristic of written discourse by Biber et al. (1999, p. 81). In both studies, the differences are relatively small, but very clear tendencies are observable for coordinators in sentence- or turn-initial position. Biber et al.'s (1999, p. 84) findings show that, in spoken language, coordinators occur at the beginning of a sentence or turn more than twice as often as in written discourse. This linguistic marker can therefore be used as a representation of medium.

Out of all coordinators, the dominant word is *and*, which makes up 77.25% of this word class. *But* and *or* contribute another 13.8% and 7.13% respectively, which means that all other relevant words together only amount to 1.82%. Looking at the overall distribution of coordinators, we can once again see more diversity among the domains (χ^2=465.74, df=4, p<0.000) than among the regions (χ^2=123.46, df=4, p<0.000), and previous trends are again confirmed.

Table 13 Relative frequencies of coordinators (General and sentence-initial)

		AUS	HK	KEY	UK	USA	domain	range
ECO	Coord.	2.7	2.6	2.88	2.61	2.56	2.66	0.32
	Sent.-init.	0.17	0.13	0.05	0.27	0.2	0.17	0.22
HN	Coord.	3.11	2.85	2.76	3.03	2.84	2.92	0.35
	Sent.-init.	0.07	0.1	0.06	0.17	0.1	0.11	0.11
LIFE	Coord.	3.71	3.6	3.42	3.53	3.45	3.54	0.29
	Sent.-init.	0.2	0.2	0.19	0.33	0.22	0.23	0.14
POL	Coord.	2.75	2.69	2.71	2.87	2.6	2.72	0.27
	Sent.-init.	0.18	0.12	0.1	0.21	0.22	0.17	0.12
SPO	Coord.	3.09	2.95	2.73	3.15	2.95	2.99	0.42
	Sent.-init.	0.17	0.16	0.12	0.31	0.29	0.22	0.19
variety	Coord.	3.12	3	2.98	3.07	2.92	3.01	
	Sent.-init.	0.17	0.15	0.12	0.27	0.21	0.19	
range	Coord.	1.01	1	0.71	0.92	0.89		1.15
	Sent.-init.	0.13	0.1	0.14	0.16	0.19		0.28

With regard to the overall frequencies of coordinators, the varieties are quite similar, but for sentence-initial ones, we can see a clear distinction between the native and the L2 varieties. Australia and the USA, and most explicitly the UK, all use coordinators in a way that is typical of spoken language, whereas Hong Kong and Kenya show a more written use of this feature.

This difference is clearly visible in all domains except hard news, where the numbers are closer together in general. Here, the formal style which was indicated in the analyses for social distance is confirmed. Politics and economy, too, seem similar again, whereas lifestyle and sports stand out with a use of coordinators closer to the spoken language style.

9.1.3 Contractions

The use of contractions is usually connected to spoken language (Biber et al., 1999, pp. 1128–32), but it also signals a more direct style and, in doing so, is related to the factor of social distance as much as to medium. When we look at the distribution of contracted forms in the dataset, they appear very similar to what we just saw for sentence-initial coordinators in the previous section (Figure 15).

For lifestyle and sports news, the tendency to use spoken style is confirmed, because the domains contain comparatively high numbers of contractions. The other three domains do not display many differences, so hard news is not as divergent as it was for other features. All domains show internal variation, however, with Kenyan news the most varied of all. The median for news from this region is 0 in all domains except lifestyle, which shows that Kenyan articles are very standardized and oriented towards written medium in terms of contractions. The three native varieties are quite similar to each other, although the median for the USA is highest in all fields. In terms of overall use, the discrepancies between differences on the regional on the one hand, and functional level on the other hand, are less expressed than for other features: the regional differences are significant at $\chi^2=3154.44$ (df=4, p<0.000), the functional ones at $\chi^2=3597.59$ (df=4, p<0.000).

9.1.4 Nominalizations

As a last operationalization for the medium, we will examine the amount of nominalizations, a mechanism that is characteristic of written language. We already saw in Chapter 8 that this linguistic feature has implications for the social distance that is created in a text, because it offers the possibility of omitting information. Independent of such functions, we are now interested

MODE OF DISCOURSE 125

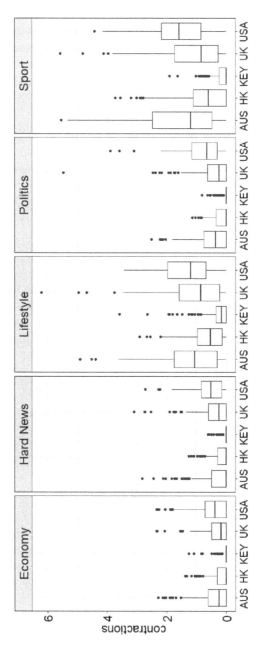

Figure 15 Distribution of contractions

solely in the frequencies, which confirm most of the observations related to the other factors of medium.

Of the varieties, the UK stands out as containing the fewest nominalizations, and also the least internal variation. Between sports, which contains the fewest nominalizations, and politics with the most, there is a difference of only 1.37%. News from the UK, therefore, once again appears in a very spoken style. The L2 varieties show the highest values for nominalizations, which is in line with the previous findings that they tend towards written style, but Kenya displays the biggest internal difference (2.48% between economy and sports news). The news from this region therefore seems less standardized in its use of nominalizations, which is especially due to the relatively large amount of nominalized items in economy (3.89%).

For the domains, too, our assumptions based on the other linguistic features are confirmed. Lifestyle and sports, which were shown to construct low social distance and spoken style, contain the fewest nominalizations. The language in these news items seems to be colloquial to a higher degree than in the other domains. This is possible because the topics covered here are not as serious and dramatic, which makes a less formal presentation more appropriate than it would be in articles dealing with crimes or deaths.

Interestingly, the domains of politics and economy, which in terms of the other features for medium were very similar, are clearly set apart in their use of nominalizations. Politics contains an average of 3.22%, economy only 2.82%. The values in politics are highest for the L2 varieties, which are also weakest in terms of press freedom. This indicates that the effect of nominalizations for medium is not as clear as that of the other linguistic features, but that its meaning for the social distance is very strong.

9.1.5 Lexical density/Distribution of word classes

For the last analysis in this study, we will take another look at lexical density. The values for the individual categories and the distribution across the texts have already been discussed as an operationalization for the experiential domain. In that context, it was taken as a reflection of the complexity of the topic a text deals with. At this point, in relation to medium, we are interested in this feature because a low lexical density is typical of spoken discourse (Neumann, 2013, p. 76). This logically follows from other linguistic markers analyzed before: nominalizations, which are characteristic of written language, are content words, whereas pronouns, which count as function words, are more frequent in spoken discourse. The lexical density is in a way a summary of that, but a look at the distribution of the main word classes adds further insights.

We will first focus on a comparison between the domains (see Figure 16). Among the content words, nouns and verbs are the dominant word classes in every field, but their difference is largest in economic news. Economy puts a clear focus on nouns and, as was seen in the previous chapter, on nominalizations as well, whereas it contains the fewest verbs. From this, we can conclude that the high lexical density values for this domain originate from the dominance of nouns. In hard news and politics on the other hand, verbs and proper nouns are responsible for the high lexical density values. For all three, a tendency towards the written medium can be concluded.

In general, proper names are the third most frequent content word class in all domains except lifestyle, which is not surprising since the keywords analysis and the examination of pronouns already showed that this domain works more on the pronominal level.

The function words also pattern across the domains. Prepositions and determiners clearly make up the majority in this area, and their numbers are similar in all domains. Pronouns are third in every case, but their numbers vary more and are highest in lifestyle and sports articles, once more reflecting the more personal and informal style of these categories (Figure 16).

If we look at the varieties and the distributions of the word classes, we can see that, once again, the differences are less pronounced on this axis, but they, too, reflect what has been found before.

Nouns and verbs are the dominant content word classes again. The biggest difference here is between Hong Kong, which works mainly with nouns, and the UK, which relies more on verbs. The UK stood out before as having very low degrees of lexical density, and we can now see that that can be traced back to a comparatively rare use of proper names combined with many pronouns. Among the function words, prepositions and determiners are again very constant and the most frequent word classes. Relating this to the subdimension of medium, we can confirm previous results, especially for the spoken style used in the UK and the opposite trend towards written style for the L2 varieties, most notably for Hong Kong (Figure 17).

9.2 Summary

In contrast to the parameters of field and tenor, for which we analyzed two subdimensions each, the mode of discourse is represented in this study by only one subdimension, the medium. The operationalization contained five

128 NEWS ACROSS FIVE CONTINENTS

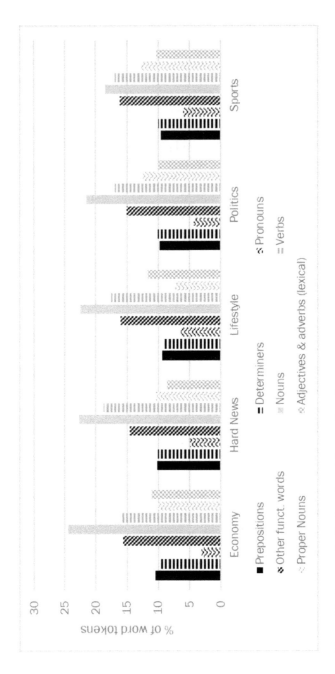

Figure 16 Average distribution of word classes – Domains

MODE OF DISCOURSE 129

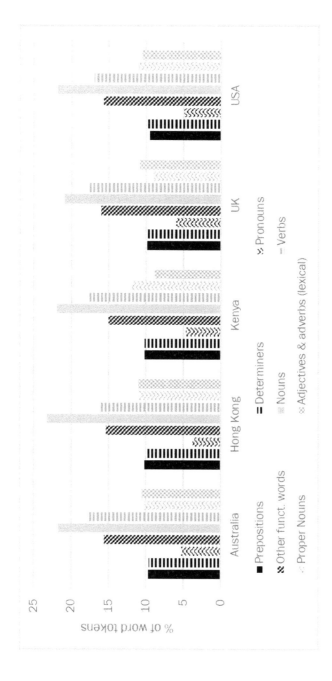

Figure 17 Average distribution of word classes – Regions

features, pronominal use, sentence-initial coordinators, contractions, nouns and nominalizations and lexical density, three of which had been analyzed before in the context of another parameter. Their results therefore not only contribute to an understanding of medium, but also show how closely related the parameters and their subdimensions are.

In this sense, the analysis of medium first of all confirms a number of assumptions resulting from the preceding analyses. Again, more variation can be found between the domains than between the varieties, and particularly sports and lifestyle news show the clearest orientation towards the spoken medium.

Among the varieties, although the values were generally closer together, we find some characteristics which support the distinction between the native and the L2 varieties. News from the UK tends towards spoken style, reflected in many pronouns and sentence-initial coordinators, a low lexical density and comparatively few nouns and nominalizations. Hong Kong, in contrast, contains the fewest personal pronouns and the highest lexical density on average. Kenya and Hong Kong have similarly low results regarding sentence-initial coordinators and contractions, and both varieties demonstrate a frequent use of nouns and nominalizations.

The mode of discourse is the third and last parameter of the situational context as defined in the register framework. During the analyses, the features were explained and we offered some explanation for the results. In the next chapter, we will now move back to a more general level of interpretation and return to our original research goals and questions, connecting our results to the concept of press freedom.

10 Regional and functional variation – What do we learn?

In the last chapter, we analyzed our dataset in terms of three parameters of context, the field, tenor and mode of discourse. They represent the overall topic, the interpersonal relations between the participants and the use of language, and conclusions for these individual aspects and their subdimensions were already drawn. In this chapter, we will bring them together and discuss the meanings of the results for the broader research goals: How can analyses of regional and functional variation benefit each other? What can we learn about these two dimensions from the combined analyses? What can we say about the media discourse in the five regions? And can we see a correlation between language use and freedom of the press?

10.1 Functional variation – Characteristics of newspaper writing

The five domains that we included in this book were chosen because they appear as separate sections in all newspapers, and can therefore be seen as essential parts of newspaper publications in all five regions. The categorization of the sampled articles into the domains – economy, hard news, lifestyle, politics and sports – was not conducted by us on the basis of the content, but was taken over from the newspapers' websites.

Although the categories are obviously a working mechanism in the reality of newspapers, they are not usually considered separately in journalistic manuals or guidelines. If anything, features and news are dealt with on their own, but it appears that the majority of writing advice is intended to be generalizable. The analyses in terms of register parameters revealed some crucial differences between the domains, however, which allow conclusions regarding their purposes and production context.

Throughout all analyses, it became clear that there is more variation on the functional than on the regional level. This is not surprising, because the domains are a more artificial categorization than the regional varieties, so the discrepancies are naturally greater. For our results, this means that there is more variation within the regional varieties (i.e. between the domains within a region) than within the domains (i.e. within one domain across all regions). For every feature that was analyzed quantitatively, we determined two overall values for every region and domain: (1) the difference between highest and lowest value (range), reflecting the level of internal variation, and (2) the deviation from the category's average value, indicating how standardized the news items are. Figure 18 shows these two for the domains, always across all five regions.[1]

Of course, the domains differed regarding the field of discourse; this was to be expected, because the terminology used in the respective news articles reflect the relevant topics of their area. We found lifestyle news to stand out in this respect due to its frequent use of pronouns, indicating a very interpersonal angle. The other analyses, especially the tenor of discourse, confirmed this by showing that this domain constructs low levels of distance and hierarchy as well.

It seems that for lifestyle news to be categorized as such, the human interest angle is crucial, whereas the topics are not specific. This is interesting because it shows that the news value of human interest (Bednarek & Caple, 2014) can be implemented in any topic or, in other words, that any topic can become a lifestyle article. Since the items also feature a very informal and rather spoken style, they are very accessible for a broad readership. This way, topics that would otherwise be more complex or require expertise can be made available to a much wider target group.

This effect is strengthened even further by a very high degree of adaptability of the domain; lifestyle news shows the highest internal variation and lowest degree of standardization. The language use is very flexible, and can be tuned to match the topic at hand, which allows the authors of these articles a lot more room for different means of presenting content and adapting the degrees of reader-oriented writing. A curiosity in our dataset is that large parts of the deviations and ranges in lifestyle originate from Kenyan news – we will look into this more closely in the next chapter dealing with regional variation.

Sports news was found to be very similar to lifestyle news in many aspects, especially regarding the medium and the social distance. In terms of deviations, though, we can see that it appears to be a lot more standardized around average language use, and the internal variation is the second lowest of all domains. This makes sense if we consider that the range of topics in this domain is fairly restricted, which showed in the keywords. The low TTR furthermore proves that although different sports have sets of specific terminology, there is a kind of overarching sports vocabulary which is nearly exclusive to this domain, yet relevant for most topics within it (e.g. items such as *league*, *season*,

---

[1] See appendix 3 for an overview of all values, ranges and deviations.

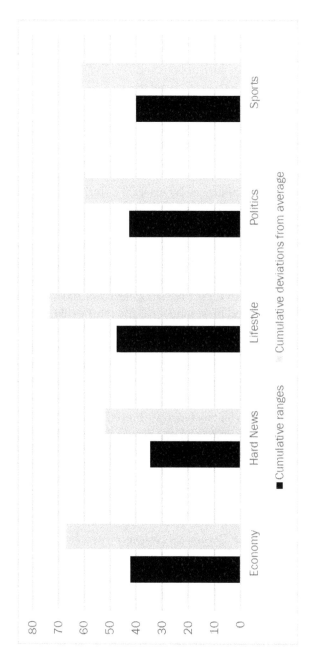

Figure 18 Cumulative ranges and deviations from average – Domains

match, team etc.). Sports news definitely requires more expertise from its readers than lifestyle articles, but shares with lifestyle the characteristic that news here is constructed as less serious and more open to evaluation. This shows not only in the amounts of boosters and minimizers, but also in the low frequencies of passive constructions and nominalizations, both of which are mechanisms that can be used to avoid giving a clear stance or opinion.

In contrast to these two domains, hard news was found to work on a very formal and distanced level and emphasizes the informative purpose most of all. This is reflected in the internal variation and deviations. The domain is extremely standardized, much more than the other four, and does not vary much across the regions either. The keywords, especially the significance of *police*, showed that it is highly influenced by external criteria on the content level. This makes it the opposite of lifestyle news, where the given content is less relevant and the news value that is constructed within the article is more crucial.

All in all, hard news items appear closest to what is described in writing textbooks and journalism manuals – they are, in a way, the stereotypical news. Topics from this area – crime, accidents, natural disasters – are also the most common examples in these books (e.g. Harcup, 2005, pp. 108–9; Keeble, 2006, pp. 94–108), and most guidelines are most easily applied to these stories because, at first sight, there are almost no ideological implications in the events described here. For most crimes or accidents, the roles of "good" and "bad" are clearly assigned to victim and criminal or attacker, respectively. These roles are predefined by our moral standards, and do not need to be expressed or justified explicitly by the journalist. The ideal of news being objective therefore seems to be most easily achieved for such stories.

However, as our analyses showed, the picture is not quite so clear-cut. Although hard news promotes an informative and distanced style, constructing the impression of objectivity, it was found to contain more passive constructions than any other domain. In this aspect it contradicts common journalistic guidelines. This characteristic can be attributed to some degree to passive formulations which omit the actor simply because it is obvious or not relevant; in statements like *The injured passenger was taken to the nearest hospital*, readers can assume from the content that an ambulance was involved and carried out the act of transporting the injured. Of course, the focus is shifted from ambulance to passenger by constructing the sentence in passive voice and omitting the actor, but this does not carry much in terms of evaluation. There are other uses of the passive voice though, namely to shift or omit blame or responsibility (Bohner, 2001; Dijk, 1998; Fowler, 1991), and the amounts of passives used in hard news suggest that we have to assume evaluative instances which negate the construction of objectivity.

Lastly, the domains of economy and politics are the hardest to tell apart. Of course, the topics in these areas often overlap – economic matters are often commented on by policians, or involve political actors or decisions, and politics in turn deals with business matters or related people frequently. The keyword analysis shows that there are differences regarding the experiential domain, but the other analyses, especially that of medium and goal orientation, show scant differences between the two categories.

So how can we distinguish between these two domains? The main respect in which they differ was found in the subdimension of social hierarchy, more specifically in terms of modality. Political news contains more modals than any other domain, and although we have to attribute them to some degree to direct quotes, the effect remains that the news items here involve more vagueness and speculation. At the same time, they contain more keywords than news from economy, indicating a slightly more specialized terminology. Political news also shows a higher degree of standardization than items from economy, so the higher threshold of accessibility created by the required expertise seems to be the norm in this domain.

10.2 Regional variation – The differences between the varieties

From the results regarding the functional variation, we can draw conclusions about the varieties, too, and many of these can be explained by the regions' historical and geographical backgrounds and language policies. This becomes most evident in the cases of the L2 varieties. To put the results into perspective, we will again draw on the ranges and deviations, as shown in Figure 19.

News articles from Kenya and Hong Kong have a lot in common, most particularly that they construct a higher distance between author and reader and draw less on boosters and minimizers than the native varieties do. Also, they are both oriented towards a more written style, which reflects that English is not the dominant medium of everyday communication, but is mainly found in restricted, official contexts in which the written channel and medium are more relevant (E. W. Schneider, 2007, p. 196). In many advanced and endonormatively stabilized varieties, written norms have been found to be highly influential on language use in general (Mesthrie & Bhatt, 2008, p. 114), so we can assume this effect in Kenya and Hong Kong to originate from this more general trend, at least to some degree.

Despite these similarities, we can see some very clear and interesting differences between the L2 varieties. In Hong Kong, the degree of interpersonal closeness that is constructed is minimal and the impression of objectivity

136 NEWS ACROSS FIVE CONTINENTS

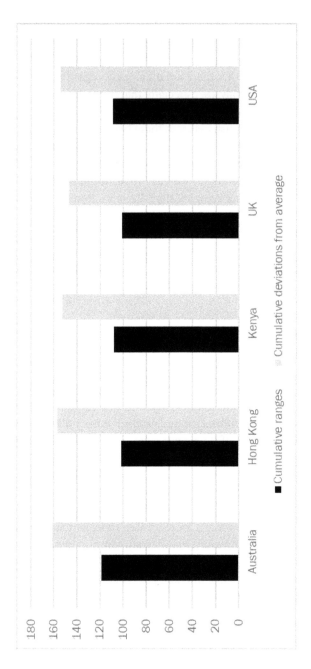

Figure 19 Cumulative ranges and deviations from average – Regions

and informativeness is emphasized strongly, which matches the unique political situation of that region. Although it is officially a part of China, Hong Kong holds an autonomous status and, due to its strategic position as a hub for trade and economy, it is oriented towards international partners. Nevertheless, the political system of China is influential on publications in Hong Kong (F. L. Lee & Chan, 2008; F. L. Lee & Lin, 2006) and, as a result, Hong Kong's press freedom has seen a mixed, but generally negative development since the first ranking in 2002 (RSF, 2020; see also Figure 1 in chapter 3.2). In addition, news here has been found to be heavily influenced by self-censorship (C.-C. Lee, 1998; F. L. Lee & Chan, 2008; F. L. Lee & Lin, 2006). Low degrees of evaluative content and frequent use of passive constructions and nominalizations as strategies to omit bits of information reflect these restrictions on news production.

News from Kenya appears a little less standardized in terms of language. Although the difference is small, this is nonetheless surprising because, in Kenya especially, English is an official but not a dominant language. In contrast to Hong Kong, where proficiency in English has long been connected to professional success and was supported by the British during their colonial rule, it was kept intentionally low in Kenya and has not been established as a requirement to such a degree, although the importance of English in the country is increasing (E. W. Schneider, 2007, p. 193).

This would suggest that Kenyan English is more limited in its functional variation than Hong Kong English, and that texts would be highly standardized, but the variety contains a higher internal variation than the sample from Hong Kong. Looking at the values, we can see that the extreme domains, hard news and lifestyle, are responsible for this, but that Kenyan lifestyle, especially, stands out from the whole dataset. Lifestyle items from this region produce extreme (that is, highest or lowest) values for seven linguistic features when compared to the same news category from elsewhere, and for 12 features in the variety-internal perspective. Additionally, the articles are the longest on average.

What is it that makes these articles so characteristic? From the analyses we can see that Kenya as a whole tends towards written style, and informative and formal writing, but that the opposite is true for the lifestyle domain. It is characterized by a relatively low level of distance and hierarchy and a low accessibility, and puts a strong focus on a human interest angle. The same trends are visible in the other regions, but the discrepancies between lifestyle on the one hand, and the remaining domains on the other, are not that great.

We concluded earlier that lifestyle articles offer a platform for any topic, as long as the news value of human interest is foregrounded. Comparing Kenyan lifestyle news to the others from the same domain, the top twenty keywords include four names of politicians and the term *government*, whereas the other regions focus on softer topics like health, beauty, technical gadgets etc. This suggests that political and social topics are more frequent in this domain in Kenya, and that they are discussed in more detail, resulting in longer articles. The emphasis on the news value of human interest might work as a mechanism to publish critical and evaluative content in a less regulated environment, a place where more serious issues are covered, but are hidden in informal and colloquial style and a more accessible form. This might be a strategy to circumvent restrictions of press freedom, but disguising topics in such a way could also be interpreted as a new mechanism of self-censorship. Based on our research, we cannot draw more detailed conclusions on this, but the results indicate implications for press freedom at this point. The quantitative results hint at a similar strategy in Hong Kong – here, too, the lifestyle domain is set apart from the others, although not as clearly. The keyword list for this category does not confirm any political leaning though; Hong Kong lifestyle news seems to be more flexible and less restricted simply because it covers less critical content.

With these insights into functional variation in the different regions, what do we gain for variational linguistics? We set out with the assumption that the two dimensions of variation interact, and that a combined analysis can benefit both angles. Based on this, we can formulate some more general conclusions for the varieties included here, more concretely on the developmental status of the L2 varieties and the degree to which they relate to the individual native ones.

Regarding the developmental status of Kenyan and Hong Kong English, the comparison with each other as well as to the different native standards shows that the two L2 varieties have features in common, some of which, like the tendency towards written medium, are characteristic of developing varieties in general. However, they are different to such a degree that a categorization in any given model is difficult, because categorizing them alike heavily foregrounds the similarities and obscures the differences.

In the models by McArthur (1987) and Görlach (1990) Kenyan and Hong Kong English are both placed in the outer rings of the respective wheel structures, and B. B. Kachru (1996, 2006) assigns both to the outer circle of norm-developing varieties. E. W. Schneider (2007, pp. 133–9, 189–97) offers a more detailed description; he, too, categorizes Hong Kong and Kenyan English alike, both as being in the third phase of nativization of his model, but he predicts different developments for the two cases.

For Kenya, he assumes that English is unlikely to become a symbol of national identity. Instead, he predicts that a conflict between support and opposition from within the country will cause Kenyan English to move to the fourth phase of endonormative stabilization, but be very homogeneous. For Hong Kong, he points out that the future of English depends on "economic, sociological, and political developments" in both Hong Kong and China, which makes it particularly hard to predict (E. W. Schneider, 2007, p. 139). Because of its necessity for business and trade, English is considered an important factor in the education of young people (Bolton, 2000, p. 271; E. Chan, 2002, p. 271; Pennington & Yue, 1994, p. 2), and its status is accordingly somewhat secure. However, an increasing influence from China could lead to different scenarios: on the one hand, English could become a distinguishing factor of Hong Kongers and a symbol of identity, should the Chinese government attempt to forcefully impose a political direction unwelcome to the people in the city (Joseph, 2004, pp. 159–61; E. W. Schneider, 2007, p. 139). On the other hand, a more ideological and less forceful exertion of influence, in combination with China's growing economic dominance, could lead to English becoming less important, so that the contexts in which it is used decrease gradually.

The results that we presented in this study cannot confirm or refute these general hypotheses with regard to the future of the two varieties – a diachronic perspective would be required to trace trends and, especially in Hong Kong, the current political events are likely to have a long-lasting effect on the developmental course of English which cannot yet be predicted. Still, the analyses show that there are differences between Kenyan and Hong Kong English which are not in line with approaches that categorize them alike. In particular, the aspect of homogeneity in Kenya cannot be confirmed in the present study; the variety demonstrates more internal variation as represented by the cumulative ranges than Hong Kong and even the UK.

The comparatively low levels of infrastructure and the resulting restrictions for communication might be a factor for a stronger differentiation of regional English varieties; in addition, Kenya is home to dozens of native languages which are spoken in different areas and have varying influences on English. This certainly explains much of the country-internal variation and will continue to do so in the future, and it naturally limits the level of homogeneity English can reach in the country. As the analysis of lifestyle news shows, though, there is more to the variation in Kenya than that; we have to conclude that in addition to regional divergence, Kenyan English has developed a characteristic functional register for very specific social purposes, and that this register, being present in the major English-speaking newspapers in the country, is understood by most people who speak the language.

Of course, local influences are not the only relevant ones for English varieties around the world. Digitalization allows us to access resources from all over the world at any time, and popular culture as well as political and economic power have a strong impact on who and what influences us. Despite the above-mentioned restrictions in infrastructure in Kenya especially, many people in the country have access to the internet, which means that this external impact has to be considered in all cases and leads us to the second aspect addressed above, that of native influence. For both L2 varieties, the origin is the UK – British colonial rule brought English to Kenya and Hong Kong. But which native variety is most influential today?

The results are a bit diverse in this regard. In terms of medium, there is some variation between the linguistic features; but overall the results indicate that the USA and Australia are most similar to each other, whereas news from the UK strongly tends towards spoken style. Taking into consideration the other parameters of tenor and field, Australia is positioned further apart from Kenya and Hong Kong. Especially regarding tenor, it clusters more clearly with the UK, with both producing indicators for a low distance between author and readers. The USA, on the other hand, remains moderate throughout most features and can therefore be seen as the closest reference point for the L2 varieties in general. However, all these links are weak. It seems that Hong Kong and Kenyan English have reached a point in their developmental status where a strong influence from one particular native standard is no longer distinguishable.

10.3 Newspaper language and press freedom

The particularities that these news domains display are to some degree logical and can be explained with the different foci of the topics, represented in the contextual parameter of field. But variations in the tenor and the mode are less easily explained. We saw in Chapter 3.2 that the freedom of press varies greatly between the regions, and that official and external criteria are often complemented by self-censorship. Apart from differences in history and language policy, this should therefore be taken into account. Since the degree of press freedom is part of the production context of news, it can be expected to manifest in the language, too, and in this chapter, we will look at potential links between the two levels.

Figure 20 gives an overview of the significances of the correlations between all linguistic features that could be quantified adequately (i.e. excluding lexical items and the keyword analysis). In addition, the press freedom rank (*PF*, last row) as defined in the ranking by RSF (2020) has been added by using the value of the region and publication year for every individual article.

	LD	TTR	PT	I-I	PN-3	PN-12	Mod.	B-M	PV	Nom.	Coord.	Contr.	PF
LD													
TTR	0.37												
PT	0.04	0.14											
I-I	-0.2	-0.11	-0.25										
PN-3	-0.46	-0.18	0.15	0.08									
PN-12	-0.48	-0.25	-0.22	0.33	0.29								
Mod.	-0.16	0.08	-0.39	0.1		0.16							
B-M	-0.21	-0.17	-0.23	0.13	0.08	0.25	0.05						
PV	0.19	0.17	0.12	-0.13	-0.17	-0.29	0.06	-0.25					
Nom.	0.28	0.05	-0.05	-0.12	-0.29	-0.27	0.09	-0.13	0.13				
Coord.	-0.24	-0.12	-0.15	0.16	0.14	0.19	0.09	0.2	-0.18	-0.13			
Contr.	-0.34	-0.21	-0.26	0.25	0.3	0.57	0.14	0.29	-0.29	-0.29	0.24		
PF	0.11			-0.06	-0.13	-0.11	-0.05	-0.18	0.09	0.22	-0.2	-0.32	

LD – Lexical density
TTR – Type-token-ratio
PT – Past tense
I-I – Interrogatives & imperatives
PN-3 – 3rd person pronouns
PN-12 – 1st & 2nd person pronouns
Mod. – Modality
B-M – Boosters & minimizers
PV – Passive voice
Nom. – Nominalizations
Coord. – Sentence-initial coordinators
Contr. – Contractions
PF – Press freedom rank

Figure 20 Correlations of linguistic features and press freedom

All significance levels are based on p=0.01, and statistically not significant relations are indicated with *x*.

Some of the features in this matrix show strong correlations because they depend on each other for syntactic or morphological reasons, for example pronouns and lexical density. Such correlations are of course logical and not of any further interest for our analysis. Leaving these obvious cases aside, we can see that the press freedom rank shows a rough pattern based on the register parameters. A low degree of press freedom shows strong negative correlations with contractions, sentence-initial coordinators and boosters and minimizers, and slightly weaker correlations with pronouns, non-declarative mood and modality. This means that markers of spoken style and low distance are more likely to occur in news produced with a high degree of freedom.

In contrast to this, press freedom correlates positively with a high lexical density, passive voice and nominalizations, which are linguistic indicators of high distance, written and formal style and an emphasis on information. In particular, passive voice and nominalizations can be assumed to reflect not only press freedom restrictions that are obvious and officially rooted in political and legal frameworks, but also self-censorship. Via these linguistic features, authors can circumvent the necessity of assigning responsibility or blame, something which they might want to avoid if they have to expect sanctions for offending the wrong people. Interestingly, alongside this, both features were found in the analysis to hold the potential to subtly include opinions and attitudes – in this function, they could work as a strategy for authors to express their opinion in a less obvious and thereby less risky way.

In general terms, we can see that press freedom is most strongly reflected in the tenor of discourse. Variation within a variety, meaning more diverse values for features across the texts, shows that the respective region is less dependent on any external norms. More flexibility is an indicator of more freedom of expression and less standardization. For the varieties analyzed here, this correlation is reflected for Australia and the USA, which have relatively high press freedom values and also large internal variation. Journalists in Kenya and Hong Kong, on the other hand, face more restrictions, and the respective varieties show low internal ranges. However, due to the general trend for developing varieties to be influenced by written norms that we discussed in the previous chapter, it is impossible at this point to determine whether the low diversity of the L2 varieties originates from the external factor of press restrictions in the regions or from the status English holds. A large-scale comparison of more L2 varieties with different press freedom backgrounds would be the only way to come to more definite results regarding this aspect of varietal variation.

11 Concluding remarks

In the course of the analyses of the individual parameters of situational context, this study answered questions and also opened up new ones. In particular, the external factor of press freedom holds a lot of potential for future linguistic work and application, but we have seen that the method, too, can be improved and adapted further. To finish this work, we will briefly recapitulate our findings and reflect on methodological aspects.

11.1 A brief summary

This study set out to combine three different fields of linguistics: variational linguistics, SFL and media discourse. Its aim was to conduct an analysis with the potential to contribute to the understanding of all three and to reach insights into newspaper language, the development of regional varieties and the applicability of a functional approach to these two forms of variation.

We began the study by discussing the individual frameworks and disentangling research trends and terminologies. A detailed look at various models of the linguistic variation of the English language showed that visual representations can contain a lot of detail, but the complexity of a language as widespread as English, and especially of the diverse group of so-called New Englishes, is difficult to cover in a model that aims at being a simplified representation.

Based on this, we formulated the assumption that a functional perspective might be more promising in describing varieties and their developmental status, and we outlined the operationalization of the systemic functional concept of register, drawing on a variety of previous work and ongoing discussions about the exact parameters and subdimensions which can be regarded as reflecting the context of situation. Some suggestions for linguistic features were found to be suitable for our analysis, whereas others were redefined to be more adequate for an analysis of newspaper language. This means that a one-to-one comparison with other research is restricted and the linguistic markers used in this study are not necessarily useful for an examination of other discourse fields; however, generalized operationalizations would be limited to very few features, and for a concise analysis of one particular discourse, specific functions of linguistic characteristics should be taken into account in order to represent the parameters of register properly.

Having defined the exact linguistic markers that provided the basis for the analysis, we briefly introduced our dataset. The corpus we used was designed along the principle of even stratification, meaning that all domains and varieties are represented by equal amounts of texts. Additionally, the structure of the collection was based on external criteria – all articles included were sampled for the domain under which they had been published by their respective newspaper.

In this format, the dataset offered two dimensions of comparison, namely along functional and regional variation. For both directions, differences and similarities between the individual subsets could be found, but the degree of functional variation surpassed that of regional diversity substantially, so that linguistic characteristics can be said to be more dependent on the domain than the region. Nonetheless, the range of variation between the domains and their degree of specificity differed greatly among the varieties, reflecting the societies' media background and traditions.

Such functional differences between varieties are difficult to represent in a model, and since they are also very fine-grained, many of them would probably prove elusive in a study relying on a broader dataset like the ICE. A discourse-specific corpus provides more precise results and makes it possible to trace characteristics on a fine level, but of course it also means that we need to accept certain limitations.

For the results at hand, this implies that they are particular to the field of news discourse, and statements made about the developmental status of the varieties are projections based on this perspective. Although the language used in news reaches many people and is influential on language in general (A. Bell, 1998, p. 65; Conboy, 2007, p. 4; Fowler, 1991, p. 7), it cannot claim to represent an entire variety. At this point, the approach to determine regional variation via functional diversity either has to leave the level of individual discourses, losing the detailed focus, or undertake massive efforts to provide empirical results from various discourses and varieties for comparison.

With regard to the assumption for which we argue, that functional variation reflects the developmental status of a regional variety, such an approach would require the clarification of certain theoretical concepts, most importantly of the notion of "developmental status". For this study, it was taken to represent an abstract value, something that can be defined for a variety and in terms of which it is comparable to others. We looked towards the presented models for this concept and, despite the inclusion of functional variation, stayed on the same level by treating every variety as a whole.

However, we saw in the analysis that language is strongly affected by discourse-specific factors like press freedom, in other words external factors that shape the situational context for this discourse, but not necessarily for others. Because of this, varieties differ in their functional variation depending on the discourse that is being investigated. For news language, we can conclude that the external factor of press freedom holds a lot of potential for future linguistic research and application. In this discourse field, Kenyan English has to be regarded as more broadly developed than Hong Kong English, but results for a different discourse field could lead to the opposite conclusion. The same applies to the relation they display towards the native varieties, and even for comparisons among them all.

These trains of thought lead to some more detailed reflections on the method that was applied in this study. The analyses and results not only give insights into the data, they also uncover advantages and disadvantages of the operationalization and its application. In the following section, we will summarize these aspects and revisit the method with suggestions for future development.

11.2 Methodological considerations

Register is defined as language in use (e.g. Halliday, 1974, p. 32; Halliday, McIntosh, & Strevens, 1964, p. 87), so it can be said that an empirical approach is the one that stays truest to the concept itself. Since we aimed at analyzing both regional and functional variation on a large scale, a quantitative approach was most suitable because it allows the comparison of register parameters between large numbers of texts and categories (Lukin et al., 2011, p. 206; Neumann, 2013, p. 3).

Because of the amount of data, quantitative analyses always imply the need to generalize; for every linguistic feature that we investigated, the results may contain instances in which the feature is used differently or in a way that is not relevant for the respective subdimension after all. These erroneous hits can only be filtered out by a qualitative analysis of individual occurrences, which is often impossible due to the size of the dataset, but effective queries ensure that their numbers are small and that they are compensated by the mass of results and data points. The design of this study, namely the connection of linguistic features to concrete subdimensions of one contextual parameter, further counteracts the negative effect of wrong hits; of course, the results still contain irrelevant instances, but since every feature was analyzed with the focus on one specific function relating to one clearly defined aspect of the context, problematic features were more easily traceable.

This procedure does not only have advantages, though. One problem with the concept of operationalization is that it is difficult to account for different, sometimes even contrary, functions one linguistic feature can have within one subdimension. In our analysis, we saw this for interrogatives, which alternatively functioned as teasers, puns or rhetorical questions. Although we had included it as an operationalization of only one subdimension, the social role relationship, it stands to reason that not all of its functions contribute to this aspect to the same degree or in the same way.

Although we did not find many linguistic features with such contradictory or diverse functions, the possibility has to be considered, and quantifying such features would mean a very high error rate and lead to questionable interpretations. Instead, they are valuable as indicators of starting points for future research – a linguistic characteristic which is used with such flexibility is certainly worth investigating in more detail in order to understand the discourse strategies at work.

Another problem that we have to deal with when working with operationalization-based analyses is that a linguistic feature can represent different dimensions of context. This was observable for a number of features investigated here and was briefly discussed in Chapter 5 and the respective sections of the analysis. In principle, assigning a linguistic feature to more than one parameter is logical since field, mode and tenor influence each other and have many points of contact. To make sure that this does not become a problem during the interpretation, it is important to narrow down the focus to what is relevant for the respective subdimension. Additionally, it needs to be considered when looking at statistical representations; ideally, all linguistic features subsumed under one subdimension would show a significant correlation in the end, proving that their assignment and grouping was appropriate. In practice, this is rather unrealistic – on the one hand, the potentially diverse functions of a feature within one dimension, as discussed above, make this unlikely. On the other hand, a multiple operationalization of one feature would then mean that strong correlations would happen across all parameters it is assigned to, which would make the distinction between the subdimensions redundant.

Despite this complication, it is of course necessary to include a linguistic feature for all subdimensions for which it is promising or has been found to be representative. Restricting every feature to one parameter would be to ignore the complexity of language and its users. To avoid this, an inductive approach would have to be chosen, for which features are not operationalized based on any theory, but are pooled and used to let patterns emerge. However, such an analysis does not offer the opportunity to trace the differences between texts back to their source in the discourse situation; clear connections to the parameters of field, tenor and mode, in contrast, have this potential, and the intermediate step of the operationalization relating to their respective subdimensions ensures that the transfer from abstract variable of context to concrete linguistic markers is comprehensible and reproducible.

The theoretically guided nature of this approach has proven very valuable for an analysis into regional variation. The developmental status of a variety does not only depend on general differences between text domains, but has to be considered more widely, taking into account where the differences come from. From this perspective, trends become evident which relativize or emphasize regional or functional differences, like the tendency towards informal and spoken style in lifestyle and sports news, or towards formal and written medium in the varieties from Kenya and Hong Kong, and interpretations of such characteristics can be related to the societies and environments more clearly. In summary, we can say that although a deductive approach has limitations in terms of the issues mentioned above, these disadvantages are outweighed by the concise nature of the results, which in turn makes it a promising tool in variational linguistics to tackle the question of developmental status.

Appendix 1: Top ten keywords

Table 14 Keywords – Domain-internal comparison

Economy

Australia		Hong Kong		Kenya		UK		USA	
Word	Keyness	Word	Keyness	Word	Keyness	Word	Keyness	Word	Keyness
Australian	459	China	1,173	Sh	1,523	bn	431	U	317
Australia	435	Yuan	655	Kenya	1,492	UK	422	S	184
cent	341	HK	568	Africa	395	Britain	274	Gazprom	124
per	307	percent	380	Nairobi	305	pc	194	Dow	119
US	218	mainland	348	African	290	p	179	CEO	113
WA	157	Kong	338	county	231	London	125	Apple	106
iron	152	Hong	325	Kenyan	213	chancellor	114	stocks	103
Queensland	149	Li	254	farmers	158	Lloyds	112	wall	97
mining	133	Chinese	233	sugar	155	British	99	street	91
Mr	125	Beijing	219	Kenyans	142	FTSE	96	Netflix	88

Hard News

Australia		Hong Kong		Kenya		UK		USA	
Word	Keyness	Word	Keyness	Word	Keyness	Word	Keyness	Word	Keyness
Brisbane	176	Kong	362	Kenya	344	her	180	Boston	198
Australian	139	China	352	Nairobi	330	miss	161	Dutschke	190
man	128	Hong	352	Sh	298	British	151	Curtis	179
Melbourne	123	Chinese	255	county	281	she	150	attorney	151
Ms	118	Beijing	190	Mombasa	273	Philpott	143	Texas	141
Perth	110	HK	190	the	237	London	138	Dorner	134
NSW	106	Yuan	150	Boda	149	cannabis	134	FBI	108
Queensland	106	province	139	hawkers	145	Berezovsky	131	York	105
robbery	102	percent	134	investigations	145	I	121	snow	99
armed	95	Chen	130	land	119	Manchester	108	federal	99

APPENDIX 1: TOP TEN KEYWORDS   149

Lifestyle

Australia		Hong Kong		Kenya		UK		USA	
Word	Keyness	Word	Keyness	Word	Keyness	Word	Keyness	Word	Keyness
Australia	417	Kong	756	Kenya	716	Marina	136	s	203
Australian	325	Hong	753	Sh	635	I	123	York	193
Sydney	150	China	403	Nairobi	307	monkeys	106	Manhattan	99
you	150	Chinese	361	Moi	225	Britain	97	brain	92
your	131	HK	295	he	195	Conny	81	acne	90
WA	128	Beijing	244	him	173	garden	80	new	84
skin	108	Romney	193	African	163	UK	80	breast	78
au	105	Yuan	168	Kenyans	145	sugar	75	game	74
Perth	97	mainland	135	was	145	Ulrike	74	a	71
Melbourne	92	Shanghai	133	county	141	we	71	apnea	70

Politics

Australia		Hong Kong		Kenya		UK		USA	
Word	Keyness	Word	Keyness	Word	Keyness	Word	Keyness	Word	Keyness
labor	800	China	1,002	Kenya	799	labour	504	Berlusconi	282
Abbott	645	Hong	480	county	652	Blair	385	Obama	279
Gillard	533	Chinese	452	Ruto	608	Britain	300	gun	275
Rudd	483	Kong	419	ICC	580	Cameron	275	sen	220
Australia	426	Leung	298	Uhuru	521	Brown	151	Weiner	210
Queensland	394	Beijing	274	cord	504	EU	148	Quinn	180
Australian	326	Japan	239	jubilee	443	UK	140	s	159
WA	222	Li	231	ODM	422	Lib	134	Italy	158
Mr	220	HK	218	Sh	419	Tory	126	mediaset	155
federal	208	Chan	154	Kenyatta	372	Russia	125	senate	135

(Continued)

Table 14 (Continued)

Sports (see also Fest 2017)

Australia		Hong Kong		Kenya		UK		USA	
Word	Keyness	Word	Keyness	Word	Keyness	Word	Keyness	Word	Keyness
Sydney	305	Mr	697	Kenya	1,424	England	379	Knicks	263
Australian	263	China	670	Gor	497	Hamilton	200	Giants	240
Australia	257	Chinese	448	Nairobi	462	I	167	Yankees	214
Melbourne	246	Hong	404	Sh	432	Froome	142	Boston	199
wallabies	197	Kong	395	Leopards	307	Capello	119	Mets	192
Perth	194	sport	282	Mahia	307	Britain	110	playoff	191
Brisbane	190	Li	197	sevens	261	Mclaren	108	Jeter	188
AF	161	sumo	192	Thika	212	Wiggins	107	playoffs	164
blacks	134	soccer	190	marathon	207	his	102	Harvey	155
WA	131	Asian	149	Sofapaka	204	Mercedes	97	Cruz	149

Table 15 Keywords – Variety-internal comparison

Australia

Economy		Hard News		Lifestyle		Politics		Sports	
Word	Keyness	Word	Keyness	Word	Keyness	Word	Keyness	Word	Keyness
per	843	police	1,071	you	724	labor	956	game	655
cent	827	man	481	your	658	Mr	900	players	515
market	656	robbery	366	can	275	minister	843	coach	472
its	383	court	360	skin	264	election	769	season	459
company	367	was	356	says	263	government	733	league	330
business	312	armed	299	or	194	Rudd	658	club	297
bank	275	crime	299	are	188	Gillard	637	his	288
prices	273	charged	277	women	187	Abbott	611	win	276
us	264	murder	250	children	187	prime	511	rugby	262
dollar	259	crash	219	exercise	141	coalition	348	team	254

APPENDIX 1: TOP TEN KEYWORDS   151

Hong Kong

Economy		Hard News		Lifestyle		Politics		Sports	
Word	Keyness	Word	Keyness	Word	Keyness	Word	Keyness	Word	Keyness
market	845	police	1,118	says	779	minister	822	sport	677
billion	505	fire	310	you	411	party	684	team	666
cent	399	crime	288	fashion	261	election	600	game	572
per	369	were	243	your	204	government	445	players	493
trading	369	killed	222	I	194	political	398	games	493
Yuan	345	court	197	style	188	prime	309	sports	382
funds	337	arrested	190	can	162	vote	211	league	351
China	323	was	183	music	157	democratic	184	golf	338
investors	293	accident	182	like	155	votes	165	tournament	293
percent	279	trial	158	she	152	Rudd	155	cup	280

Kenya

Economy		Hard News		Lifestyle		Politics		Sports	
Word	Keyness	Word	Keyness	Word	Keyness	Word	Keyness	Word	Keyness
billion	522	police	1,256	I	655	election	615	team	659
per	502	were	331	you	603	party	573	league	614
cent	469	officers	310	your	485	president	514	club	504
Sh	442	killed	259	her	333	ICC	511	match	476
tax	353	arrested	209	says	329	cord	467	coach	466
market	307	suspects	202	my	328	Ruto	430	Gor	460
financial	299	accident	191	she	316	ODM	381	cup	402
bank	292	said	191	hair	230	Uhuru	358	players	379
shares	244	investigations	181	child	196	MP	342	marathon	374
sector	242	fire	179	it	193	jubilee	330	win	351

(Continued)

Table 15 (Continued)

UK

Economy		Hard News		Lifestyle		Politics		Sports	
Word	Keyness	Word	Keyness	Word	Keyness	Word	Keyness	Word	Keyness
bank	664	police	1,038	you	312	Cameron	481	team	630
its	528	was	447	my	280	labour	469	England	547
shares	484	her	420	your	231	Mr	449	players	374
market	484	crime	378	I	197	election	445	cup	366
bn	467	murder	304	women	182	Obama	428	game	366
p	439	officers	271	she	176	Blair	416	I	354
stock	383	death	260	sugar	172	minister	411	season	340
per	370	accident	250	food	169	party	396	match	279
cent	342	court	235	hair	147	EU	370	his	278
investors	324	robbery	219	garden	141	prime	311	he	264

USA

Economy		Hard News		Lifestyle		Politics		Sports	
Word	Keyness	Word	Keyness	Word	Keyness	Word	Keyness	Word	Keyness
stock	602	police	1,250	says	633	Obama	530	season	695
billion	589	said	523	your	407	President	493	game	681
investors	553	murder	377	you	403	Berlusconi	477	team	581
market	441	was	370	brain	227	party	457	play	389
bank	404	were	272	women	204	election	434	I	330
its	385	authorities	272	researchers	194	senate	424	win	320
stocks	383	death	255	sleep	187	Mr	402	Yankees	308
shares	380	arrested	254	or	184	political	375	Knicks	300
index	380	officers	243	art	184	Merkel	311	Giants	292
company	351	Dutschke	233	cancer	169	vote	308	playoff	282

Appendix 2: Top 20 place references per variety

Table 16 Popular place references per variety

Australia

No.	Item	Freq.	%	No.	Item	Freq.	%
1	Australia	716	0.19	11	NSW	77	0.02
2	US	289	0.08	12	England	74	0.02
3	Sydney	278	0.07	13	Adelaide	63	0.02
4	WA	262	0.07	14	New Zealand	60	0.02
5	Melbourne	242	0.06	15	Japan	58	0.02
6	Queensland	233	0.06	16	India	51	0.01
7	Perth	192	0.05	17	World	47	0.01
8	Brisbane	178	0.05	18	Asia	43	0.01
9	China	113	0.03	19	Canberra	43	0.01
10	Victoria	97	0.03	20	Europe	41	0.01

Σ 3,157 0.82%

Hong Kong

No.	Item	Freq.	%	No.	Item	Freq.	%
1	China	1,598	0.37	11	Korea	128	0.03
2	Hong Kong	789	0.18	12	Singapore	120	0.03
3	US	535	0.12	13	Taiwan	109	0.03
4	Beijing	377	0.09	14	London	93	0.02
5	Japan	276	0.06	15	Germany	87	0.02
6	Shanghai	175	0.04	16	EU	86	0.02
7	Asia	170	0.04	17	Tokyo	78	0.02
8	India	166	0.04	18	Guangdong	75	0.02
9	World	149	0.03	19	France	68	0.02
10	Australia	141	0.03	20	Thailand	61	0.01

Σ 5,281 1.22%

Kenya

No.	Item	Freq.	%	No.	Item	Freq.	%
1	Kenya	1,432	0.37	11	Rwanda	47	0.01
2	Nairobi	466	0.12	12	Nigeria	40	0.01
3	Africa	293	0.08	13	London	39	0.01
4	Mombasa	194	0.05	14	China	37	0.01
5	World	151	0.04	15	Sudan	37	0.01
6	Uganda	101	0.03	16	India	36	0.01
7	US	88	0.02	17	France	34	0.01
8	Tanzania	84	0.02	18	UK	32	0.01
9	Westgate	64	0.02	19	Turkana	29	0.01
10	Rome	48	0.01	20	Europe	26	0.01

Σ 3,278 0.84%

(Continued)

Table 16 (Continued)

UK								
No.	Item	Freq.	%	No.	Item	Freq.	%
1	Britain	434	0.09	11	Germany	93	0.02
2	UK	380	0.08	12	Manchester	88	0.02
3	London	354	0.08	13	America	87	0.02
4	England	351	0.07	14	Scotland	84	0.02
5	US	339	0.07	15	China	72	0.02
6	EU	206	0.04	16	Japan	68	0.01
7	Europe	162	0.03	17	Italy	65	0.01
8	World	122	0.03	18	Spain	65	0.01
9	France	120	0.03	19	Wales	64	0.01
10	Russia	105	0.02	20	Africa	60	0.01
			Σ 3,319 0.71%				

USA								
No.	Item	Freq.	%	No.	Item	Freq.	%
1	US	670	0.14	11	Texas	89	0.02
2	New York	345	0.07	12	Manhattan	87	0.02
3	Boston	224	0.05	13	America	75	0.02
4	Europe	208	0.04	14	Brooklyn	73	0.02
5	Italy	196	0.04	15	Japan	68	0.01
6	Germany	148	0.03	16	London	68	0.01
7	Washington	132	0.03	17	World	68	0.01
8	France	128	0.03	18	Georgia	67	0.01
9	China	121	0.03	19	Greece	64	0.01
10	EU	115	0.02	20	California	63	0.01
			Σ 3,009 0.63%				

Appendix 3: Ranges and deviations

Table 17 Ranges and deviations for individual features

Australia

Linguistic Feature	Values					Ø Range	Deviations from category's average					|Σ|
	ECO	HN	LIFE	POL	SPO		ECO	HN	LIFE	POL	SPO	
Boosters / Minimizers	0.84	0.49	1.06	0.64	1.02	0.57	0.03	-0.32	0.25	-0.17	0.21	0.98
Contractions	0.51	0.48	1.45	0.52	1.67	1.19	-0.42	-0.45	0.52	-0.41	0.74	2.54
Declaratives	98.84	98.92	93.50	98.71	98.68	5.42	1.11	1.19	-4.23	0.98	0.95	8.46
Imperatives	0.56	0.81	3.67	0.59	0.43	3.24	-0.65	-0.40	2.46	-0.62	-0.78	4.92
Interrogatives	0.60	0.27	2.83	0.71	0.89	2.56	-0.46	-0.79	1.77	-0.35	-0.17	3.54
Lexical density	60.10	60.35	58.98	61.03	58.00	3.03	0.41	0.66	-0.71	1.34	-1.69	4.81
Modality	1.10	0.88	1.35	1.67	1.41	0.79	-0.18	-0.40	0.07	0.39	0.13	1.17
Nominalizations	2.80	1.56	1.76	3.41	1.19	2.22	0.66	-0.58	-0.38	1.27	-0.95	3.84
Nouns	24.15	22.39	22.25	21.71	18.03	6.12	2.44	0.68	0.54	0.00	-3.68	7.35
Passive voice	10.07	18.39	8.20	12.37	8.72	10.19	-1.48	6.84	-3.35	0.82	-2.83	15.32
Past tense	50.00	72.09	27.33	48.07	47.38	44.76	1.03	23.12	-21.64	-0.90	-1.59	48.28
Pronouns (1st & 2nd p.)	0.82	0.98	3.11	1.57	2.42	2.29	-0.96	-0.80	1.33	-0.21	0.64	3.94
Pronouns (3rd p. / all)	74.93	80.85	53.71	72.56	63.39	27.14	5.84	11.76	-15.38	3.47	-5.70	42.15
Pronouns (all)	3.43	5.17	6.75	4.41	6.62	3.32	-1.85	-0.11	1.47	-0.87	1.34	5.64
Sent.-initial coordinators	0.17	0.07	0.20	0.18	0.17	0.13	0.01	-0.09	0.04	0.02	0.01	0.18
TTR	44.40	46.49	40.98	42.88	42.61	5.51	0.93	3.02	-2.49	-0.59	-0.86	7.89

(Continued)

Table 17 (Continued)

Hong Kong

Linguistic Feature	Values							Deviations from category's average					
	ECO	HN	LIFE	POL	SPO	Ø	Range	ECO	HN	LIFE	POL	SPO	|Σ|
Boosters / Minimizers	0.67	0.59	0.92	0.61	0.88	0.73	0.33	-0.06	-0.14	0.19	-0.12	0.15	0.66
Contractions	0.25	0.28	0.73	0.22	0.85	0.47	0.63	-0.22	-0.19	0.26	-0.25	0.38	1.30
Declaratives	99.47	99.46	97.02	99.22	98.84	98.80	2.45	0.67	0.66	-1.78	0.42	0.04	3.56
Imperatives	0.29	0.10	1.37	0.09	0.40	0.45	1.28	-0.16	-0.35	0.92	-0.36	-0.05	1.84
Interrogatives	0.23	0.44	1.62	0.69	0.77	0.75	1.39	-0.52	-0.31	0.87	-0.06	0.02	1.78
Lexical density	62.64	61.22	60.57	61.71	59.14	61.06	3.50	1.58	0.16	-0.49	0.65	-1.92	4.80
Modality	1.11	0.83	1.04	1.31	1.15	1.09	0.48	0.02	-0.26	-0.05	0.22	0.06	0.61
Nominalizations	3.09	2.45	2.01	3.99	1.81	2.67	2.18	0.42	-0.22	-0.66	1.32	-0.86	3.48
Nouns	25.33	23.93	23.88	22.63	20.27	23.21	5.06	2.12	0.72	0.67	-0.58	-2.94	7.03
Passive voice	8.75	16.92	8.59	12.02	8.61	10.98	8.33	-2.23	5.94	-2.39	1.04	-2.37	13.97
Past tense	41.67	72.08	26.71	51.51	40.00	46.39	45.37	-4.72	25.69	-19.68	5.12	-6.39	61.60
Pronouns (1st & 2nd p.)	0.34	0.38	1.63	0.49	1.44	0.86	1.29	-0.52	-0.48	0.77	-0.37	0.58	2.72
Pronouns (3rd p. / all)	85.65	87.70	66.46	84.89	70.65	79.07	21.24	6.58	8.63	-12.61	5.82	-8.42	42.06
Pronouns (all)	2.37	3.17	4.92	3.31	4.94	3.74	2.57	-1.37	-0.57	1.18	-0.43	1.20	4.75
Sent.-initial coordinators	0.13	0.10	0.20	0.12	0.16	0.14	0.10	-0.01	-0.04	0.06	-0.02	0.02	0.15
TTR	42.30	45.77	40.26	43.19	42.79	42.86	5.51	-0.56	2.91	-2.60	0.33	-0.07	6.47

APPENDIX 3: RANGES AND DEVIATIONS 157

Kenya

Linguistic Feature	Values						∅	Range	Deviations from category's average					|Σ|
	ECO	HN	LIFE	POL	SPO	∅	Range	ECO	HN	LIFE	POL	SPO	|Σ|
Boosters / Minimizers	0.54	0.36	0.78	0.35	0.49	0.50	0.43	0.04	-0.14	0.28	-0.15	-0.01	0.62
Contractions	0.08	0.06	0.29	0.07	0.22	0.14	0.23	-0.06	-0.08	0.15	-0.07	0.08	0.44
Declaratives	99.28	98.97	95.51	98.44	98.35	98.11	3.77	1.17	0.86	-2.60	0.33	0.24	5.20
Imperatives	0.25	0.74	1.95	0.45	0.78	0.83	1.70	-0.58	-0.09	1.12	-0.38	-0.05	2.23
Interrogatives	0.47	0.29	2.54	1.12	0.88	1.06	2.25	-0.59	-0.77	1.48	0.06	-0.18	3.08
Lexical density	61.06	60.38	57.55	60.34	60.90	60.05	3.51	1.01	0.33	-2.50	0.29	0.85	4.99
Modality	1.12	0.81	1.20	1.31	1.20	1.13	0.50	-0.01	-0.32	0.07	0.18	0.07	0.65
Nominalizations	3.89	2.57	2.29	3.53	1.41	2.74	2.48	1.15	-0.17	-0.45	0.79	-1.33	3.89
Nouns	24.66	23.11	22.05	20.21	19.37	21.88	5.29	2.78	1.23	0.17	-1.67	-2.51	8.36
Passive voice	13.96	20.19	11.42	14.83	9.91	14.06	10.28	-0.10	6.13	-2.64	0.77	-4.15	13.79
Past tense	40.00	75.00	32.22	53.95	50.26	50.29	42.78	-10.29	24.71	-18.07	3.66	-0.03	56.76
Pronouns (1st & 2nd p.)	0.71	0.78	2.62	0.87	1.59	1.31	1.91	-0.60	-0.53	1.31	-0.44	0.28	3.16
Pronouns (3rd p. / all)	73.91	83.23	62.32	78.90	66.46	72.96	20.91	0.95	10.27	-10.64	5.94	-6.50	34.30
Pronouns (all)	2.76	4.72	7.07	4.17	4.77	4.70	4.31	-1.94	0.02	2.37	-0.53	0.07	4.93
Sent.-initial coordinators	0.05	0.06	0.19	0.10	0.12	0.10	0.14	-0.05	-0.04	0.09	0.00	0.02	0.20
TTR	43.13	45.39	37.69	41.87	43.39	42.29	7.70	0.84	3.10	-4.60	-0.42	1.10	10.06

(Continued)

Table 17 (Continued)

UK

Linguistic Feature	Values						Range	Deviations from category's average					
	ECO	HN	LIFE	POL	SPO	Ø		ECO	HN	LIFE	POL	SPO	|Σ|
Boosters / Minimizers	0.81	0.63	1.08	0.68	0.93	0.83	0.45	-0.02	-0.20	0.25	-0.15	0.10	0.72
Contractions	0.33	0.46	1.20	0.50	1.16	0.73	0.87	-0.40	-0.27	0.47	-0.23	0.43	1.80
Declaratives	97.42	98.72	93.82	97.73	97.67	97.07	4.90	0.35	1.65	-3.25	0.66	0.60	6.50
Imperatives	0.68	0.28	1.58	0.41	0.45	0.68	1.30	0.00	-0.40	0.90	-0.27	-0.23	1.80
Interrogatives	1.90	1.05	4.59	1.85	1.88	2.25	3.54	-0.35	-1.20	2.34	-0.40	-0.37	4.67
Lexical density	60.16	58.75	57.58	59.34	56.62	58.49	3.54	1.67	0.26	-0.91	0.85	-1.87	5.56
Modality	1.37	0.92	1.34	1.38	1.43	1.29	0.51	0.08	-0.37	0.05	0.09	0.14	0.74
Nominalizations	2.25	1.53	1.48	2.56	1.19	1.80	1.37	0.45	-0.27	-0.32	0.76	-0.61	2.41
Nouns	23.83	21.38	21.38	20.94	17.02	20.91	6.81	2.92	0.47	0.47	0.03	-3.89	7.78
Passive voice	10.50	19.01	9.58	11.77	8.12	11.80	10.89	-1.30	7.21	-2.22	-0.03	-3.68	14.43
Past tense	42.21	68.93	35.24	44.91	42.86	46.83	33.69	-4.62	22.10	-11.59	-1.92	-3.97	44.20
Pronouns (1st & 2nd p.)	0.80	1.32	3.18	1.36	2.57	1.85	2.38	-1.05	-0.53	1.33	-0.49	0.72	4.12
Pronouns (3rd p. / all)	77.84	79.63	56.87	73.40	64.41	70.43	22.76	7.41	9.20	-13.56	2.97	-6.02	39.16
Pronouns (all)	3.61	6.54	7.42	5.15	7.25	5.99	3.81	-2.38	0.55	1.43	-0.84	1.26	6.46
Sent.-initial coordinators	0.27	0.17	0.33	0.21	0.31	0.26	0.16	0.01	-0.09	0.07	-0.05	0.05	0.27
TTR	43.92	42.47	40.19	43.98	41.65	42.44	3.79	1.48	0.03	-2.25	1.54	-0.79	6.09

APPENDIX 3: RANGES AND DEVIATIONS   159

USA

Linguistic Feature	Values						Range	Deviations from category's average					
	ECO	HN	LIFE	POL	SPO	Ø		ECO	HN	LIFE	POL	SPO	|Σ|
Boosters / Minimizers	0.77	0.52	0.99	0.67	0.90	0.77	0.47	0.00	-0.25	0.22	-0.10	0.13	0.70
Contractions	0.56	0.52	1.90	0.59	1.88	1.09	1.38	-0.53	-0.57	0.81	-0.50	0.79	3.20
Declaratives	98.57	98.86	94.49	98.42	97.69	97.61	4.37	0.96	1.25	-3.12	0.81	0.08	6.23
Imperatives	0.73	0.28	2.11	0.38	0.75	0.85	1.83	-0.12	-0.57	1.26	-0.47	-0.10	2.52
Interrogatives	0.70	0.85	3.40	1.20	1.56	1.54	2.70	-0.84	-0.69	1.86	-0.34	0.02	3.75
Lexical density	61.37	60.90	60.09	61.22	57.26	60.17	4.11	1.20	0.73	-0.08	1.05	-2.91	5.97
Modality	1.06	0.73	1.10	1.27	1.14	1.06	0.54	0.00	-0.33	0.04	0.21	0.08	0.66
Nominalizations	2.30	2.20	1.62	2.73	1.08	1.99	1.65	0.31	0.21	-0.37	0.74	-0.91	2.54
Nouns	24.36	22.54	22.69	21.49	17.78	21.77	6.58	2.59	0.77	0.92	-0.28	-3.99	8.55
Passive voice	7.33	14.10	7.52	8.52	6.38	8.77	7.72	-1.44	5.33	-1.25	-0.25	-2.39	10.66
Past tense	50.00	73.61	27.53	49.64	43.67	48.89	46.08	1.11	24.72	-21.36	0.75	-5.22	53.16
Pronouns (1st & 2nd p.)	0.63	0.96	2.26	0.96	2.12	1.39	1.63	-0.76	-0.43	0.87	-0.43	0.73	3.22
Pronouns (3rd p. / all)	79.55	80.40	60.14	77.93	67.18	73.04	20.26	6.51	7.36	-12.90	4.89	-5.86	37.52
Pronouns (all)	3.13	4.95	5.72	4.36	6.49	4.93	3.36	-1.80	0.02	0.79	-0.57	1.56	4.74
Sent.-initial coordinators	0.20	0.10	0.22	0.22	0.29	0.21	0.19	-0.01	-0.11	0.01	0.01	0.08	0.22
TTR	42.55	43.06	39.46	45.16	39.08	41.86	6.08	0.69	1.20	-2.40	3.30	-2.78	10.37

Glossary

Annotation
Adding additional information to a corpus/dataset. Also called tagging. (Baker, Hardie, & McEnery, 2006, p. 13)

Boxplot
Boxplots display information on the distribution of data points. The whiskers show the smallest and largest observation in a category, the box itself shows the first three **quartiles** and the **interquartile range**, and the line in the box indicates the **median**. Points outside the box represent outliers, which are data points clearly set apart from the rest. (Neumann & Fest, 2016, p. 207)

Chi-Square test / χ²
A test for statistical significance; the result of the test is presented as $χ^2$.

Correlation
Measures how much two variables correlate with each other. Positive correlation means that variable A increases as variable B does. Negative correlation means that variable A decreases as variable B increases. The coefficient (r) is between −1 and +1, with the correlation being stronger the farther away the value is from 0. (Winter, 2019, p. 89)

Header
A block with metadata that precedes the actual body of the text. A header is formatted so that it can be recognized and processed by a computer/corpus software and thereby help to query the data more efficiently. Which metadata is included varies greatly, and concrete information on this can usually be found in the description of the corpus. (Baker, Hardie, & McEnery, 2006, pp. 81–3).

Interquartile range
The difference between the first and the third **quartile** (Q1 and Q3). (Winter, 2019, p. 59)

Keyword
A word which appears statistically significantly more often in one corpus or text when compared to another than would be expected by chance. (Baker, Hardie, & McEnery, 2006, p. 97)

Lexical density
A process to calculate the proportion of content and function words in a corpus or text, usually by dividing the number of content words by the number of all words. However, other ways of calculating lexical density have been used (see Baker, Hardie, & McEnery, 2006, p. 106, for a description).

Mean
Represents the sum of all data points divided by the number of data points. Also called arithmetic mean.

Median
Represents the halfway point of all data points. 50% of all data points are below the median, and 50% are above it. The median is always the second **quartile** (Q2). (Winter, 2019, p. 59)

Part of speech-tagging
A form of annotation which defines a grammatical category for every token in the corpus and attaches it in the form of a machine-readable code (called tag). Especially on large datasets, part of speech (POS)-tagging is usually done automatically with the help of a tagger. See also: **tagset**. (Baker, Hardie, & McEnery, 2006, p. 128)

Quartile
Values which indicate where a certain amount of data points are located. The first quartile (Q1) covers 25% of all data points. 50% fall under the second quartile (Q2), and the third quartile (Q3) is the value under which 75% of all data points can be found. Q2 always equals the **median**. The quartiles Q1, Q2 and Q3 are visualized in a **boxplot** by the lower, middle and upper lines of the box. (Winter, 2019, p. 59)

Range
The difference between the smallest and largest point in a given dataset. (Winter, 2019, p. 58)

Tagset
A clearly defined set of tags/codes which is used for annotation, e.g. **part of speech-tagging**. (Baker, Hardie, & McEnery, 2006, p. 155)

Token
Every individual item; the number of tokens represents the total number of linguistic units in a text or corpus. (cf. Baker, Hardie, & McEnery, 2006, pp. 159–60, 162)

Type

Every unique item in a text or corpus. If an item is repeated, the type count is not increased (in contrast to the **token** count). There are different definitions of the exact meaning of *type* – it can be defined as a unique word (e.g. Baker, Hardie, & McEnery, 2006, p. 162) or based on lemmata (e.g. Francis & Kučera, 1982; Thorndike & Lorge, 1944; see also Youmans, 1990).

Type/token ratio

A measurement of lexical repetition in a text or corpus, achieved by dividing the number of **types** by the number of **tokens**. A ratio calculated on the basis of treating **types** as lemmata is also sometimes called lemma/token ratio. (cf. Baker, Hardie, & McEnery, 2006, p. 162)

References

Abbott, G. (1981). Editorial. *World Englishes*, *1*(1), 1–4. https://doi.org/10.1111/j.1467-971X.1981.tb00438.x

Abdulaziz, M. H. (1982). Patterns of Language Acquisition and Use in Kenya: Rural–Urban Differences. *International Journal of the Sociology of Language*, *34*, 95–120. https://doi.org/10.1515/ijsl.1982.34.95

Abdulaziz, M. H. (1991). East Africa (Tanzania and Kenya). In J. Cheshire (Ed.), *English around the World: Sociolinguistic Perspectives* (pp. 391–404). Cambridge: Cambridge University Press.

Adewunmi, B. (2013, January 22). The sexual politics of hair – are all cuts created equally? *Guardian*.

Aguilar-Sánchez, J. (2005). English in Costa Rica. *World Englishes*, *24*(2), 161–72. https://doi.org/10.1111/j.1467-971X.2005.00401.x

Ajala, A. (1983). The Nature of African Boundaries. *Africa Spectrum*, *18*(2), 177–89.

Alliance for Audited Media (2013). Top 25 U.S. Newspapers for March 2013. Retrieved from http://auditedmedia.com/news/research-and-data/top-25-us-newspapers-for-march-2013.aspx

Allsopp, R. (2003). *Dictionary of Caribbean English Usage*. Oxford: Oxford University Press.

Alméciga, W. Y. E., & Evans, R. (2014). Mentor Texts and the Coding of Academic Writing Structures: A Functional Approach. *HOW: A Colombian Journal for Teachers of English*, *21*(2), 94–111.

Anthony, L. (2019). AntConc (Version 3.5.8) [Computer software]. Tokyo: Waseda University. Retrieved from https://www.laurenceanthony.net/software/antconc/

Asante, M. Y. (2012). Variation in Subject–Verb Concord in Ghanaian English. *World Englishes*, *31*(2), 208–25. https://doi.org/10.1111/j.1467-971X.2012.01751.x

Audit Bureau of Circulations (2013). AdNews ABC Circulation Results Nov 2013. Retrieved from http://yaffacdn.s3.amazonaws.com/live/adnews/files/dmfile/ABCNEWS.pdf

Axler, M., Yang, A., & Stevens, T. (1998). Current Language Attitudes of Hong Kong Chinese Adolescents and Young Adults. In M. Pennington (Ed.), *Language in Hong Kong at Century's End* (pp. 329–38). Hong Kong: Hong Kong University Press.

Bailey, R. W. (1985). The Idea of World English. *English Today*, *1*(1), 3–6. https://doi.org/10.1017/S0266078400013018

Baker, P., Hardie, A., & McEnery, T. (2006). *A Glossary of Corpus Linguistics*. Edinburgh: Edinburgh University Press.

Banda, F. (2010). Critical Review of Media Development Measurements: What Are We Measuring? In A. S. Jannusch & T. R. Lansner (Eds.), *Measuring Change II: Expanding Knowledge on Monitoring and Evaluation in Media Development* (pp. 39–52). Aachen: Catholic Media Council.

Banda, F., & Berger, G. (2008). How to Assess Your Media Landscape. Retrieved from https://archive.ccrvoices.org/cdn.agilitycms.com/centre-for-communication-rights/Images/Articles/pdf/how-to-assess-your-media-landscape-2008.pdf

Barés, G. M., & Llurda, E. (2013). Internationalization of Business English Communication at University: A Threefold Needs Analysis. *Ibérica, 26*, 151–69.

Barnett, E. (2012, August 30). For sleep's sake have a screen break before bed. *Daily Telegraph*.

Bartsch, S. (2009). Corpus Studies of Register Variation: An Exploration of Academic Registers. *International Journal of English Studies, 20*(1), 105–24.

Bateman, J., Delin, J., & Henschel, R. (2007). Mapping the Multimodal Genres of Traditional and Electronic Newspapers. In T. D. Royce & W. L. Bowcher (Eds.), *New Directions in the Analysis of Multimodal Discourse* (pp. 147–72). New Jersey: Lawrence Erlbaum.

Beaugrande, R.-A. de, & Dressler, W. (1981). *Einführung in die Textlinguistik. Konzepte der Sprach- und Literaturwissenschaft: Vol. 28*. Tübingen: Niemeyer.

Becker, L. B., Vlad, T., & Nusser, N. (2007). An Evaluation of Press Freedom Indicators. *International Communication Gazette, 69*(1), 5–28. https://doi.org/10.1177/1748048507072774

Bednarek, M. (2006). *Evaluation in Media Discourse: Analysis of a Newspaper Corpus*. London: Continuum.

Bednarek, M. (2007). Local Grammar and Register Variation: Explorations in Broadsheet and Tabloid Newspaper Discourse. *Empirical Language Research Journal, 1*(1).

Bednarek, M. (2008). *Emotion Talk across Corpora*. Basingstoke: Palgrave Macmillan.

Bednarek, M., & Caple, H. (2012a). 'Value Added': Language, Image and News Values. *Discourse, Context & Media, 1*(2–3), 103–13. https://doi.org/10.1016/j.dcm.2012.05.006

Bednarek, M., & Caple, H. (2012b). *News Discourse*. London: Continuum.

Bednarek, M., & Caple, H. (2014). Why do News Values Matter? Towards a New Methodological Framework for Analysing News Discourse in Critical Discourse Analysis and Beyond. *Discourse & Society, 25*(2), 135–58. https://doi.org/10.1177/0957926513516041

Begi, N. (2014). Use of Mother Tongue as a Language of Instruction in Early Years of School to Preserve the Kenyan Culture. *Journal of Education and Practice, 5*(3), 37–49.

Bell, A. M. (1888). Volapük. *Science, 11*(260), 39–40. https://doi.org/10.1126/science.ns-11.260.39

Bell, A. (1984). Language Style as Audience Design. *Language in Society, 13*(2), 145–204. https://doi.org/10.1017/S004740450001037X

Bell, A. (1991). *The Language of News Media. Language in Society: Vol. 17*. Oxford: Blackwell.

Bell, A. (1995). Language and the Media. *Annual Review of Applied Linguistics, 15*, 23–41. https://doi.org/10.1017/S0267190500002592

Bell, A. (1998). The Discourse of Structure of News Stories. In A. Bell & P. Garrett (Eds.), *Approaches to Media Discourse* (pp. 64–104). Oxford: Blackwell.

Benamara, F., Cesarano, C., Picariello, A., Reforgiato, D., & Subrahmanian, V. S. (2007). Sentiment Analysis: Adjectives and Adverbs Are Better than Adjectives Alone. *Proceedings of the International Conference on Weblogs and Social Media.*

Benson, P. (2002). Hong Kong Words: Variation and Context. In K. Bolton (Ed.), *Hong Kong English: Autonomy and Creativity* (pp. 161–70). Aberdeen: Hong Kong University Press.

Berns, M. (2005). Expanding on the Expanding Circle: Where Do WE Go from here? *World Englishes*, *24*(1), 85–93. https://doi.org/10.1111/j.0883-2919.2005.00389.x

Bhatia, V. K. (1993). *Analysing Genre: Language Use in Professional Settings.* London: Longman.

Biber, D. (1985). Investigating Macroscopic Textual Variation through Multifeature/Multidimensional Analyses. *Linguistics*, *23*(2), 337–60. https://doi.org/10.1515/ling.1985.23.2.337

Biber, D. (1988). *Variation across Speech and Writing.* Cambridge: Cambridge University Press.

Biber, D. (1993). Representativeness in Corpus Design. *Literary and Linguistic Computing*, *8*(4), 243–57.

Biber, D. (1995). *Dimensions of Register Variation: A Cross-Linguistic Comparison.* Cambridge: Cambridge University Press.

Biber, D., & Conrad, S. M. (2009). *Register, Genre, and Style.* Cambridge, UK: Cambridge University Press.

Biber, D., Johansson, S., Leech, G., Conrad, S. M., & Finegan, E. (1999). *Longman Grammar of Spoken and Written English.* Harlow: Longman.

Black, R. (2011, January 3). People who wear glasses are seen as smarter and more professional, study finds. *Daily News.*

Bobda, A. S. (2003). The Formation of Regional and National Features in African English Pronunciation: An Exploration of Some Non-interference Factors. *English World-Wide*, *24*(1), 17–42. https://doi.org/10.1075/eww.24.1.03sim

Bobda, A. S. (2009). The Meaning of English Words across Cultures, with a Focus on Cameroon and Hong Kong. *Journal of Multilingual and Multicultural Development*, *30*(5), 375–89. https://doi.org/10.1080/01434630802147882

Bochenski, N. (2013, January 20). 16-year-old charged over violent city robbery. *Sydney Morning Herald.*

Bohner, G. (2001). Writing about Rape: Use of the Passive Voice and other Distancing Text Features as an Expression of Perceived Responsibility of the Victim. *British Journal of Social Psychology*, *40*(4), 515–29. https://doi.org/10.1348/014466601164957

Bolt, P., & Bolton, K. (1996). The International Corpus of English in Hong Kong. In S. Greenbaum (Ed.), *Comparing English Worldwide: The International Corpus of English* (pp. 197–214). Oxford: Clarendon Press.

Bolton, K. (2000). The Sociolinguistics of Hong Kong and the Space for Hong Kong English. *World Englishes*, *19*(3), 265–85. https://doi.org/10.1111/1467-971X.00179

Bolton, K. (2006). World Englishes Today. In B. B. Kachru, Y. Kachru, & C. L. Nelson (Eds.), *Blackwell Handbooks in Linguistics. The Handbook of World Englishes* (pp. 240–69). Malden, Mass: Blackwell.

Bolton, K., & Kwok, H. (1990). The Dynamics of the Hong Kong Accent: Social Identity and Sociolinguistic Description. *Journal of Asian Pacific Communication, 1*(1), 147–72.

Bond, M. H. (1985). Language as a Carrier of Ethnic Stereotypes in Hong Kong. *The Journal of Social Psychology, 125*(1), 53–62. https://doi.org/10.1080/00224545.1985.9713508

Bonfadelli, H. (2004). *Medienwirkungsforschung I: Grundlagen und theoretische Perspektiven* (3rd ed.). Konstanz: UVK Verl.-Ges.

Bongartz, C. M., & Buschfeld, S. (2011). English in Cyprus: Second Language Variety or Learner English? In J. Mukherjee & M. Hundt (Eds.), *Exploring Second-Language Varieties of English and Learner Englishes: Bridging a Paradigm Gap* (pp. 35–54). Amsterdam: John Benjamins.

Böttger, C. (2007). *Lost in Translation? An Analysis of the Role of English as the 'Lingua Franca' of Multilingual Business Communication*. Verlag Dr. Kovač, Hamburg.

Bowcher, W. L. (1999). Investigating Institutionalization in Context. In M. Ghadessy (Ed.), *Current Issues in Linguistic Theory: Vol. 169. Text and Context in Functional Linguistics* (pp. 141–76). Amsterdam: John Benjamins.

Boyd, A., Stewart, P., & Alexander, R. (2008). *Broadcast Journalism: Techniques of Radio & Television News* (6th ed.). Amsterdam: Elsevier.

Boykoff, M. T., & Boykoff, J. M. (2004). Balance as Bias: Global Warming and the US Prestige Press. *Global Environmental Change, 14*(2), 125–36. https://doi.org/10.1016/j.gloenvcha.2003.10.001

Boykoff, M. T., & Boykoff, J. M. (2007). Climate Change and Journalistic Norms: A Case-Study of US Mass-Media Coverage. *Geoforum, 38*(6), 1190–1204. https://doi.org/10.1016/j.geoforum.2007.01.008

Bradley, M. (2013, July 9). New Premier Is Named in Egypt. *Wall Street Journal Asia*.

Brinker, K., Cölfen, H., & Pappert, S. (2014). *Linguistische Textanalyse: Eine Einführung in Grundbegriffe und Methoden* (8th ed.). Berlin: Erich Schmidt Verlag.

Brown, R., & Gilman, A. (1960). The Pronouns of Power and Solidarity. In T. A. Seboek (Ed.), *Style in Language* (pp. 253–76). Cambridge, MA: MIT Press.

Brysbaert, M., New, B., & Keuleers, E. (2012). Adding Part-of-Speech Information to the SUBTLEX-US Word Frequencies. *Behavior Research Methods, 44*(4), 991–7. https://doi.org/10.3758/s13428-012-0190-4

Budohoska, N. (2014). *English in Kenya or Kenyan English?* Frankfurt am Main, New York: Peter Lang.

Bull, P., & Fetzer, A. (2006). Who Are We and Who Are You?: The Strategic Use of Forms of Address in Political Interviews. *Text & Talk, 26*(1), 3–37. https://doi.org/10.1515/TEXT.2006.002

Buregeya, A. (2006). Grammatical Features of Kenyan English and the Extent of their Acceptability. *English World-Wide, 27*(2), 199–216.

Buregeya, A. (2019). *Kenyan English. Dialects of English: Vol. 14*. Boston: De Gruyter Mouton.

Burger, H. (2005). *Mediensprache: Eine Einführung in Sprache und Kommunikationsformen der Massenmedien* (3rd ed.). Berlin: De Gruyter.

Burgess, J. (2010). Evaluating the Evaluators: Media Freedom Indexes and What They Measure. Retrieved from http://repository.upenn.edu/cgcs_monitoringandeval_videos/1

Butt, D., & Wegener, R. (2007). The Work of Concepts: Context and Metafunction in the Systemic Functional Model. In R. Hasan, C. M. I. M. Matthiessen, & J. Webster (Eds.), *Continuing Discourse on Language: A Functional Perspective (Vol. 2)* (pp. 589–618). London: Equinox.

Caple, H. (2010). Doubling-up: Allusion and Bonding in Multi-Semiotic News Stories. In M. Bednarek & J. R. Martin (Eds.), *New Discourse on Language: Functional Perspectives on Multimodality, Identity, and Affiliation* (pp. 111–33). London, New York: Continuum.

Caple, H., & Bednarek, M. (2015). Rethinking News Values: What a Discursive Approach Can Tell Us about the Construction of News Discourse and News Photography. *Journalism*, 2, 1–22. https://doi.org/10.1177/1464884914568078

Carpenter, S. (2007). U.S. Elite and Non-elite Newspapers' Portrayal of the Iraq War: A Comparison of Frames and Source Use. *Journalism & Mass Communication Quarterly*, 84(4), 761–76. https://doi.org/10.1177/107769900708400407

Chambers, J. K. (2004). Dynamic Typology and Vernacular Universals. In B. Kortmann (Ed.), *Dialectology Meets Typology. Dialect Grammar from a Crosslinguistic Perspective* (pp. 127–45). Berlin: De Gruyter Mouton.

Chan, B. H.-S. (2009). English in Hong Kong Cantopop: Language Choice, Code-Switching and Genre. *World Englishes*, 28(1), 107–29. https://doi.org/10.1111/j.1467-971X.2008.01572.x

Chan, E. (2002). Beyond Pedagogy: Language and Identity in Post-Colonial Hong Kong. *British Journal of Sociology of Education*, 23(2), 271–85.

Chan, J. [Jim] (2013). Contextual Variation and Hong Kong English. *World Englishes*, 32(1), 54–74. https://doi.org/10.1111/weng.12004

Chan, J. M., & Lee, F. L. (2011). The Primacy of Local Interests and Press Freedom in Hong Kong: A Survey Study of Professional Journalists. *Journalism*, 12(1), 89–105. https://doi.org/10.1177/1464884910385189

Chen, Y., Conroy, N. J., & Rubin, V. L. (2015). Misleading Online Content. In M. Abouelenien, M. Burzo, R. Mihalcea, & V. Pérez-Rosas (Eds.), *Proceedings of the 2015 ACM on Workshop on Multimodal Deception Detection* (pp. 15–19). New York: ACM Press. https://doi.org/10.1145/2823465.2823467

Chevillet, F. (1993). English or Englishes? *English Today*, 9(4), 29–33. https://doi.org/10.1017/S0266078400007288

Childs, B., & Wolfram, W. (2004). Bahamian English: Phonology. In B. Kortmann, E. W. Schneider, K. Burridge, R. Mesthrie, & C. Upton (Eds.), *A Handbook of Varieties of English* (Vol. 1, pp. 435–49). Berlin: De Gruyter Mouton.

Christie, P. (1989). Questions of Standards and Intra-Regional Differences in Caribbean Examinations. In O. García & R. Otheguy (Eds.), *English across Cultures, Cultures across English*. Berlin: De Gruyter Mouton.

Christophersen, P. (1988). 'Native Speakers' and World English. *English Today*, 4(3), 15–18. https://doi.org/10.1017/S0266078400003473

Churchill, W. (1956–1958). *A History of the English-Speaking Peoples*. London: Cassell.

Coetzee-Van Rooy, S., & Rooy, B. van (2005). South African English: Labels, Comprehensibility and Status. *World Englishes*, 24(1), 1–19. https://doi.org/10.1111/j.0883-2919.2005.00384.x

Conboy, M. (2006). *Tabloid Britain: Constructing a Community through Language*. London: Routledge.

Conboy, M. (2007). *The Language of the News*. London: Routledge.

Cooper, R. (2011, December 23). Now 20 business leaders declare Cameron's veto a 'diplomatic coup' as Clegg vows to get own way at next summit. *Daily Mail*.

Craig, D. (1983). Toward a Description of Caribbean English. In B. B. Kachru (Ed.), *The Other Tongue: English across Cultures* (1st ed., pp. 198–209). Oxford: Pergamon Press.

Crawford, E. (2009). A New Sort of Democracy?: The Opinion Pages in the Scottish Daily Quality Press. *Journalism*, 10(4), 451–72. https://doi.org/10.1177/1464884909104951

Crystal, D. (1985). How Many Millions? The Statistics of English Today. *English Today*, 1(1), 7–9. https://doi.org/10.1017/S026607840001302X

Crystal, D. (2003). *English as a Global Language* (2nd ed.). Cambridge: Cambridge University Press.

Cummings, P. J., & Wolf, H.-G. (2011). *A Dictionary of Hong Kong English: Words from the Fragrant Harbor*. Hong Kong: Hong Kong University Press.

Curran, J., Iyengar, S., Brink Lund, A., & Salovaara-Moring, I. (2009). Media System, Public Knowledge and Democracy: A Comparative Study. *European Journal of Communication*, 24(1), 5–26. https://doi.org/10.1177/0267323108098943

Deterding, D., Wong, J., & Kirkpatrick, A. (2008). The Pronunciation of Hong Kong English. *English World-Wide*, 29(2), 148–75.

Devonish, H., & Otelemate, H. G. (2004). Jamaican Creole and Jamaican English: Phonology. In B. Kortmann, E. W. Schneider, K. Burridge, R. Mesthrie, & C. Upton (Eds.), *A Handbook of Varieties of English* (Vol. 1, pp. 450–80). Berlin: De Gruyter Mouton.

Dijk, T. van (1985). Structures of News in the Press. In T. van Dijk (Ed.), *Discourse and Communication* (pp. 69–93). Berlin: De Gruyter.

Dijk, T. van (1998). Opinions and Ideologies in the Press. In A. Bell & P. Garrett (Eds.), *Approaches to Media Discourse* (pp. 21–63). Oxford: Blackwell.

Dinmore, G. (2006, March 30). Bush Enters Debate on Freedom in Iran. *Financial Times*.

Diwersy, S., Evert, S., & Neumann, S. (2014). A Weakly Supervised Multivariate Approach to the Study of Language Variation. In B. Szmrecsanyi & B. Wälchli (Eds.), *Lingua & Litterae: Vol. 28. Aggregating Dialectology, Typology, and Register Analysis: Linguistic Variation in Text and Speech*. Berlin: De Gruyter. https://doi.org/10.1515/9783110317558.174

Drasovean, A., & Tagg, C. (2015). Evaluative Language and Its Solidarity-Building Role on TED.com: An Appraisal and Corpus Analysis. *Language@Internet*, 12.

Dreyfus, S., & Jones, S. C. (2010). Constructing Sports Stars: Appliable Linguistics and the Language of the Media. In A. Mahboob & N. Knight (Eds.), *Appliable Linguistics: Reclaiming the Place of Language in Linguistics* (pp. 114–29). London: Continuum.

Du-Babcock, B. (2013). English as Business Lingua Franca: A Comparative Analysis of Communication Behavior and Strategies in Asian and European Contexts. *Ibérica*, 26, 99–130.

Dunning, E. (1999). *Sport Matters: Sociological Studies of Sport, Violence, and Civilization*. London: Routledge.

Eco, U. (1995). *The Search for the Perfect Language*. Oxford: Blackwell.

Edelman, A. (2013, April 14). Schumer silent on potential Weiner mayoral run. *Daily News*.

Eggins, S. (1994). *An Introduction to Systemic Functional Linguistics*. New York: Continuum.

Eggins, S., & Martin, J. R. (1997). Genres and Registers of Discourse. In T. van Dijk (Ed.), *Discourse as Structure and Process* (pp. 230–56). London: Sage Publications.

Engel, U. (1988). *Deutsche Grammatik*. Heidelberg: Julius Groos.

Ethnologue (2016). Ethnologue: Languages of the World. Retrieved from www.ethnologue.com

Evans, S. (2009). The Evolution of the English-Language Speech Community in Hong Kong. *English World-Wide*, 30(3), 278–301.

Evans, S., & Green, C. (2001). Language in Post-Colonial Hong Kong: The Roles of English and Chinese in the Public and Private Sectors. *English World-Wide*, 22(2), 247–68.

Evert, S., & Neumann, S. (2021). A Register Variation Perspective on Varieties of English. In E. Seoane & D. Biber (Eds.), *Corpus Based Approaches to Register Variation* (pp. 143–78). Amsterdam: Benjamins.

Fest, J. (2011). *A Corpus-Based Analysis of Register Features in British Football Journalism* (MA Thesis). RWTH Aachen University, Aachen.

Fest, J. (2015a). Corpora in the Social Sciences – How Corpus-based Approaches can Support Qualitative Interview Analyses. *Revista De Lenguas Para Fines Específicos*, 21(2), 48–69.

Fest, J. (2015b). Defining Endings in Newspaper Writing – A Case Study on Football Coverage. In G. Hopps, S. Neumann, S. Strasen, & P. Wenzel (Eds.), *Aachen British and American Studies: Vol. 19. Last Things: Essays on Ends and Endings* (pp. 53–64). Frankfurt am Main: Peter Lang.

Fest, J. (2016). *News in the Context of Regional and Functional Variation: A Corpus-based Analysis of Newspaper Domains across Varieties of English*. RWTH Aachen University, Aachen. Retrieved from http://publications.rwth-aachen.de/record/678439/files/678439.pdf

Fest, J. (2017). Sports News around the World – A Quantitative Study of Register Features in Newspaper Sports Coverage. In D. Caldwell, J. Walsh, E. W. Vine, & J. Jureidini (Eds.), *Routledge Studies in Sociolinguistics. The Discourse of Sport: Analyses from Social Linguistics* (pp. 190–208). London, New York: Routledge.

Fest, J. (2021). Commitment in Newspaper Coverage of Climate Change: A Corpus-based Analysis of Print News from the USA and Australia. In W. Kreisel, P. H. Marsden, & T. Reeh (Eds.), *Die Landschaft interpretieren: Interdisziplinäre Ansätze/Interpreting Landscape: Interdisciplinary approaches* (pp. 275–300). Göttingen: Universitätsverlag Göttingen.

Firth, J. R. (1950). Personality and Language in Society. *The Sociological Review, a42*(1), 37–52. https://doi.org/10.1111/j.1467-954x.1950.tb02460.x

Fishman, J. A. (1996). Introduction: Some Empirical and Theoretical Issues. In J. A. Fishman, A. W. Conrad, & A. Rubal-Lopez (Eds.), *Post-Imperial English: Status Change in Former British and American Colonies, 1940–1990* (pp. 3–12). New York: De Gruyter Mouton. https://doi.org/10.1515/9783110872187.3

Fishman, J. A., Conrad, A. W., & Rubal-Lopez, A. (Eds.) (1996). *Post-Imperial English: Status Change in Former British and American Colonies, 1940–1990*. New York: De Gruyter Mouton.

Ford, C. A. (2010). *The Mind of Empire: China's History and Modern Foreign Relations*. Lexington: University Press of Kentucky.

Fowler, R. (1991). *Language in the News: Discourse and Ideology in the Press*. London: Routledge.

Francis, W. N., & Kučera, H. (1982). *Frequency Analysis of English Usage: Lexicon and Grammar*. Boston: Houghton Mifflin.

Freedom House (2021). *Freedom of the Press Index*. Retrieved from https://freedomhouse.org/

Ghadessy, M. (1988a). The Language of Written Sports Commentary: Soccer: A Description. In M. Ghadessy (Ed.), *Registers of Written English: Situational Factors and Linguistic Features* (pp. 17–51). London: Pinter Publishers.

Ghadessy, M. (Ed.) (1988b). *Registers of Written English: Situational Factors and Linguistic Features*. London: Pinter Publishers.

Gillen, J., & Merchant, G. (2013). Contact Calls: Twitter as a Dialogic Social and Linguistic Practice. *Language Sciences, 35*, 47–58. https://doi.org/10.1016/j.langsci.2012.04.015

Gilquin, G., & Granger, S. (2011). From EFL to ESL: Evidence from the International Corpus of Learner English. In J. Mukherjee & M. Hundt (Eds.), *Exploring Second-Language Varieties of English and Learner Englishes: Bridging a Paradigm Gap* (pp. 55–78). Amsterdam: John Benjamins.

Gisborne, N. (2002). Relative Clauses in Hong Kong English. In K. Bolton (Ed.), *Hong Kong English: Autonomy and Creativity* (pp. 141–60). Aberdeen: Hong Kong University Press.

Gisborne, N. (2009). Aspects of the Morphosyntactic Typology of Hong Kong English. *English World-Wide, 30*(2), 149–69. https://doi.org/10.1075/eww.30.2.03gis

Goldwert, L. (2012, June 26). Men obsessed with their muscles are more sexist, more likely to believe thin women are more attractive. *Daily News*.

Görlach, M. (1989). Word-Formation and the ENL: ESL: EFL Distinction. *English World-Wide, 10*(2), 279–313.

Görlach, M. (1990). *Studies in the History of the English Language*. Heidelberg: Winter.

Granato, L. (2002). *Newspaper Feature Writing*. Sydney: University of New South Wales Press in Association with Deakin University Press.

Gray, J. (2002). *Rebellions and Revolutions: China from the 1800s to 2000* (2nd ed.). Short Oxford History of the Modern World. Oxford: Oxford University Press.

Greenbaum, S. (1990). Standard English and the International Corpus of English. *World Englishes, 9*(1), 79–83. https://doi.org/10.1111/j.1467-971X.1990.tb00688.x

Grice, H. P. (1979). Logik und Konversation. In G. Meggle (Ed.), *Handlung, Kommunikation, Bedeutung* (pp. 243–65). Frankfurt am Main: Suhrkamp.

Gut, U. (2011). Studying Structural Innovations in New Englishes. In J. Mukherjee & M. Hundt (Eds.), *Exploring Second-Language Varieties of English and Learner Englishes: Bridging a Paradigm Gap* (pp. 101–24). Amsterdam: John Benjamins.

Guz, W. (2009). English Affixal Nominalizations across Language Registers. *Poznań Studies in Contemporary Linguistics, 45*(4), 461–85. https://doi.org/10.2478/v10010-009-0030-6

Haase, C. (2004). Conceptualization Specifics in East African English: Quantitative Arguments from the ICE-East Africa Corpus. *World Englishes, 23*(2), 261–8. https://doi.org/10.1111/j.0883-2919.2004.00350.x

Haase, F.-A. (2013). A Contrastive Study of Essay Writing in German and English and Its Tradition of Rhetoric: The School Essay, Essay as Academic Writing, and the Essay as an Artificial Literary Product. *Linguistica E Letteratura, 38*(1–2), 299–321.

Halliday, M. A. K. (1961). Categories of the Theory of Grammar. *Word, 17*(3), 241–92.

Halliday, M. A. K. (1974). *Language and Social Man*. London: Longman.

Halliday, M. A. K. (1975). *Learning How to Mean – Explorations in the Development of Language*. London: Edward Arnold.

Halliday, M. A. K., & Hasan, R. (1976). *Cohesion in English*. London: Longman.

Halliday, M. A. K., & Hasan, R. (1985). *Language, Context, and Text: Aspects of Language in a Social-Semiotic Perspective*. Oxford: Oxford University Press.

Halliday, M. A. K., & Matthiessen, C. M. I. M. (1999). *Construing Experience through Meaning: A Language-Based Approach to Cognition. Open Linguistics Series*. London: Cassell.

Halliday, M. A. K., & Matthiessen, C. M. I. M. (2014). *An Introduction to Functional Grammar* (4th ed.). London: Edward Arnold.

Halliday, M. A. K., McIntosh, A., & Strevens, P. (1964). *The Linguistic Sciences and Language Teaching*. London: Longman.

Hancock, I. F., & Angogo, R. (1986). English in East Africa. In R. W. Bailey & M. Görlach (Eds.), *English as a World Language* (4th ed., pp. 306–23). Ann Arbor: The University of Michigan Press.

Hänsel, E. C., & Deuber, D. (2013). Globalization, Postcolonial Englishes, and the English Language Press in Kenya, Singapore, and Trinidad and Tobago. *World Englishes, 32*(3), 338–57. https://doi.org/10.1111/weng.12035

Harcup, T. (2005). *Journalism: Principles and Practice*. London: Sage Publications.

Hart, S. (2013, April 10). Heather Watson remains hopeful of making French Open in May after being laid low by glandular fever. *Daily Telegraph*.

Hasan, R. (1978). Text in the Systemic-Functional Model. In W. Dressler (Ed.), *Research in Text Theory: Vol. 2. Current Trends in Textlinguistics* (pp. 228–46). Berlin: De Gruyter.

Hasan, R. (1999). Speaking with Reference to Context. In M. Ghadessy (Ed.), *Current Issues in Linguistic Theory: Vol. 169. Text and Context in Functional Linguistics* (pp. 219–328). Amsterdam: John Benjamins.

Hasan, R. (2009a). The Place of Context in a Systemic Functional Model. In M. A. K. Halliday & J. Webster (Eds.), *Continuum Companion to Systemic Functional Linguistics* (pp. 166–89). London: Continuum.

Hasan, R. (2009b). A View of Pragmatics in a Social Semiotic Perspective. *Linguistics and the Human Sciences*, 5(3), 251–79. https://doi.org/10.1558/lhs.v5i3.251

Haynes, L. (1983). Caribbean English: Form and Function. In B. B. Kachru (Ed.), *The Other Tongue: English across Cultures* (1st ed., pp. 210–26). Oxford: Pergamon Press.

Heine, B. (1977). Sprachen und Sprachprobleme in Kenia. In W. Leifer (Ed.), *Kenia: Geographie, Vorgeschichte, Geschichte, Gesellschaft, Kultur, Erziehung, Gesundheitswesen, Wirtschaft, Entwicklung* (pp. 251–67). Tübingen: Horst Erdmann Verlag.

Herman, E. S., & Chomsky, N. (1988). *Manufacturing Consent: The Political Economy of the Mass Media*. London: Vintage.

Hiraga, Y. (2005). British Attitudes towards Six Varieties of English in the USA and Britain. *World Englishes*, 24(3), 289–308. https://doi.org/10.1111/j.0883-2919.2005.00411.x

Holzknecht, S. (1989). Sociolinguistic Analysis of a Register: Birthday Notices in Papua New Guinea Post Courier. *World Englishes*, 8(2), 179–92. https://doi.org/10.1111/j.1467-971X.1989.tb00653.x

Hong Kong Census and Statistics Department (1982). Preliminary Results of the 1981 Population Census.

Hong Kong Department of Justice (2015). The Basic Law. Retrieved from https://www.basiclaw.gov.hk/filemanager/content/en/files/basiclawtext/basiclaw_full_text.pdf

Huang, K. (2001). American Business and the China Trade Embargo in the 1950s. *Essays in Economic & Business History*, 19, 33–48.

Hundt, M., & Vogel, K. (2011). Overuse of the Progressive in ESL and Learner Englishes – Fact or Fiction? In J. Mukherjee & M. Hundt (Eds.), *Exploring Second-Language Varieties of English and Learner Englishes: Bridging a Paradigm Gap* (pp. 145–66). Amsterdam: John Benjamins. https://doi.org/10.1075/scl.44.08vog

Hützen, N. (2015). *Shell Nouns in Academic Journal Articles: Differences and Similarities across Eight Disciplines* (PhD Thesis). RWTH Aachen University, Aachen.

Hyland, K. (1997). Language Attitudes at the Handover: Communication and Identity in 1997 Hong Kong. *English World-Wide*, 18(2), 191–210.

Hyland, K. (2002). Authority and Invisibility. *Journal of Pragmatics*, 34(8), 1091–112. https://doi.org/10.1016/S0378-2166(02)00035-8

ICE Project (2016). International Corpus of English. Retrieved from http://ice-corpora.net/ice/index.html

IREX (2020). Media Sustainability Index (MSI). Retrieved from https://www.irex.org/resource/media-sustainability-index-msi

Johnson, H. M. (1966). *Sociology: A Systematic Introduction*. New Delhi: Allied Publishers.

Johnson, R. K. (1994). Language Policy and Planning in Hong Kong. *Annual Review of Applied Linguistics*, 14, 177. https://doi.org/10.1017/S0267190500002889

Joseph, J. (2004). *Language and Identity: National, Ethnic, Religious*. Houndmills: Palgrave Macmillan.

Kachru, B. B. (1981). The Pragmatics of Non-Native Varieties of English. In L. E. Smith (Ed.), *English for Cross-Cultural Communication* (pp. 15–39). London: Palgrave Macmillan.

Kachru, B. B. (1983a). *The Indianization of English: The English Language in India*. Delhi: Oxford University Press.

Kachru, B. B. (1983b). Introduction: The Other Side of English. In B. B. Kachru (Ed.), *The Other Tongue: English across Cultures* (1st ed., pp. 1–12). Oxford: Pergamon Press.

Kachru, B. B. (1983c). Meaning in Deviation: Toward Understanding Non-Native English Texts. In B. B. Kachru (Ed.), *The Other Tongue: English across Cultures* (1st ed., pp. 325–50). Oxford: Pergamon Press.

Kachru, B. B. (1983d). Models for Non-Native Englishes. In B. B. Kachru (Ed.), *The Other Tongue: English across Cultures* (1st ed., pp. 31–57). Oxford: Pergamon Press.

Kachru, B. B. (1985). Standards, Codification and Sociolinguistic Realism: The English in the Outer Circle. In R. Quirk & H. G. Widdowson (Eds.), *English in the World: Teaching and Learning the Language and Literatures* (pp. 11–30). Cambridge: Cambridge University Press.

Kachru, B. B. (1988). The Sacred Cows of English. *English Today*, 4(4), 3–8. https://doi.org/10.1017/S0266078400000973

Kachru, B. B. (1990). *The Alchemy of English: The Spread, Functions, and Models of Non-Native Englishes*. Urbana and Chicago: University of Illinois Press.

Kachru, B. B. (1991). Liberation Linguistics and the Quirk Concern. *English Today*, 7(1), 3–13. https://doi.org/10.1017/S026607840000523X

Kachru, B. B. (1992). Teaching World Englishes. In B. B. Kachru (Ed.), *The Other Tongue: English across Cultures* (2nd ed., pp. 355–65). Urbana, Chicago: University of Illinois Press.

Kachru, B. B. (1996). World Englishes: Agony and Ecstasy. *Journal of Aesthetic Education*, 30(2), 135–55. https://doi.org/10.2307/3333196

Kachru, B. B. (1997). World Englishes and English-Using Communities. *Annual Review of Applied Linguistics*. (17), 66–87. https://doi.org/10.1017/s0267190500003287

Kachru, B. B. (2006). English: World Englishes. In K. Brown (Ed.), *Encyclopedia of Language and Linguistics* (Vol. 4, pp. 195–202). Amsterdam: Elsevier.

Kachru, B. B., & Quirk, R. (1981). Introduction. In L. E. Smith (Ed.), *English for Cross-Cultural Communication* (pp. xiii–xx). London: Palgrave Macmillan.

Kachru, B. B., & Smith, L. E. (1985). Editorial. *World Englishes*, 4(2), 209–12. https://doi.org/10.1111/j.1467-971X.1985.tb00408.x

Kachru, Y., & Nelson, C. L. (2006). *World Englishes in Asian Contexts. Asian Englishes Today*. Hong Kong: Hong Kong University Press.

Kanyoro, M. R. A. (1991). The Politics of the English Language in Kenya and Tanzania. In J. Cheshire (Ed.), *English around the World: Sociolinguistic Perspectives* (pp. 402–19). Cambridge: Cambridge University Press.

Katzenberger, S. (1999). *Komplementäre Kommunikation lokaler Medien: Hörfunk und Presse: intermediale Profile, programmliche Pools, publizistische Performanz. Aktuelle Medien- und Kommunikationsforschung: Vol. 9.* Münster: LIT Verlag.

Keeble, R. (2006). *The Newspapers Handbook* (4th ed.). London: Routledge.

Kenyon, J. S. (1924). *American Pronunciation.* Ann Arbor: George Wahr.

KhosraviNik, M. (2009). The Representation of Refugees, Asylum Seekers and Immigrants in British Newspapers during the Balkan Conflict (1999) and the British General Election (2005). *Discourse & Society, 20*(4), 477–98. https://doi.org/10.1177/0957926509104024

Kleinnijenhuis, J., Schultz, F., Utz, S., & Oegema, D. (2015). The Mediating Role of the News in the BP Oil Spill Crisis 2010: How U.S. News Is Influenced by Public Relations and in Turn Influences Public Awareness, Foreign News, and the Share Price. *Communication Research, 42*(3), 1–21. https://doi.org/10.1177/0093650213510940

Knox, J. S. (2009a). *Multimodal Discourse on Online Newspaper Home Pages: A Social-Semiotic Perspective* (PhD Thesis). University of Sydney, Sydney.

Knox, J. S. (2009b). Punctuating the Home Page: Image as Language in an Online Newspaper. *Discourse & Communication, 3*(2), 145–72. https://doi.org/10.1177/1750481309102450

Kolodzy, J. (2006). *Convergence Journalism: Writing and Reporting across the News Media.* Lanham, Oxford: Rowman & Littlefield.

Kortmann, B., & Szmrecsanyi, B. (2004). Global Synopsis: Morphological and Syntactic Variation in English. In B. Kortmann, E. W. Schneider, K. Burridge, R. Mesthrie, & C. Upton (Eds.), *A Handbook of Varieties of English* (Vol. 2, pp. 1142–1202). Berlin: De Gruyter Mouton.

Krings, C. (2003). *Zur Typologie des Erzählschlusses in der englischsprachigen Kurzgeschichte. Aachen British and American Studies.* Frankfurt am Main: Peter Lang.

Lamb, K. (2013, January 4). Australian stabbed during Bali robbery. *Sydney Morning Herald.*

Lamb, S. (1991). Acts without Agents: An Analysis of Linguistic Avoidance in Journal Articles on Men Who Batter Women. *American Journal of Orthopsychiatry, 61*(2), 250–57. https://doi.org/10.1037/h0079243

Lawton, D. L. (1986). English in the Caribbean. In R. W. Bailey & M. Görlach (Eds.), *English as a World Language* (4th ed., pp. 251–80). Ann Arbor: The University of Michigan Press.

Le Pelley, M. (2013). The African Media Barometer – Not just another Media Index. *Rhodes Journalism Review, 2013*(33), 52–4.

Lee, C.-C. (1998). Press Self-Censorship and Political Transition in Hong Kong. *Harvard International Journal of Press/Politics, 3*(2), 55–73. https://doi.org/10.1177/1081180X98003002005

Lee, D. (2001). Genres, Registers, Text Types, Domains and Styles: Clarifying the Concepts and Navigating a Path through the BNC Jungle. *Language Learning and Technology, 5*(3), 37–72. https://doi.org/10.1163/9789004334236_021

Lee, F. L., & Chan, J. M. (2008). Organizational Production of Self-Censorship in the Hong Kong Media. *The International Journal of Press/Politics, 14*(1), 112–33. https://doi.org/10.1177/1940161208326598

Lee, F. L., & Lin, A. (2006). Newspaper Editorial Discourse and the Politics of Self-Censorship in Hong Kong. *Discourse & Society*, *17*(3), 331–58. https://doi.org/10.1177/0957926506062371

Lee, J. F. K., & Collins, P. (2004). On the Usage of 'have', 'dare', 'need', 'ought' and 'used to' in Australian English and Hong Kong English. *World Englishes*, *23*(4), 501–13. https://doi.org/10.1111/j.0083-2919.2004.00374.x

Leifer, W. (1977). Von den Uranfängen bis zur Gegenwart. In W. Leifer (Ed.), *Kenia: Geographie, Vorgeschichte, Geschichte, Gesellschaft, Kultur, Erziehung, Gesundheitswesen, Wirtschaft, Entwicklung* (pp. 103–61). Tübingen: Horst Erdmann Verlag.

Leith, W. (2012, March 27). The bitter truth about sugar. *Daily Telegraph*.

Lewis, M. P., Simons, G. F., & Fennig, C. D. (2015). *Ethnologue: Languages of Kenya*. Dallas: SIL International.

Li, D. C. S. (2000). Cantonese-English Code-Switching Research in Hong Kong: A Y2K Review. *World Englishes*, *19*(3), 305–22. https://doi.org/10.1111/1467-971X.00181

Liu, F. (2018). Lexical Metaphor as Affiliative Bond in Newspaper Editorials: A Systemic Functional Linguistics Perspective. *Functional Linguistics*, *5*(1). https://doi.org/10.1186/s40554-018-0054-z

Llewellyn, J., Hancock, G., Kirst, M., & Roeloffs, K. (1982). *A Perspective on Education in Hong Kong: Report by a Visiting Panel*. Hong Kong: Government Printer.

Louwerse, M., McCarthy, P. M., McNamara, D. S., & Graesser, A. C. (2004). Variation in Language and Cohesion across Written and Spoken Registers. In K. Forbus, D. Gentner, & T. Regier (Eds.), *Proceedings of the 26th Annual Meeting of the Cognitive Science Society* (pp. 843–8). Mahwah, NJ: Lawrence Erlbaum.

Lowenberg, P. H. (1992). Testing English as a World Language: Issues in Assessing Non-Native Proficiency. In B. B. Kachru (Ed.), *The Other Tongue: English across Cultures* (2nd ed., pp. 108–21). Urbana, Chicago: University of Illinois Press.

Lüger, H.-H. (1995). *Pressesprache* (2nd ed.). *Germanistische Arbeitshefte: Vol. 28*. Tübingen: Niemeyer.

Luhmann, N. (2000). *The Reality of the Mass Media*. Stanford: Stanford University Press.

Luke, K. K. (1998). Why Two Languages Might Be Better Than One: Motivations of Language Mixing in Hong Kong. In M. Pennington (Ed.), *Language in Hong Kong at Century's End* (pp. 145–59). Hong Kong: Hong Kong University Press.

Luke, K. K., & Richards, J. C. (1982). English in Hong Kong: Functions and Status. *English World-Wide*, *3*(1), 47–64.

Lukin, A. (2010). 'News' and 'Register': A Preliminary Investigation. In A. Mahboob & N. Knight (Eds.), *Appliable Linguistics: Reclaiming the Place of Language in Linguistics* (pp. 92–113). London: Continuum.

Lukin, A., Moore, A., Herke, M., Wegener, R., & Wu, C. (2011). Halliday's Model of Register Revisited and Explored. *Linguistics and the Human Sciences*, *4*(2), 187–213. https://doi.org/10.1558/lhs.v4i2.187

Mahlberg, M., & O'Donnell, M. B. (2008). A Fresh View of the Structure of Hard News Stories. In S. Neumann & E. Steiner (Eds.), *Online Proceedings of the 19th European Systemic Functional Linguistics Conference and Workshop, Saarbrücken, 23–25 July 2007*.

Maley, A. (1985). The Most Chameleon of Languages. *English Today*, *1*(1), 30–33. https://doi.org/10.1017/S0266078400013122

Malinowski, B. (1935). *Coral Gardens and Their Magic: A Study of the Methods of Tilling the Soil and of Agricultural Rites in the Trobriand Islands Vol 2: The Language of Magic and Gardening*. London: Allen & Unwin.

Martin, J. R. (1992). *English Text: System and Structure*. Philadelphia: John Benjamins.

Martin, J. R. (2004). Positive Discourse Analysis: Solidarity and Change. *Revista Canaria De Estudios Ingleses*, *49*, 179–200.

Martin, J. R., & White, P. R. R. (2005). *The Language of Evaluation: Appraisal in English*. Basingstoke: Palgrave Macmillan.

Matsuda, A., & Friedrich, P. (2011). English as an International Language: A Curriculum Blueprint. *World Englishes*, *30*(3), 332–44. https://doi.org/10.1111/j.1467-971X.2011.01717.x

Matsumoto, D., Hwang, H. C., & Sandoval, V. A. (2015). Cross-Language Applicability of Linguistic Features Associated with Veracity and Deception. *Journal of Police and Criminal Psychology*, *30*(4), 229–41. https://doi.org/10.1007/s11896-014-9155-0

Mazrui, A. [Alamin], & Mazrui, A. [Ali] (1996). A Tale of Two Englishes: The Imperial Language in Post-Colonial Kenya and Uganda. In J. A. Fishman, A. W. Conrad, & A. Rubal-Lopez (Eds.), *Post-Imperial English: Status Change in Former British and American Colonies, 1940–1990* (pp. 271–302). New York: De Gruyter Mouton.

McArthur, T. (1987). The English Languages? *English Today*, *3*(3), 9–13. https://doi.org/10.1017/S0266078400013511

Meade, A. (2013, April 5). Bitcoins explained: A viable future currency, or an accident waiting to happen? *Daily Mail*.

Mesthrie, R., & Bhatt, R. M. (2008). *World Englishes: The Study of New Linguistic Varieties*. Cambridge: Cambridge University Press.

Michieka, M. M. (2005). English in Kenya: A Sociolinguistic Profile. *World Englishes*, *24*(2), 173–86. https://doi.org/10.1111/j.1467-971X.2005.00402.x

Michieka, M. M. (2009). Expanding Circles within the Outer Circle: The Rural Kisii in Kenya. *World Englishes*, *28*(3), 352–64. https://doi.org/10.1111/j.1467-971X.2009.01597.x

Moag, R. (1983). The Life Cycle of Non-Native Englishes: A Case Study. In B. B. Kachru (Ed.), *The Other Tongue: English across Cultures* (1st ed., pp. 270–88). Oxford: Pergamon Press.

Modiano, M. (1999). International English in the Global Village. *English Today*, *15*(2), 22–8. https://doi.org/10.1017/S026607840001083X

Moise, E. E. (1986). *Modern China: A History*. London: Longman.

Mollin, S. (2007). New Variety or Learner English? Criteria for Variety Status and the Case of Euro-English. *English World-Wide*, *28*(2), 167–85.

Mouton, A. (2013, July 15). Will consumers embrace wearable tech? *USA Today*.

Mufwene, S. (1994). New Englishes and Criteria for Naming Them. *World Englishes*, *13*(1), 21–31. https://doi.org/10.1111/j.1467-971X.1994.tb00280.x

Mufwene, S. (2015). Colonization, Indigenization, and the Differential Evolution of English: Some Ecological Perspectives. *World Englishes*, *34*(1), 6–21. https://doi.org/10.1111/weng.12129

Munger, K., Luca, M., Nagler, J., & Tucker, J. (2020). The (Null) Effects of Clickbait Headlines on Polarization, Trust, and Learning. *Public Opinion Quarterly*, *84*(1), 49–73. https://doi.org/10.1093/poq/nfaa008

Nabea, W. (2009). Language Policy in Kenya: Negotiation with Hegemony. *The Journal of Pan African Studies*, *3*(1), 121–38.

Nelson, G. (2006). The Core and Periphery of World Englishes: A Corpus-Based Exploration. *World Englishes*, *25*(1), 115–29. https://doi.org/10.1111/j.0083-2919.2006.00450.x

Neumann, S. (2012). Applying Register Analysis to Varieties of English. In M. Fludernik & B. Kohlmann (Eds.), *Anglistentag 2011 Freiburg: Proceedings* (pp. 75–94). Trier: WVT.

Neumann, S. (2013). *Contrastive Register Variation: A Quantitative Approach to the Comparison of English and German*. Berlin: De Gruyter Mouton.

Neumann, S. (2020). On the Interaction between Register Variation and Regional Varieties in English. *Language, Context and Text. The Social Semiotics Forum*, *2*(1), 121–44. https://doi.org/10.1075/langct.00023.neu

Neumann, S., & Fest, J. (2016). Cohesive Devices across Registers and Varieties: The Role of Medium in English. In C. Schubert & C. Sanchez-Stockhammer (Eds.), *Topics in English Linguistics: Vol. 90. Variational Text Linguistics: Revisiting Register in English* (pp. 195–220). Berlin: De Gruyter Mouton. https://doi.org/10.1515/9783110443554-010

O'Donnell, S. (2013, September 29). The truth about travelling alone as a woman. *Courier Mail*.

Oxford English Dictionary (2016). OED Online. Retrieved from http://www.oed.com/

Pape, S., & Featherstone, S. (2005). *Newspaper Journalism: A Practical Introduction*. London: Sage Publications.

Papper, R. A. (2013). *Broadcast News and Writing Stylebook* (5th ed.). Boston: Pearson.

Pennington, M. (1995). Language Diversity in Bilingualism: Preliminary Speculations on Varieties of Hong Kong English. *Language in Education Journal*, *1*(1), 1-19.

Pennington, M. (1998a). Colonial's Aftermath in Asia: A Snapshot View of Bilingualism in Hong Kong. *Hong Kong Journal of Applied Linguistics*, *3*(1), 1–6.

Pennington, M. (1998b). Introduction: Perspectives on Language in Hong Kong at Century's End. In M. Pennington (Ed.), *Language in Hong Kong at Century's End* (pp. 3–40). Hong Kong: Hong Kong University Press.

Pennington, M., & Yue, F. (1994). English and Chinese in Hong Kong: Pre-1997 Language Attitudes. *World Englishes*, *13*(1), 1–20.

Pennycook, A. (1994). The Politics of Pronouns. *English Language Teaching Journal*, *48*(2), 173–8. https://doi.org/10.1093/elt/48.2.173

Pierson, H. D., & Bond, M. H. (1982). How Do Chinese Bilinguals Respond to Variations of Interviewer Language and Ethnicity? *Journal of Language and Social Psychology*, *1*(2), 123–39. https://doi.org/10.1177/0261927X8200100203

Platt, J. (1986). English in Singapore, Malaysia, and Hong Kong. In R. W. Bailey & M. Görlach (Eds.), *English as a World Language* (4th ed., pp. 384–414). Ann Arbor: The University of Michigan Press.

Platt, J., Weber, H., & Ho, M. L. (1984). *The New Englishes*. London, Boston, Melbourne, Henley: Routledge and Kegan Paul.

Poon, A. Y. K. (2009). A Review of Research in English Language Education in Hong Kong in the Past 25 Years: Reflections and the Way forward. *Educational Research Journal*, *24*(1), 7–40.

Population By-census Office (2016). Results. Retrieved from https://www.bycensus2016.gov.hk/en/bc-mt.html

Potts, A., Bednarek, M., & Caple, H. (2015). How Can Computer-Based Methods Help Researchers to Investigate News Values in Large Datasets? A Corpus Linguistic Study of the Construction of Newsworthiness in the Reporting on Hurricane Katrina. *Discourse & Communication*, *9*(2), 149–72. https://doi.org/10.1177/1750481314568548

Poynton, C. (1989). *Language and Gender: Making the Difference*. Oxford: Oxford University Press.

Price, M. E., Abbott, S., & Morgan, L. (Eds.) (2011). *Measures of Press Freedom and Media Contributions to Development. Evaluating the Evaluators*. New York: Peter Lang.

Pyykkö, R. (2002). Who Is 'Us' in Russian Political Discourse. In A. Duszak (Ed.), *Pragmatics & Beyond New Series: Vol. 98. Us and Others: Social Identities across Languages, Discourses and Cultures* (pp. 233–48). Amsterdam: John Benjamins. https://doi.org/10.1075/pbns.98.14pyy

Quirk, R. (1981). International Communication and the Concept of Nuclear English. In L. E. Smith (Ed.), *English for Cross-Cultural Communication* (pp. 151–65). London: Palgrave Macmillan.

Quirk, R., Greenbaum, S., Leech, G., & Svartvik, J. (1985). *A Comprehensive Grammar of the English Language* (2nd ed.). Harlow: Longman.

Raguseo, C. (2010). Twitter Fiction: Social Networking and Microfiction in 140 Characters. *Teaching English as a Second or Foreign Language*, *13*(4).

Randall, D. (2000). *The Universal Journalist* (2nd ed.). London: Pluto Press.

Reinemann, C., Stanyer, J., Scherr, S., & Legnante, G. (2012). Hard and Soft News: A Review of Concepts, Operationalizations and Key Findings. *Journalism*, *13*(2), 221–39. https://doi.org/10.1177/1464884911427803

Reporters without Borders (2020). Press Freedom Index 2020. Retrieved from https://rsf.org/en/ranking

Richards, J. C., & Tay, M. (1981). Norm and Variability in Language Use and Language Learning. In L. E. Smith (Ed.), *English for Cross-Cultural Communication* (pp. 40–56). London: Palgrave Macmillan.

Richards, S. (1998). Learning English in Hong Kong: Making Connections between Motivation, Language Use, and Strategy Choice. In M. Pennington (Ed.), *Language in Hong Kong at Century's End* (pp. 303–28). Hong Kong: Hong Kong University Press.

Rojas, J. P. F. (2012, November 30). Ukip takes second place in by-elections. *Daily Telegraph*.

Romaine, S. (1992). English: From Village to Global Village. In T. Machan & C. Scott (Eds.), *English in Its Social Contexts: Essays in Historical Sociolinguistics* (pp. 253–60). Oxford: Open University Press.

Rooy, B. van, Terblanche, L., Haase, C., & Schmied, J. J. (2010). Register Differentiation in East African English: A Multidimensional Study. *English World-Wide, 31*(3), 311–49. https://doi.org/10.1075/eww.31.3.04van

Rosenthal, J. (2007a, November 6). The Reporters Without Borders Press Freedom Index: Independent Assessment or EU Propaganda? (Part I). *World Politics Review*. Retrieved from https://www.worldpoliticsreview.com/articles/1312/the-reporters-without-borders-press-freedom-index-independent-assessment-or-eu-propaganda-part-i

Rosenthal, J. (2007b, November 14). The Reporters Without Borders Press Freedom Index: Independent Assessment or EU Propaganda? (Part II). *World Politics Review*. Retrieved from https://www.worldpoliticsreview.com/articles/1350/the-reporters-without-borders-press-freedom-index-independent-assessment-or-eu-propaganda-part-ii

Santorini, B. (1991). Part-of-Speech Tagging Guidelines for the Penn Treebank Project.

Schmid, H. (1994). *Probabilistic Part-of-Speech Tagging Using Decision Trees*. Proceedings of International Conference on New Methods in Language Processing, Manchester, UK.

Schmid, H. (1995). *Improvements in Part-of-Speech Tagging with an Application to German*. Proceedings of the ACL SIGDAT-Workshop, Dublin, Ireland.

Schmied, J. J. (1989a). English in East Africa: Theoretical, Methodological and Practical Issues. In J. J. Schmied (Ed.), *Bayreuth African Studies Series: Vol. 15. English in East and Central Africa I* (pp. 7–37). Altendorf: Gräbner.

Schmied, J. J. (1989b). Second-Language Varieties across the Indian Ocean. In J. J. Schmied (Ed.), *Bayreuth African Studies Series: Vol. 15. English in East and Central Africa I* (pp. 85–97). Altendorf: Gräbner.

Schmied, J. J. (1991a). *English in Africa: An Introduction*. London: Longman.

Schmied, J. J. (1991b). National and Subnational Features in Kenyan English. In J. Cheshire (Ed.), *English around the World: Sociolinguistic Perspectives* (pp. 420–32). Cambridge: Cambridge University Press.

Schmied, J. J. (2006). East African Englishes. In B. B. Kachru, Y. Kachru, & C. L. Nelson (Eds.), *Blackwell Handbooks in Linguistics. The Handbook of World Englishes* (pp. 188–202). Malden, Mass: Blackwell.

Schneider, E. W. (2003). The Dynamics of New Englishes: From Identity Construction to Dialect Birth. *Language, 79*(2), 233–81. https://doi.org/10.1353/lan.2003.0136

Schneider, E. W. (2007). *Postcolonial English: Varieties around the World*. Cambridge: Cambridge University Press.

Schneider, E. W. (2014). New Reflections on the Evolutionary Dynamics of World Englishes. *World Englishes, 33*(1), 9–32. https://doi.org/10.1111/weng.12069

Schneider, K. (1999). Exploring the Roots of Popular English News Writing: A Preliminary Report on a Corpus-Based Project. In H.-J. Diller, E. Otto, & G. Stratmann (Eds.), *Anglistik und Englischunterricht: Vol. 62. English via Various Media* (pp. 201–22). Heidelberg: Universitätsverlag C. Winter.

Schneider, K. (2000). The Emergence and Development of Headlines in English Newspapers. In F. Ungerer (Ed.), *Pragmatics & Beyond New Series: Vol. 80. English Media Texts – Past and Present* (pp. 45–65). Amsterdam: John Benjamins.

SCMP (1986, November). Language Project Deserves Applause. *South China Morning Post*.

SCMP (1989, February). 'Worst' English Tag Should Be Eliminated. Editorial. *South China Morning Post*.

Scott, C. E. (2011). Exploring Diachronic Register Change in Reports of Armistice 1902–2003. *Linguistics and the Human Sciences, 4*(3), 241–64. https://doi.org/10.1558/lhs.v4i3.241

Seargeant, P. (2005). Globalisation and Reconfigured English in Japan. *World Englishes, 24*(3), 309–19. https://doi.org/10.1111/j.0083-2919.2005.00412.x

Seargeant, P. (2012). *Exploring World Englishes: Language in a Global Context*. London: Routledge.

Sewell, A., & Chan, J. [Jason] (2010). Patterns of Variation in the Consonantal Phonology of Hong Kong English. *English World-Wide, 31*(2), 138–61.

Sharma, D. (2009). Typological Diversity in New Englishes. *English World-Wide, 30*(2), 170–95. https://doi.org/10.1075/eww.30.2.04sha

Shoemaker, P. J., & Cohen, A. A. (2006). *News around the World: Content, Practitioners, and the Public*. London: Routledge.

Sin, K., & Roebuck, D. (1996). Language Engineering for Legal Transplantation: Conceptual Problems in Creating Common Law Chinese. *Language & Communication, 16*(3), 235–54. https://doi.org/10.1016/0271-5309(96)00017-1

Skandera, P. (1999). What Do We Really Know about Kenyan English? A Pilot Study in Research Methodology. *English World-Wide, 20*(2), 217–36. https://doi.org/10.1075/eww.20.2.02ska

Skandera, P. (2003). *Drawing a Map of Africa*. Tübingen: Narr.

Smith, E. (2008, September 27). Obama faces off against McCain. *Sun*.

Smith, L. E. (1992). Spread of English and Issues of Intelligibility. In B. B. Kachru (Ed.), *The Other Tongue: English across Cultures* (2nd ed., pp. 75–90). Urbana, Chicago: University of Illinois Press.

So, D. (1992). Language-Based Bifurcation of Secondary Education in Hong Kong: Past, Present and Future. In K. K. Luke (Ed.), *Into the Twenty First Century: Issues of Language and Education in Hong Kong* (pp. 69–95). Hong Kong: Linguistic Society of Hong Kong.

Stamou, A. (2001). The Representation of Non-Protesters in a Student and Teacher Protest: A Critical Discourse Analysis of News Reporting in a Greek Newspaper. *Discourse & Society, 12*(5), 653–80. https://doi.org/10.1177/0957926501012005005

The State of the News Media (2012). Who Owns the Media: Top Newspaper Companies.

Steiner, E. (2004). *Translated Texts: Properties, Variants, Evaluations*. Frankfurt am Main: Peter Lang.

Strang, B. (1970). *A History of English*. London: Methuen.

Strevens, P. (1980). *Teaching English as an International Language: From Practice to Principle*. Oxford: Pergamon Press.

Strevens, P. (1981). Forms of English: An Analysis of the Variables. In L. E. Smith (Ed.), *English for Cross-Cultural Communication* (pp. 1–14). London: Palgrave Macmillan.

Sure, K. (1989). Attitudes towards English among Kenyan Students. In J. J. Schmied (Ed.), *Bayreuth African Studies Series: Vol. 15. English in East and Central Africa I* (pp. 39–61). Altendorf: Gräbner.

Sweeting, A., & Vickers, E. (2005). On Colonizing 'Colonialism': The Discourses of the History of English in Hong Kong. *World Englishes*, 24(2), 113–30. https://doi.org/10.1111/j.1467-971X.2005.00397.x

Szmrecsanyi, B., & Kortmann, B. (2011). Typological Profiling: Learner Englishes versus Indigenized L2 Varieties of English. In J. Mukherjee & M. Hundt (Eds.), *Exploring Second-Language Varieties of English and Learner Englishes: Bridging a Paradigm Gap* (pp. 167–87). Amsterdam: John Benjamins.

Taguchi, N. (2002). A Comparative Analysis of Discourse Markers in English Conversational Registers. *Issues in Applied Linguistics*, 13(1), 41–69. https://doi.org/10.5070/l4131005052

Tay, M. (1991). Southeast Asia and Hong Kong. In J. Cheshire (Ed.), *English around the World: Sociolinguistic Perspectives* (pp. 319–32). Cambridge: Cambridge University Press.

Teo, P. (2000). Racism in the News: A Critical Discourse Analysis of News Reporting in Two Australian Newspapers. *Discourse & Society*, 11(1), 7–49. https://doi.org/10.1177/0957926500011001002

Thomas, R. (1985). Plain English and the Law. *Statute Law Review*, 6(1), 139–51. https://doi.org/10.1093/slr/6.1.139

Thompson, E. A., White, P. R. R., & Kitley, P. (2008). 'Objectivity' and 'Hard News' Reporting across Cultures: Comparing the News Report in English, French, Japanese and Indonesian Journalism. *Journalism Studies*, 9(2), 212–28. https://doi.org/10.1080/14616700701848261

Thorndike, E. L., & Lorge, I. (1944). *The Teacher's Word Book of 30,000 Words*. New York: Teachers College, Columbia University.

Trappel, J., & Maniglio, T. (2009). On Media Monitoring – The Media for Democracy Monitor (MDM). *Communications*, 34(2), 169–201. https://doi.org/10.1515/COMM.2009.012

UK Audit Bureau of Circulations (2015). National Newspapers Report.

UNESCO (2019). Media Development Indicators (MDIs). Retrieved from https://unesdoc.unesco.org/ark:/48223/pf0000163102

UNESCO Institute for Statistics (2021). Kenya. Retrieved from http://uis.unesco.org/en/country/ke

Vestergaard, T. (1999). Free Adjuncts in Newspaper Discourse. In H.-J. Diller, E. Otto, & G. Stratmann (Eds.), *Anglistik und Englischunterricht: Vol. 62. English via Various Media* (pp. 89–105). Heidelberg: Universitätsverlag C. Winter.

Weeks, D. (2013, March 1). What's got interim? *Sun*.

Wegener, R. (2011). *Parameters of Context: From Theory to Model and Application* (PhD Thesis). Macquarie University, Sydney.

Welch, M., Fenwick, M., & Roberts, M. (1997). Primary Definitions of Crime and Moral Panic: A Content Analysis of Experts' Quotes in Feature Newspaper Articles on Crime. *Journal of Research in Crime and Delinquency*, 34(4), 474–94. https://doi.org/10.1177/0022427897034004004

Wenzel, P. (2015). Endings in Literature: A Survey. In G. Hopps, S. Neumann, S. Strasen, & P. Wenzel (Eds.), *Aachen British and American Studies: Vol. 19. Last Things: Essays on Ends and Endings* (pp. 19–34). Frankfurt am Main: Peter Lang.

White, P. R. R. (1997). Death, Disruption and the Moral Order: The Narrative Impulse in Mass Media 'Hard News' Reporting. In J. R. Martin & F. Christie (Eds.), *Genre and Institutions. Social Processes in the Workplace and School* (pp. 101–33). London: Cassell.

White, P. R. R. (2004). Subjectivity, Evaluation and Point of View in Media Discourse. In C. Coffin & K. O'Halloran (Eds.), *Applying English Grammar: Functional and Corpus Approaches* (pp. 229–46). London, New York: Edward Arnold.

White, P. R. R. (2006). Evaluative Semantics and Ideological Positioning in Journalistic Discourse: A New Framework for Analysis. In I. Lassen, J. Strunck, & T. Vestergaard (Eds.), *Mediating Ideology in Text and Image: Ten Critical Studies* (pp. 37–67). Amsterdam: John Benjamins.

White, P. R. R. (2012). Exploring the Axiological Workings of 'Reporter Voice' News Stories – Attribution and Attitudinal Positioning. *Discourse, Context & Media*, 1(2–3), 57–67. https://doi.org/10.1016/j.dcm.2012.10.004

Widdowson, H. G. (1994). The Ownership of English. *TESOL Quarterly*, 28(2), 377–89. https://doi.org/10.2307/3587438

Widdowson, H. G. (1997). EIL, ESL, EFL: Global Issues and Local Interests. *World Englishes*, 16(1), 135–46. https://doi.org/10.1111/1467-971X.00054

Winter, B. (2019). *Statistics for Linguists: An Introduction Using R*. New York: Routledge.

Xiao, R. (2009). Multidimensional Analysis and the Study of World Englishes. *World Englishes*, 28(4), 421–50. https://doi.org/10.1111/j.1467-971X.2009.01606.x

Yao, X., & Collins, P. (2012). The Present Perfect in World Englishes. *World Englishes*, 31(3), 386–403. https://doi.org/10.1111/j.1467-971X.2012.01756.x

Yoshikawa, H. (2005). Recognition of World Englishes: Changes in Chukyo University Students' Attitudes. *World Englishes*, 24(3), 351–60. https://doi.org/10.1111/j.0083-2919.2005.00416.x

Youmans, G. (1990). Measuring Lexical Style and Competence: The Type-Token Vocabulary Curve. *Style*, 24(4), 584–99.

Zappavigna, M. (2011). Ambient Affiliation: A Linguistic Perspective on Twitter. *New Media & Society*, 13(5), 788–806. https://doi.org/10.1177/1461444810385097

Zuengler, J. E. (1983). Kenyan English. In B. B. Kachru (Ed.), *The Other Tongue: English across Cultures* (1st ed., pp. 112–24). Oxford: Pergamon Press.

Index

Agentive roles 48, 50, 92
Annotation 62, 63
Channel (as a parameter of **register**) 54, 55, 122, 136
Concentric circles of English (Kachru) 9, 15, 24
    Expanding circle 9, 15
    Inner circle 9, 10, 15, 16
    Outer circle 9, 10, 15, 16, 19, 26, 138
Content words 44, 68, 80, 82, 126, 127
Developmental status 4, 138, 140, 143, 144, 147
Dynamic Model (Schneider) 18, 19, 24, 26, 58, 138, 139
EFL 12–17
EIL 10, 11, 16
ENL 3, 10, **12–17**, 38
English as a first language > see L1
English as a foreign language > see EFL
English as a native language > see ENL
English as a second language > see L2
ESL > see L2
Experiential domain **43–45**, 56, **68–83**, 126, 135
Function words 44, 63, 80, 126, 127

Goal orientation **43–48**, 52, 56, **83–90**
Header 62
Headline 28, 29, 62, 63, 73, 95, 96
    Subheadline 62, 63
ICE 10, 18, 22, 24, 39, 144
International Corpus of English > see ICE
L1 12, 13, 15
L2 3, **12–17**, 25, 26, 32, 57, 58, 59, 61, 71, 82, 85, 118, 120, 124, 126, 127, 130, 135, 138, 140, 142
Language role 54, 121
Lexical words > see Content words
Mark-up 46, 62
Media Development Indicators (UNESCO) 31
Media Sustainability Index 31
Medium (as a parameter of **register**) 54, **55**, 56, **121–127**, 130, 132, 135, 138, 140, 147
Multidimensional analysis 39
News value 5, 37, 47, 52, 59, 61, 68, 71, 77, 106, 111, 132, 134, 137, 138
    Human interest 89, 132, 137, 138
    Proximity 52, 61, 71, 111
    Recency 77
    Superlativeness 106
Newsworthiness 29, 68, 106

Operationalization 36, 40, **43–56**, 58, 67, 80, 85, 88, 96, 100, 103, 117, 124, 126, 127, 143, 145, 146, 147

Press freedom 5, 27, **30–33**, 46, 126, 130, 137, 138, **140–142**, 143, 145

Press Freedom Index 5, 31, 32, 33, 137, 140, 141

Recency 29, 73, 75, 90

Register 3, 4, 11, 19, **34–36**, 37, 38, 39, 40, **43–56**, 130, 131, 139, 142, 143, 144, 145

Reporters without Borders 5, 31, 32, 33, 137, 140

RSF > see Reporters without Borders

Self-censorship 5, 31, 32, 118, 137, 138, 140, 142

SFL > see Systemic functional linguistics

Social distance 48, 49, **51–54**, 56, 83, 92, 96, **103–119**, 121, 124, 126, 132

Social role relationship **49–51**, 52, 85, 88, **92–102**, 119, 146

Systemic functional linguistics 34, 39, 52